Family rhythms

MANCHESTER
1824

Manchester University Press

Family rhythms

The changing textures of family life in Ireland

Jane Gray, Ruth Geraghty
and David Ralph

Manchester University Press

Published by Manchester University Press
Altrincham Street, Manchester M1 7JA

www.manchesteruniversitypress.co.uk

British Library Cataloguing-in-Publication Data
A catalogue record for this book is available from the British Library

Library of Congress Cataloging-in-Publication Data applied for

ISBN   978 0 7190 9151 3   hardback

ISBN   978 0 7190 9152 0   paperback

First published 2016

Typeset in 10/12 Photina by
Servis Filmsetting Ltd, Stockport, Cheshire
Printed in Great Britain by
Bell & Bain Ltd, Glasgow

Contents

Figures

Photographs

Panels

Preface

We had a number of goals in mind when we embarked on the project of writing this book. First, there has been a huge growth in output within the field of Irish family sociology in recent years, thanks to the availability of funding for the analysis of major new data sources such as the *Growing Up in Ireland: The National Longitudinal Study of Children.* We believed that there was an unfilled need to bring these findings together in a student-friendly book that placed them in the context of national and international sociological theory and research on families, and that drew together some emerging policy implications.

Second, there is a wealth of 'classical' research on Irish families dating back to the early decades of the twentieth century, the value of which has been under-estimated in explanations of contemporary family change. We saw an opportunity to highlight for both students and general readers the contributions these studies have made, alongside an appreciation of contemporary scholarship.

Third, and most importantly, the availability of substantial new qualitative datasets made it possible for us to engage with contemporary theoretical perspectives by 're-visioning' the changing rhythms and textures of Irish family life over an extended period of social change.

Jane Gray was a co-principal investigator, together with Professor Seán Ó Riain, on the project funded by the Irish Research Council to develop an infra-structural database of qualitative life history narratives from three cohorts of Irish people, born in different historical periods, whose lives have traversed many social, cultural and economic changes since the earliest decades of the state. These *Life Histories and Social Change* interviews have been deposited in the Irish Qualitative Data Archive (IQDA), where they are available for re-use by researchers and educators.

Growing Up in Ireland: The National Longitudinal Study of Children is a government funded panel study that is tracking two cohorts of Irish children over time: a 'child cohort' that joined the study at nine years of age, and an 'infant cohort' that is being followed from birth. As part of the first wave of interviews with the nine-year-olds and their parents, and also with the infants' parents, researchers from the *Growing Up in Ireland* study carried out qualitative interviews with a selected group of participants. In the case of the child cohort, 120 children and their families were interviewed. The transcripts from these interviews are also now available through IQDA to academic researchers and students.

Thanks to a second grant from the Irish Research Council, Ruth Geraghty and David Ralph joined Jane Gray in the *Family Rhythms* project at Maynooth University. *Family Rhythms* was designed to act as a demonstrator and knowledge-exchange project for the analysis of archived qualitative data, using the *Life Histories and Social Change* interviews and the interviews from the *Growing Up in Ireland* child cohort. This book is one of the principal outputs from that project. We believe it is unique in bringing a comprehensive overview of existing sociological knowledge about family change into dialogue with original analysis of qualitative data to develop a new understanding of the changing contours of Irish family life. The rich memories, reflections and descriptions that we have included throughout provide context and depth to the quantitative data and abstract ideas that also inform our analysis. More significantly, they have allowed us to develop new insights into the motives, feelings and rationalities behind Irish peoples' family practices and experiences in changing social contexts – aspects of the explanation of social change that are not so easily captured in quantitative data.

We would like to acknowledge the generosity of the Irish Research Council in funding the research towards this book and to extend our thanks to researchers from the *Growing Up in Ireland* team for their assistance with the data. We are grateful, also, to the Maynooth University Research Development Office for providing support through their Publications Fund. The National Institute for Regional and Spatial Analysis at Maynooth University provided a congenial home to the *Family Rhythms* project. Thanks to Professors Rob Kitchin and Mark Boyle who supported us in their capacity as Directors of the Institute and to Rhona Bradshaw and Orla Dunne for their assistance in managing the project.

The IQDA plays a key role in making qualitative data available for sharing and re-use. It has been funded by the Irish Government as part of the Irish Social Science Platform under the fourth Programme for Research in Third Level Institutions (PRTLI4), and as a participant in the inter-institutional consortium that has developed the Digital Repository of Ireland (DRI) with the assistance of government funding under PRTLI5. The *Life Histories and Social Change* dataset forms the basis for a demonstrator project on enhanced qualitative social science data (Irish Lifetimes) in the DRI.

This book forms part of the emerging knowledge available to researchers, students and the public, thanks to the up-scaling of new social science research data in Ireland. It demonstrates the value of 'big' qualitative data for enhancing our understanding of social change and for informing policy. Prospective qualitative research will continue to play an important role in the future. We hope that future waves of the *Growing Up in Ireland* project will include qualitative modules as part of that endeavour.

Finally, we would like to acknowledge the Irish people of many different ages and backgrounds who contributed the narratives that inspired this work. Jane Gray would like to thank Paul, Rebecca and Adam for their patience and love as she worked on this project and to acknowledge how Lewis Gray's wisdom helped her to understand the textures of Irish life across the generations. Ruth Geraghty would like to thank her family, especially Frank, Mary, Will, David, Marianne, Gordon, Deirdre, Alannah, Cara and Tom for their constant support, encouragement and love.

Introduction:
Irish families in the sociological imagination

In an interview carried out in 2007, Rose (born in the 1950s) told research-ers from Maynooth University how, when she was a teenager, her older unmarried sister had become pregnant:

> Now this ... wasn't the done thing back in [the late 1960s] [...] you were sent away [...] but my mother and father took the child and legally adopted her and although she is technically my niece she's my sister, she was reared as a sister to the rest of us [...] and then after that she was just a sister [...] Then my mother went on to have another child. (Rose, b. 1950s, LHSC)

Including the adopted niece, Rose had nine siblings altogether. When she was in her early twenties, Rose married her first serious boyfriend with whom she had been going out for five years. Using the 'Billings' method of family planning they postponed having their first child for a couple of years while both worked and shared domestic tasks at home. However, when her first child came along Rose gave up her job to concentrate on raising her family.

Rose and her husband began to experience difficulties in their relationship and when her youngest was born they separated, although they have never legally divorced. Once her youngest child started secondary school Rose went back to education and later secured a part-time job. A number of years before her interview, Rose's daughter had an unexpected pregnancy:

> Oh it broke my heart, oh devastated I was, just you get over these things but, so she lives here with her little fella ... Very hard time now, it took us all by shock. It took me a long time to come to terms with it. I think it was because she was so young. I mean, the others had had babies by then but she's not with the father now anymore, she has another boyfriend now, they're engaged, lovely lad. It just didn't work out with her and the father.

1

At the time of her interview, Rose's daughter was still living at home with her child, although she was engaged to marry and was looking for work, having completed her Leaving Certificate (final exam). Now that her grandchild was old enough to go to school, Rose planned to mind the child in the afternoons after she herself had finished work. Her other children were either married or living with their partners. To the best of their ability, Rose and her ex-husband had provided them with financial help to set up in their own homes.

Rose's story illustrates just some of the continuities, changes and diversity in Irish family lives that are explored throughout this book. As we go to press, Ireland prepares to introduce significant legislative changes to address the changing character of Irish family lives. According to Minister for Justice and Equality, Frances Fitzgerald, the new *Child and Family Relationships Bill* 'responds to a world where children are reared within married families, within lone parent households, in blended families, households headed by same-sex couples or by grandparents and other relatives', and where children are conceived through assisted human reproduction.[1] On 22 May 2015, the Irish people voted in a referendum to extend civil marriage rights to same-sex couples.

In some respects the changes prompting this new legislation have occurred in a very short space of time. In other respects, as Rose's story illustrates, there have been continuities in the challenges families faced across the generations. This book aims to document and explain the changing rhythms, textures and meanings of Irish family life from a sociological perspective through an innovative **qualitative longitudinal approach**, drawing on two major datasets newly available through the Irish Qualitative Data Archive (www.iqda.ie): *Life Histories and Social Change* and *Growing Up in Ireland*. **See Panel i.1 below for a detailed description of the datasets and how they are used throughout the book.** These datasets are described as qualitative because they are based on semi-structured interviews that encouraged people to talk about their lives in an open-ended way, rather than giving information through the 'box-ticking' method that we are familiar with from participating in surveys and questionnaires, such as the Census. They are **longitudinal** in the sense that they allow us to examine how people's lives changed as they grew up, formed families of their own, and aged in different historical periods from the 1930s through to the present. By including original qualitative data we aim to bring these changes to life and to provide readers with a front-row view of research on family change in Ireland. Before describing the plan of the book in more detail, we begin with a discussion of what is distinctive about sociological perspectives on family life.

---

1   Address by the Minister for Justice and Equality, Frances Fitzgerald TD at the Children's Rights Alliance Seminar on the Children and Family Relationships Bill 2015, Dublin Castle, 2 March 2015. http://childrensrights.ie/sites/default/files/conferenceproceedings/files/MinJusticeCFRBillSeminar020315.pdf. Accessed 16 March 2015.

Panel i.1   Description of the data

Throughout this book you will find quotations and narratives drawn from the following two datasets: *Life Histories and Social Change* (2007) – This database comprises 100 in-depth life history interviews with respondents from three birth cohorts, whose lives traversed the twentieth century. The database also includes life history calendars and retrospective social network schedules. These data provide a **retrospective** view on social change, because they are based on the individual life stories recounted to the interviewers; *Growing Up in Ireland* (2008) – This is a national mixed-method **panel study** centred on a child cohort (beginning at nine years) and an infant cohort (beginning at nine months). Panel studies provide **prospective** information on social change, by following a group of people through time. To date, the first qualitative waves of the nine-year-old 'child' cohort and the nine-month-old 'infant' cohort have been made available. This book focuses on qualitative data from the child cohort. These qualitative data include in-depth interviews with children and parents, and 'time capsules' incorporating a range of items including drawings, writings and images.

Together, these datasets allow us to track and compare the changing family experiences of people born before 1935, between 1945 and 1954, between 1965 and 1974, and those who were nine years old when interviewed, together with their parents, between 2007 and 2009 (see Figure i.1). Extracts from the two studies are presented throughout the book as evidence or examples of each topic under discussion. Data from the *Life Histories and Social Change* study are indicated by the abbreviation 'LHSC', while data from the *Growing Up in Ireland* study are indicated by 'GUI'. Throughout the book you will see direct quotations from

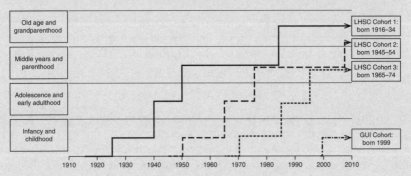

Figure i.1 Timeline showing four cohorts by life stage

Source: Life Histories and Social Change collection (2007); Growing up in Ireland collection (2008). (Timeline is based on average year of birth per cohort and is indicative only of life stage.)

participants in both studies; each participant has been given a pseudonym to protect their identity. Other potentially identifying information has been concealed or removed. In a small number of cases we have altered some personal details in order to protect participant confidentiality. **See the appendices for a list of all participants referred to in the book and for more technical descriptions of the datasets.**

When we quote an adult participant from the LHSC study we also provide their year of birth so that you can assess the **historical period** when they lived through a particular **life stage**. For example, 'Maurice (b.1966, LHSC)' indicates that the quotation is from 'Maurice', who was born in 1966, and participated in the LHSC study. When quoting a child participant from the GUI study we provide their age at the time of interview. For example, 'Frank (age 9, GUI)' indicates that the quotation is from 'Frank', who was a nine-year-old child participant in GUI.

In addition, each chapter includes panels on 'Looking at the data', in which we present a lengthier extract from either the LHSC study or the GUI study. These longer quotations are an opportunity to examine and assess **primary qualitative research data**, using the concepts and ideas that have been presented earlier in the chapter. Additional primary qualitative data, audio clips from interviews and sample questions can be accessed at www.iqda.ie/content/family-rhythms. **Refer to the appendices for technical information on the LHSC and GUI datasets.**

Families in the sociological imagination

Writing in 1959, the American sociologist C. Wright Mills used the example of marriage to illustrate what he meant by the 'sociological imagination':

> Inside a marriage a man and a woman may experience personal troubles, but when the divorce rate during the first four years of marriage is 250 out of every 1,000 attempts, this is an indication of a structural issue having to do with the institutions of marriage and the family and other institutions that bear upon them. (Mills, 2000 [1959]: 9)[2]

The promise of sociology, according to Mills, lies in its ability to trace the connections between the troubles we may experience in our daily life, and social processes that are, to some extent, outside our control. Notice that we don't say that personal problems are caused by processes outside our control. Because

---

2   Note that Mills was writing at the end of the 1950s. Divorce rates subsequently rose to much higher levels in the United States and other countries. **We discuss the Irish experience of divorce in Chapter 5.**

our private troubles may be linked to wider patterns of social change, it does not follow that we bear no responsibility for our actions, or that we cannot alter the social milieu within which those troubles arise. As shown throughout this book, the relationships between personal troubles and public issues are complex.

What makes the sociological approach different?

For many of us, the media provide much of our information about changing family trends, and thus the set of ideas with which we evaluate our individual family experience. Journalists often report and interpret general statistics about family life that have been gathered by organizations like the Central Statistics Office. They may interview 'experts' drawn from academic and research institutions, social care practice or voluntary organizations. They often include material drawn from interviews with 'ordinary people' to illustrate the family issue they are concerned with. Journalists strive to ensure that their facts and sources are accurate and reliable. They frequently refer to sociological or other scholarly research when constructing their interpretations and evaluations of the issue at hand.

So how do sociological accounts of family life differ from those of journalists? The principal differences lie in their reference to sociological theory, the systematic way in which their data are collected, and the extent to which the work is – at least initially – oriented to a professional peer audience (Ragin and Amoroso, 2010). One consequence is that sociological research often 'debunks' popular understanding of contemporary family trends. For example, year-on-year increases in the numbers of divorced people are often reported in the media in ways that imply that divorce is a growing problem in Ireland. But more systematic sociological analysis shows that the rate of divorce in Ireland is one of the lowest among western societies. Similarly, many people believe that the extended family has disappeared in Ireland, and that people no longer have the kind of support from grandparents and other relatives that they used to have in the past. However, sociological research suggests that contemporary families have as much support from grandparents as did earlier generations. **The relationships between children and their grandparents are discussed in more detail in Chapter 6.**

Another way in which many people find information with which to evaluate their own family experience is through contact with social care workers, therapists and other clinicians. The members of these professions work at the coal face of changing family patterns. In the course of their work they accumulate a wealth of information about the problems people encounter in their family lives. What can sociological research, generated within the 'ivory tower' of universities and research institutes, add to their knowledge and experience? In fact, by collecting systematic data, linking findings to theory, and making comparisons, sociology provides essential contextual information for understanding family problems.

Knowledge generated by practice-oriented research can be misleading if it is applied to society as a whole. In a classic example, widely reported research in the United States by psychologist Judith Wallerstein seemed to show that parents' divorce had very serious consequences for their children, well into adulthood (see Cherlin, 1999). Her findings were regularly cited in the debates leading up to the referendums on divorce that took place in Ireland in 1986 and 1995. However, Wallerstein's research was carried out with people who presented to her clinic – people who already felt they had problems – so it was unreliable as a source of information about the population of children whose parents had divorced. Sociological research in the United States showed that only a minority of the children of divorce experienced the kinds of problems she identified (Cherlin, 1999). In fact, Dr Wallerstein was so troubled by the use of her research by anti-divorce campaigners in Ireland that she was moved to write to them that 'I have always supported divorce as an important social remedy' (quoted by Carol Coulter in the *Irish Times*, 25 October 1995). **Sociological research on the consequences of divorce for children and children's experiences of living in a non-marital family is discussed in Chapter 3.** Knowing that a 'private trouble' is experienced by a minority of people does not trivialize the problem, or make it irrelevant, but it does contextualize it. In relation to divorce, for example, it prompts us to ask better questions about the particular circumstances under which it does cause severe problems for children, which in turn should allow us to make better interventions with those who seek help, and better social policy relating to the break-up of marriage.

The difference between knowledge generated by sociology, and knowledge created in clinical settings, illustrates both the strengths and limitations of sociology. It cannot guide practice at the level of individuals. The sociological imagination can empower us by alleviating the sense of being trapped by forces beyond our control. For example, if we know that a sizable minority of people experience violence in their family lives we may not feel so isolated and lonely, or inclined to blame ourselves. We may be motivated to make family violence a public issue, by campaigning for ways to alleviate the problem. **Domestic violence as a public issue is discussed in more detail in Chapter 5**. However, most of the time sociology will be of no direct assistance to us in solving our personal troubles: it will not tell us how to cope with a violent situation, or help a troubled child. Similarly, while sociology provides essential context for therapeutic practice, it does not provide a template for addressing the problems of individual clients. We can understand this better if we examine two logical errors that are often made with respect to the sociological imagination. Both involve confusing levels of analysis.

Avoiding mistakes when thinking sociologically

The **ecological fallacy** refers to the logical error of making inferences about individuals based on observations about groups. Suppose we find that areas of Dublin with high rates of unemployment are also areas with a high reported incidence of domestic violence, can we conclude that unemployed Dubliners are more likely to beat their spouses than employed Dubliners? When we think about this for a moment, it is clear that the answer is 'no'. There are both employed and unemployed people in the areas in question, and unless we have information about individuals, we don't know who is experiencing family violence. It could be that most of those who perpetrate violence at home are found amongst the employed people in the area, or it could be that employment status is irrelevant.

We often make this error in a more general way. For example, if we know that on average women who work full-time outside the home spend 7 to 10 more hours a week on housework than men who work full-time outside the home, can we assume that the man sitting next to us on the bus is a lazy slob who doesn't help his wife around the house? Again, the answer is 'no'. Sociological research on the division of household labour shows that there is a tendency for women to contribute a greater share; it does not claim that this phenomenon is universal.

It is also important to avoid the **individualistic fallacy**. Just because you may be a husband who shares equally in household tasks, doesn't mean that sociologists are wrong to say that most husbands don't contribute an equal share. Qualitative data, such as the quotations and stories presented throughout this book, can increase the risk of making this kind of error because they are not **statistically representative** in the way that quantitative data usually are. Consider Rose's story from the beginning of this chapter. Some aspects of her experience are 'typical' of the times she lived through, but others are not. For example, while families were certainly larger in the 1950s and 1960s than they are today, Rose's nine (or ten) siblings added up to a larger than average family for the time. While births outside marriage comprise a significant proportion of all births today (more than a third), births to teenage mothers like Rose's daughter are relatively uncommon.

Qualitative data are not intended to be representative of the population as quantitative data are. Instead, qualitative researchers seek to uncover the shared meanings and practices that give rise to the trends captured by quantitative researchers. Qualitative research can also be useful for revealing patterns that may be hidden to quantitative research. For example, we don't know how commonly births outside marriage were disguised in the past by formal or informal adoption, as in the case of Rose's niece. Both quantitative and qualitative research have an important part to play in grasping 'history and biography and the relations between the two within society' (Mills 1959: 6). What C. Wright Mills called the 'promise' of sociology lies in the space between individual and collective experience, but it is essential not to confuse the two.

Changing sociological perspectives on families

From the early twentieth century at least through the 1980s, sociologists typically thought of 'the family' as an **institution**. According to one definition (Nolan and Lenski, 1999: 8), a social institution is 'a durable answer to a persistent problem' for human societies. Conventionally, anthropologists and sociologists have viewed the requirement of caring for infants – humans need adult care for much longer than is typically the case in other species – as the problem giving rise to the institution of the family. Social institutions like the family have been thought of as comprising a set of interdependent **roles** governed by socially agreed rules of behaviour (Cherlin, 2004).

Throughout much of the twentieth century sociologists were concerned with trying to understand how the family as an institution changed over time – especially in response to wider social changes such as industrialization and urbanization. Beginning in the 1970s, feminist and Marxist sociologists began to question whether the normative family described by sociologists met the requirements of all social groups equally, suggesting that working-class people and women were disadvantaged by the roles and rules that were enforced by social convention, and in many cases also by state policy. **Learn more about sociological perspectives on the family as an institution in Chapter 1.**

Writing in 1963, sociologist William Goode noted that sociologists approached the family both as an **ideal type** – that is, an abstract statement of what were thought to be the essential features of the family as an institution – and as a set of ideals that people aspired to. Sociologists have always recognized that – for a whole range of reasons – some people may not be able to live up to the prevailing societal ideal in their family life. Beginning in the 1980s, however, it became increasingly difficult for sociologists to identify either the ideal type or the shared set of ideals that governed families in western societies. Families, and the values people held about family life, were becoming more diverse. More babies were being born outside marriage; in many countries divorce rates were increasing rapidly; and men's and women's roles were being transformed. In the latter decades of the twentieth century sociological scholarship in the West was taken up with trying to make sense of this **convergence to diversity** (Boh, 1989) in family life within and between advanced industrial countries. **We will examine these debates in detail in Chapter 2.**

More recently, however, sociologists have responded to the changes in family life by going back to basics, that is, by investigating what families look like 'on the ground' (Morgan, 2011). Instead of beginning with a set of theoretical expectations about what 'the family' ought to be like, sociologists are turning to the qualitative research tradition to examine how people 'do family' in their everyday lives. They have become interested in exploring the different configurations of relationships that make up people's family networks in practice, rather than beginning with the 'rules' of kinship and household formation (Widmer and Jallinoja, 2008). And rather than relying exclusively on survey data about family values to understand the ideals that govern family behaviour, they have begun to examine how people construct shared expectations by 'displaying family' (Finch, 2007) in different social contexts. This book is informed by these new approaches as it seeks to develop a new understanding of the transformation of Irish families since the early decades of the twentieth century.

As well as turning to qualitative approaches to understanding people's family lives, sociologists have, in recent years, renewed their interest in linking individual life paths to wider patterns of social and historical change (Elder, 1994; Hareven, 1994). The **life-course perspective** provides a number of useful concepts to help us understand the connections between personal and public issues so eloquently described by Mills. First, this perspective emphasizes the significance of **birth cohorts**. Many of us are familiar with the ways in which membership in particular social groups – such as social classes, or ethnic and racial groups – affect our **life-chances**. For example, people from poorer socio-economic backgrounds may be less likely to get a college education, which in turn may have consequences for how much they are likely to earn in their life-times. It is also true that people have shared experiences by virtue of being born around the same time, and by moving through life – and history – together.

We have become increasingly familiar with this idea in contemporary Ireland, as it has become clear that the consequences of the 'Celtic Tiger' and the 'Great Recession' varied, depending on what life stage you were at during these historical periods, and when you made key **life transitions**, such as setting up house, or starting a family. In trying to understand family change, sociologists have increasingly emphasized the importance of adopting a life-course perspective, because 'snapshot' representations of family patterns at particular historical moments can be misleading. For example, a comparatively low proportion of people marrying might mean that the practice of marriage is dying out, but it might just be that a particular cohort of people are postponing marriage to a later age. This book adopts a life course perspective on family change in Ireland, focusing on changing family patterns from the perspective of different life stages. **For more on the relationship between life course patterns and trends in demographic behaviour, see Chapter 2.**

Plan of the book

In the first part of this book, we provide an overview of the key theoretical perspectives and empirical debates that have informed the sociology of the family. Chapter 1 introduces the idea of the 'modern family' that dominated sociological scholarship during most of the twentieth century (and which had its origins in nineteenth-century perspectives). In this chapter we also introduce the idea of **demographic transition**. Chapter 2 examines how sociologists have grappled with the rapid demographic and social changes that have affected western family lives since the 1960s, and introduces the conceptual framework for Part II of our book.

Part II aims to re-vision family change in Ireland from a qualitative longitudinal perspective. This part of the book explores the changing family experience from the perspectives of different life stages, drawing on the qualitative life narratives and semi-structured interviews in the two datasets described in Panel i.1 above. We examine the following life stages: childhood (Chapter 3), early adulthood (Chapter 4), parenting in the middle years (Chapter 5) and grandparenthood (Chapter 6). While we focus on continuity and change in the practices and experiences that make up everyday family life, we do not neglect the wider socio-historical context within which these continuities and changes occur. Throughout, we show how the **micro-practices** that made up people's individual family lives were played out in the context of **macro-societal changes** in **demography**, economy and values. We also emphasize the changing role of the state in responding to family patterns and in facilitating or constraining peoples' choices and practices. Throughout, we emphasize the Irish experience of family, highlighting exemplary Irish studies.

What makes Ireland interesting?

Ireland is an interesting case study for understanding changing patterns of family life for two reasons. First, as we have already noted, Irish family trends have changed very rapidly in recent years. Some of the most significant changes include:

1. Women are giving birth to fewer children
2. A considerably greater proportion of women are having babies outside marriage
3. More unmarried people live together in intimate partnerships
4. Divorce has been legalized and has become more acceptable
5. More mothers are participating in the paid labour force
6. Civil partnership, including for same-sex couples, has been recognized in law

Compared to other European countries, in Ireland many of these changes have been compressed into a shorter time span. Ireland is interesting precisely because its family trends have often seemed out of step with those of its European neighbours. As we will describe in Chapter 1, there is a growing body of research showing that the demography of Ireland is not as distinct as scholars once thought. Nevertheless, by comparing Ireland with other countries, we can learn a lot, not just about our own family patterns, but also about the

Panel i.2   Discussion: what do we mean by 'the family'?

Many sociologists argue that families are increasingly diverse, especially compared to the recent past. As we go through our lives, more of us move in and out of a greater range of family relationships than our parents did. For example, a child might begin life living with a single parent, then spend some time living with his or her mother and a step-father, then with a divorced parent and step-siblings. **As we will see in Chapter 3, however, most children across Europe spend most of their childhoods living with both parents**. No doubt you can think of other possible sequences at different life stages. Other factors leading to increasing family diversity include the use of new reproductive technologies, growing recognition of gay and lesbian families, and transnational family relationships. These changes challenge us to think about what we mean by 'the family'.

Bunreacht na hÉireann (Constitution of Ireland, 1937) describes the family as an institution founded on marriage. Over the years, government legislation, and amendments to the Constitution, have recognized changes in the form of marriage in Irish society. **See Chapter 4 for a more detailed discussion on the 'deinstitutionalization' of marriage.** For example, legal discrimination against children born outside marriage was abolished by the Status of Children Act in 1987. Provision for divorce was introduced in 1997. Most recently, civil partnership for same-sex couples, and 'marriage-like' protections for cohabiting couples, were introduced in 2011. The Irish state has extended the right to marriage to same-sex couples, following a referendum held in May 2015.

Do you think marriage is central to the definition of the family? Ask yourself whether or not the following might be considered 'family' in different circumstances:

1. A married couple without children
2. A gay couple with children
3. Two bachelor brothers living together on a farm
4. All the relatives a bride invites to her wedding
5. An intimate friend that you see every day and who has always been there in times of trouble and sickness

In everyday life we think of 'family' both in terms of the kinds of relationships that are involved – whether or not people are married, or are connected by 'blood' – and in terms of the quality of the relationships involved – we expect relationships between family members to be characterized by affection and a regular pattern of give and take.

To make matters more complicated, we tend to include different people in our understanding of 'family' depending on the context. The 'extended' family we invite to our wedding or expect to show up at our funeral is generally larger than the 'immediate' family with whom we share our daily lives, but we do not expect our relations with extended family members to have the same quality as those with our immediate family. Indeed, as sociologists are beginning to recognize, in everyday life our relationships with friends and neighbours can sometimes be more 'family like' than those with more distant 'blood' relatives. **Chapters 1 and 2 provide an introduction to some key concepts and ideas with which to describe and explain our changing understanding of 'family'.**

likely causes of family trends throughout the western world. By making comparisons, sociologists try to identify the common factors behind shared trends, and also the factors giving rise to differences amongst countries. Throughout this book, Irish family processes will be compared with those of other countries, primarily in Europe and North America. The increased availability of qualitative longitudinal research in other countries – such as scholarship from the *Timescapes* project in the United Kingdom (Neale et al., 2012) – also makes Ireland an interesting comparative case for understanding changing meanings, practices and displays.

Finally, Ireland is interesting because there is a wealth of fascinating ethnographic, historical and survey research on family life, dating back to the early part of the twentieth century. We believe that the value of this scholarship has been underestimated both within Ireland and in comparative research on family change. Throughout this book we provide detailed accounts of landmark studies in Irish family research.

In the next chapter, we begin our journey by showing how, by the middle of the twentieth century, sociologists concluded that a particular family type, which they called the nuclear, or **conjugal family**, functioned best within modern industrial societies. While many sociologists would no longer agree with this theory, it has exerted a powerful influence within the field of family studies and continues to inform everyday assumptions about the nature of family change.

Key concepts and ideas in the Introduction

- Private troubles and public issues
- Ecological fallacy
- Convergence to diversity
- Ideal type
- How people 'do family' in their everyday lives
- How people 'display family' in different social contexts
- Qualitative longitudinal data
- Life-course perspective on family change

Part I

Questioning the modern family

1

The idea of the modern family

Traditional family unit dying away. (Quinn – *Irish Independent* 16 December 2011)
Traditional family farm under threat. (*Irish Examiner* 6 February 2014)

We are used to reading news reports and commentaries about the 'traditional family'. We also frequently come across advertisements urging us to enjoy a 'traditional family holiday' or buy produce from a 'traditional family run' firm. But what do we mean by 'traditional family'? Consider the following vignettes derived from the LHSC interviews:

Seamus (b. 1916, LHSC) grew up on a small farm in the 1910s and 1920s and met his future wife, a farmer's daughter, 'on an open platform' – that is, a dance in the open air – in the mid-1940s. Four years later they married. He was in his early thirties and she two years younger. Seamus' father made the farm over to him the previous year. The agreement included stipulations that Seamus' parents would continue living in the house and that 'you should bury them and everything like that, keep them clothed'. Although Seamus' mother died shortly after his marriage, his father lived for another twenty years and his wife's mother also came to live with them because she did not get along with her own daughter-in-law. Seamus and his wife had seven children, 'they came too fast'. He told the interviewer that there was nobody with whom you could discuss things like family planning in those days. (Seamus, b. 1916, LHSC)

John (b. 1946, LHSC) grew up on a small farm in the 1940s and 1950s and started going to dances as a teenager. He remembered 'some of the lads coming home from England ... [with] a 'French letter' [condom] and of course they would be big guys and they wouldn't even know how to use it!' At age sixteen John secured a job in the public service. He met his future wife, Sharon, at a trade union meeting. They married four years later when he was in his late twenties, 'which was old at the time for a fellow ... a lot of my friends were married at twenty-one'. Sharon

15

left work two years later and when John was promoted the two of them moved
to a large urban centre. They were four years married before the first of two children arrived. They offered to build a 'granny flat' for Sharon's mother, as Sharon
didn't want her to live in the same house because her 'husband and children came
first' and she felt that her mother would interfere in raising the children. Sharon
returned to work shortly before John retired, when their second child had finished
his education. (John, b. 1946, LHSC)

From today's perspective, both Seamus' and John's families might seem
quite traditional. However, at the middle of the last century, John's family
would have been thought rather modern. Throughout this book we will argue
that many of the assumptions we often make about the decline of the 'traditional family' are based on nostalgic and inaccurate images of family life in the
past, and 'snapshot' images that make us unduly pessimistic about families in
the present. Nevertheless, as Seamus's and John's stories illustrate, there were
significant changes in Irish family life between the 1940s and the 1970s.

Throughout most of the twentieth century, the idea that the 'modern
family' has a different size, structure and set of functions from traditional families dominated sociological thinking about family change. This chapter traces
this idea from its origins in the classical, evolutionary statements of the nineteenth century to the structural-functionalist perspective that predominated
in mid-twentieth-century sociology. The chapter also introduces the theory
of **demographic transition** and the emergence of new challenges to the idea
of the modern family that are explored further in Chapter 2. Along the way,
we introduce some key concepts in family sociology, and describe some classic
studies of Irish family life.

The nineteenth-century heritage:
classical perspectives on families and social change

During the nineteenth century European social thinkers began to accumulate
systematic evidence from around the world that seemed to show that 'the
family', as they understood it, did not exist in all societies. In trying to make
sense of these differences, they developed explanations that centred on the
idea that modern families had evolved from older or more primitive forms. The
nineteenth century was also a period of rapid social change in Europe itself,
with many families leaving the countryside to seek employment in industrial
urban centres, leading to concerns that the overthrow of long-established
social hierarchies – of generation, gender and class – would give rise to increasing disorder. These social conditions gave rise to ambivalent perspectives on
family change that have, in varying guises, persisted to the present day.

Here we will examine the ideas of two nineteenth-century thinkers who have
had considerable influence on sociological theories about families: Friedrich

Engels and Frédéric Le Play. In the course of our excursion through past ideas, we illuminate some of the concepts that are essential for thinking clearly about what we mean when we talk about 'families'. We also provide an introduction to how these concepts have been used in research on Irish families.

Kinship and marriage systems: Friedrich Engels

Friedrich Engels was, of course, Karl Marx's friend and collaborator. In 1884, after Marx's death, he published *The Origin of the Family, Private Property and the State* where, drawing on the work of anthropologist Lewis Henry Morgan, he linked the emergence of the family, as his fellow Victorians understood it, to the evolution of state ordered societies based on private property. In order to understand Engels' (1972 [1884]) argument, we need to know something about kinship systems.

Each of us is related to other people (living or dead), either through 'blood' – that is, the biological link between parent and child, brother and sister – or through the sexual connection between man and woman. The term **kin** refers to the group of living persons who are related to us, while **kindred** refers to the group of relatives we recognize through the genealogical links in our memory (Segalen, 1986: 43 and 55). **Kinship**, however, refers to a social institution that governs society to a greater or lesser extent. In some societies, the institution of kinship governs all aspects of social life, including politics, the economy and religion. From the perspective of individuals, the kinship group to which they belong may determine who they marry, and where they work and live. Moreover, societies differ as to how they identify the members of different kinship groups. A detailed account of kinship – a specialist topic within the field of anthropology – is beyond the scope of this book. However, a brief discussion of some key concepts will suffice to make sense of evolutionary perspectives on family change, and to provide the context for understanding contemporary ideas about extended family relationships. **See Chapter 2 for more on this topic.**

Kinship systems vary according to rules of **filiation** – who is considered to be your ancestor or your descendent – and according to rules of **alliance** – which persons you are permitted to marry. In contemporary Ireland the system of filiation is **undifferentiated**: we recognize both our father's and mother's ancestors as part of our kinship group, although we do have a leaning to our father's side. If you were to trace your family tree, you would probably find it easier to begin with your father's ancestors because the family name and any property are likely to have descended along your father's **line**. However, in other societies, only ancestors and descendents on *either* the father's or mother's side are recognized as relatives. This is called **unilineal** filiation.

Most commonly, in **patrilineal** (or **agnatic**) systems, names, privileges, rights and obligations are passed from father to son. A newly married couple will live with, or near, the husband's father's family (**patrilocal** residence). In some (**matrilineal**) societies, however, descent is traced from mother to daughter, and husbands tend to live with or near their wives' families (**matri-local** residence). In societies with unilineal descent systems, individuals may be identified as members of a particular descent group, or **lineage**, traced to a common ancestor. Lineages are at the heart of how such societies are organized. The term **clan** refers to descent groups where the common ancestor has become mythical, and no direct genealogical link can be traced to living individuals. Lineages may therefore be subsets of clans.

In addition to rules of filiation, all societies have rules about who a person can and cannot marry. In every society **incest** is prohibited, but the definition of incestuous relationships varies to some extent. In some societies, marriage rules not only ensure that individuals marry outside their own kinship group (**exogamy**), they also prescribe the group from which a spouse must be taken (**endogamy**). Such **elementary marriage systems** (which may seem quite complicated to us) ensure that different descent groups are socially linked through marriage. Under **complex marriage systems** – like our own – the rules specify only those people who we may not marry. In practice, however, the range of people from whom we choose a partner is not entirely open. Sociological research has shown that we tend to choose partners from within our own social class or ethnic group. For example, in Ireland, people tend to marry partners with the same average level of education as their own (Halpin and Chan, 2003). This phenomenon is called **homogamy**.

Now, having introduced some key concepts in the study of kinship, let us return to Engels' argument about the origin of the family. Synthesizing Morgan's ideas he argued that marriage systems had changed alongside the evolution of human 'modes of production'. The Marxist concept of **mode of production** refers to the major ways in which societies are organized in order to meet the material needs of their members – for food, warmth and shelter – and to ensure their continuity over time.

Engels argued that as human societies became more dependent on agriculture, rules about marriage and sexual intercourse became increasingly restrictive. In the first phase of this transformation, women and men formed partnerships, but monogamy was not strictly enforced and the marriages could be easily dissolved. Most importantly, Engels argued that the matrilineal 'clan' remained more important in everyday life than the marital relationship, because it controlled access to resources for cultivating crops or grazing animals. This meant that women and children were socially and economically dependent on the clan rather than on husbands and fathers. However, in the second phase this changed alongside the development of civilization and the state.

As agriculture became productive enough to support groups of people who were directly engaged in production, such as political rulers, priests, soldiers and craftsmen, kinship became less important for how societies were organized and governed. In state societies, agricultural production was carried out by family based households rather than by clans. According to Engels, alongside the development of civilization, the nuclear family became separated from the clan group, and there was a switch from matrilineal to patrilineal descent and patrilocal residence. This secured male dominance over women and children leading, in Engels' colourful phrase, to 'the world-historical defeat of the female sex'.

How did this happen? According to Engels, over time, the domestication of animals led to a decline in the significance of hunting for human subsistence, so that men displaced women in the fields and spent more time around the home. The accumulation of wealth by individual men led to conflict between the marital family and the matrilineal clan. Men wanted to see their property passed on to their own children, rather than having it dispersed amongst the members of their wife's clan. They therefore enforced the change to patrilineal descent and, in order to ensure that their property was passed on to their own children, insisted on monogamy for women.

Before the advent of DNA testing, enforced chastity for women was the only way that men could be absolutely certain that the children their wives gave birth to were their own. This led to the consolidation of the patriarchal, **bourgeois family**, which predominated in the England of Engels' own time. In such families the father ruled over his wife and children and acted on behalf of the household within the public sphere governed by the state. However Engels believed that the development of industrial society would lead to a further change in the family, both because the growing class of people who worked for capitalist employers had no property to protect, and because women's employment outside the home reduced their dependence on men.

Many scholars have been fascinated and inspired by Engels' extraordinary attempt to link kinship and family change to socio-economic evolution. Today, we know that both Morgan and Engels made some false inferences from their limited ethnographic knowledge. Engels, in particular, erred in confusing matrilineal descent systems with **matriarchy**. While women often do have more social influence in matrilineal systems (and such systems are indeed more commonly found in horticultural societies), women are not the dominant sex, nor do they have equal status with men (although they may have higher status than in patrilineal societies). In matrilineal societies a woman's uncles and brothers are the dominant men in her life, in contrast to patrilineal societies where fathers and husbands dominate. Despite these problems, as we will see, scholars continue to be inspired by the basic logic of Engels argument – that particular forms of family life (including patterns of power and inequality within families) – emerge in different socio-economic contexts.

Households and family systems: Frédéric Le Play

Engels tried to develop a big theory of family change, linking kinship and marriage practices to the evolution and transformation of social relations in different modes of production. By contrast Frédéric Le Play focused his attention

Panel 1.1   Landmark Irish study: *The Tory Islanders*
by Robin Fox (1978)

The anthropologist Robin Fox began his **ethnographic** study of Tory Island, a small island off the north coast of Donegal, in 1960 and continued to visit the island for the next five years. His resulting 1978 publication *The Tory Islanders* presents several aspects of the island's social structure including practices around **kinship**, inheritance and household formation. According to Fox, due to its physical and ecological isolation, by the 1960s, Tory remained relatively immune to many of the external pressures that had affected the mainland. The island offered 'in a strange sense ... a semifossilized history' (p. x) where more ancient systems of land tenure and inheritance, long gone from the rest of the country, lingered on. Some of these systems appeared distinctly pre-famine and different from those seen elsewhere in Ireland at the time. Fox's study therefore offers a counterpoint to the classic anthropological study of the rural west of Ireland by Arensberg and Kimball (2001 [1940]) (see Panel 1.2, p. 22).

In *The Tory Islanders* Fox presented the genealogies of the islanders in great detail, and uncovered how they used strings of personal names to uniquely identify each person according to his or her **lineage**, or descent group. In one example, people that were descended from a widow named Nellie Doohan were identified as either 'Liam-Nellies' or 'Eoghan-Nellies', depending on which of her sons they were descended from. The 'Eoghan-Nellies' could be further subdivided into 'John-Eoghan-Nellies' and so on. In this **cognatic descent system**, people could be identified through the names of their **patrilateral ancestors** (on their fathers' side), their **matrilateral ancestors** (on their mother's side) or both. Fox found that there was a clear overall preference amongst both men and women for identifying themselves through their father's (and father's father's) names, but that a minority of people adopted matrilateral names.

Another notable practice on the island, reported by Fox, was that in many cases after marriage men and women continued to live separately in the home of their parents rather than 'betray' the solidarity of their own families by living together in a new household. Fox also discovered remnants of the rundale system of land use on the island, a practice that was widespread in Ireland before the famine. In principle, the rundale system operates as a system of group ownership of land and other resources, and each member of the group has use rights to these resources for the duration of their lifetime.

on explaining differences in the **family systems** whereby customs, values and resources were transferred across the generations. Family systems can be defined as preferred patterns of 'recruitment' into **households** or **domestic groups**. They specify 'who should live with whom at which stages of the life course; the social, sexual, and economic rights and obligations of individuals occupying different kin positions in relation to each other; and the division of labour among kin related individuals' (Mason, 2001: 161). Le Play linked different family systems to variations in the physical environment which created the conditions for making a living (Mogey, 1955).

According to Le Play (1872: 64), in places with 'vast undivided pastures', such as the Asian steppes, the patriarchal family system predominated. Large extended families, including married sons, their wives and children, lived together (or in close proximity) under the authority of a ruling father. When the older couple died, a new patriarchal head took over. If the family became too large for the resources available to it, 'the elders will give up part of the common property in animals, equipment, and specialist personnel, and this new group will leave the ancestral hearth like a swarm of bees to settle down and found a similar colony in a new region' (Mogey, 1955: 313). For Le Play, this system had the advantage of securing the transfer of values, customs and practices across the generations. However, it tended to inhibit innovation and technological progress (Le Play, 1872: 65).

An **unstable family system** existed at the opposite extreme, according to Le Play. Characteristic of what he viewed as 'barbarous' hunting and gathering societies and the 'degraded' conditions of urban industrial settings, in unstable families sons would leave their parents' households to marry and set up on their own 'as soon as they gain any confidence in themselves' (Le Play, 1872: 41). While this system favoured innovation, it failed to ensure the transmission of custom, values and practices from one generation to another, and could lead to the isolation and abandonment of people in old age (Mogey, 1955: 313). For Le Play, the unstable family was a threat to 'social harmony'.

In between the two extremes, Le Play placed the **stem-family system** (or 'famille souche'), which he argued was typical of developed agricultural regions in western and central Europe where the land was fully occupied. Under this system, one son, whom the father thought 'most capable of fulfilling the duties marked out by custom' (Le Play, 1872: 42), was designated to inherit the family property. When he married, he moved into his parents' household (or close by). The other sons and daughters were endowed with 'the amount laid up with his earnings in one generation' (Le Play, 1872: 42) and they were then free to establish their own independent households. Le Play saw the stem-family as an ideal compromise between the patriarchal and unstable family forms: it facilitated enterprise and innovation amongst new families while preserving customary values and practices by maintaining the continuity of older families across the generations. Le Play believed that French law, which required the equal partition of property amongst all the children in a family, was contrary to the best interests of the family (and society) and he advocated returning the right to dispose of property as they wished to male household heads.

While Le Play's typology of family systems is not explicitly evolutionary, it does implicitly incorporate a theory of social change; Le Play argued that agricultural people 'abrogated' the patriarchal family system, adapting their institutions once 'the soil is completely appropriated to culture and divided into distinct properties' (Le Play, 1872: 64). Like Engels, Le Play did not believe that the most modern type of family he observed (the urban, unstable form) was an improvement on what had gone before, but in contrast to Engels he hoped for a return to a more desirable, traditional family form, rather than for a better future.

As we will see in more detail below, and in Chapter 2, Le Play's model of different family systems inspired a tradition of scholarly research that continues to be highly influential amongst those seeking to explain regional and global variations in family patterns, both in the past and in the present. This perspective has particular relevance for understanding the scholarship on Irish families (see Panel 1.6, p. 35).

Panel 1.2   Landmark Irish study: *Family and Community in Ireland* **by Conrad M. Arensberg and Solon T. Kimball (2001 [1940])**

Frederic Le Play's depiction of the **stem-family system** is of particular relevance to Ireland, because of the influence of a study undertaken in the 1930s by two American anthropologists, Conrad Arensberg and Solon Kimball, as part of the wider Harvard Irish Study. Arensberg and Kimball spent a number of years living in a small farming community in north Co. Clare and their resulting ethnography *Family and Community in Ireland* has been one of the most influential texts in twentieth-century Irish family studies.

Arensberg and Kimball depicted family life in Irish farming communities as diverging significantly from family arrangements in other parts of the world, principally because of the predominance of the stem-family system. In a practice known as **primogeniture**, the eldest or first born son inherited the entire family estate (generally between 30 and 200 acres of farmland and a homestead) upon his father's retirement. Maintaining the familial line on a farm holding was of primary concern and necessitated a strict sexual code for unmarried family members. Marriage itself was a 'crisis' that had to be carefully managed by the families involved. In a practice known as **matchmaking**, the inheriting son was matched with a suitable bride, while all non-inheriting children remained unmarried until they were dispersed from the family homestead. Money raised from the dowry passed to the groom's father who (in theory at least) used this sum to disperse his younger offspring into professions, or, as was most commonly the case, through assisting their emigration from Ireland.

What made rural Ireland such an interesting case study for the Harvard team was that it seemed to be an outlier at the time. The distinctive family practices seen in Clare, the authors argued, were largely a response to the long post-famine adjustment of the Irish economy. This adjustment involved a transition from subsistence tillage to commercial livestock agriculture, with landholdings no longer subdivided among several off-spring but instead inherited by a single successor. Securing property became a precondition for marriage in this post-famine economic system. This further explains why the age of marriage in most instances was so high, as generally the successor son was well into middle-age by the time his father retired and signed the family farm over to him.

Being the first in-depth treatment of Irish family and community life, Arensberg and Kimball's book quickly became a 'classic'; however, in the 1970s, serious challenges to their portrayal began to emerge. One critic wrote that 'on every score ... [Arensberg and Kimball's] account ranges from the inaccurate to the fictive'. Others took issue with how applicable their depiction of Irish farming families actually was, citing census data and other ethnographic work to suggest that the picture of the stem-family was only valid for the west of Ireland, and only before the 1950s. In other words, the stem-family was atypical and far from the statistical norm in Ireland. Others showed how the size of families had been declining even since the beginning of the twentieth-century, while single and no-family households were growing in number (for a com-prehensive review of the literature, see Byrne et al., 2001). We return to aspects of these debates later in this chapter, when we discuss evidence for and against the prevalence of the stem-family in north-west Europe and in Ireland.

It is clear that Arensberg and Kimball's account is meant to be an **ideal type**, of the kind we discussed in the introduction to this book. Indeed, their study reveals that many of the real families that they encountered failed to conform fully to their ideal-typical representation. Nevertheless, as we show throughout this book, the life story narratives of many of the older participants in the *Family Rhythms* study suggest that Arensberg and Kimball did indeed capture some fundamental aspects of family life in rural Ireland during the first half of the twentieth century. Their study should not be approached uncritically, but neither should it be dismissed out of hand.

The twentieth-century heritage: perspectives on modernization

During the first half of the twentieth century, social scientists and other observers began to document a significant shift away from the corporate interests of
extended family groups, such as those depicted in Arensberg and Kimball's
account, towards a new focus on the interests of parents and their children
– that is, on the nuclear or **conjugal family**. In order to understand the wider
context for these developments, we need to introduce some concepts and evidence from the field of **demography**.

Demographic transition

Demography is the scientific study of population. Demographers seek to explain
shifts in the size and structure of human populations by examining trends in
the number of births and deaths, and in patterns of ageing and migration. The
fields of demography and family sociology have evolved separately from one
another, although there are obvious and important relationships amongst
the subjects they are concerned with. Demographic changes have major consequences for family life. For example, increasing life expectancy means that,
on average, children and adolescents today have the opportunity to interact
with more of their grandparents than in the past. In turn, changes in people's
family behaviour have consequences for demography. For example, as people
choose to have fewer children the birth rate may decline. The phenomenon of
demographic transition is at the heart of contemporary population dynamics
and of the changing family patterns that concern sociologists.

When scholars like Engels and Le Play developed their ideas about family
change, most human societies were characterized by high rates of fertility (number of births per woman) and by high rates of mortality (number
of deaths per population) – especially amongst infants and young children.
However, this was about to change. First, mortality rates began to decline,
primarily because of improvements in public sanitation and hygiene. Second,
from the 1880s and 1890s, in most European countries, couples began to limit
the number of babies that they had (this occurred much earlier in France and
in the United States, see Guinnane 2011). This was not, at first, due to the
availability of new methods of contraception, although condoms made from
vulcanized rubber that were more reliable and easier to use were introduced
around the middle of the nineteenth century (Guinnane, 2011). Nevertheless,
historical demographers believe that, together with periodic abstinence, coitus
interruptus, or withdrawal, was the most widely used method of birth control
before the twentieth century.

In Ireland, there was a longstanding belief that the demographic transition did not begin until much later than in other west European countries.
However, there is evidence that many couples, particularly in urban areas –
but also in some rural areas – were taking steps to control their fertility, at least

Panel 1.3   Landmark Irish Study: *Jewish Ireland in the Age of Joyce*
by Cormac Ó Gráda (2006)

Dublin's Jewish community is rarely mentioned in social and economic histories of the city primarily due to its small size. Nevertheless, Jewish immigrants, mainly from Lithuania, began to settle in Dublin, and to a smaller extent in Cork and Belfast, at the turn of the century. Cormac Ó Gráda's *Jewish Ireland in the Age of Joyce* offers a compelling account of the Lithuanian Jews, or Litvaks, that fled pogroms in Tsarist Russia and arrived in Irish cities around the 1870s, before disappearing largely again by the early-1940s.

Using a large combination of sources, including public and private archival records, autobiographical memoirs and interviews, Ó Gráda tells the story of Irish Jewry, principally that of the three-thousand strong population of Dublin who congregated mostly around 'Little Jerusalem' – an area stretching from Portobello to Clanbrassil Street around the Grand Canal, and seeping into the middle-class suburbs of Rathgar and Terenure in the south-west of the city. Ó Gráda profiles their settlement and occupational trajectories, showing how their living and working conditions shifted from generation to generation. These shifts are largely a story of successful gentrification and a gradual move from proletarian occupations – petit trading, peddling – into the professions.

Where Ó Gráda's account becomes particularly interesting from a family studies perspective is his analysis of household-level data from decennial census returns. Using data from the 1911 Census, Ó Gráda showed that age specific Jewish marital fertility was higher amongst the first generation of Jewish immigrants than that of either Catholic or other Christians in the same urban neighbourhoods. In comparison to their non-Jewish neighbours, these Jewish immigrants married and started having children at a younger age, had more children early on in their marriage and stopped having children at a younger age. Comparing this with figures from the 1946 Census, Ó Gráda then uncovered a rapid **demographic transition** amongst the second generation of Jewish couples (the sons and daughters of these immigrants) to a pattern of low marital fertility and an accelerated lowering of child mortality rates. By the 1940s marriage fertility amongst Jews had declined to less than half that of Catholics and significantly less than that of Church of Ireland couples living in the same area, thus indicating a higher uptake of contraceptive technologies within Jewish couples.

In effect, this snapshot of Ireland's Jewish families reflects changes to family structures that were occurring in most other European societies at the time – a **demographic transition** to smaller family sizes and reduced mortality rates. This marked Jewish families out from the majority

> Christian population, who lagged behind European norms by continu-
> ing to have large families and high overall child mortality rates. But did
> the social networks between Jews and their non-Jewish neighbours have
> any impact on demographic patterns in Dublin during this period? While
> this is difficult to document, Ó Gráda states that 'given the close proxim-
> ity of one group to the other over half a century or so, it is not implausible
> to expect two-way cultural influences to have been at work' (p. 201).

by the first decade of the twentieth century, and probably earlier. This meant
that they had fewer children than if they had made no attempt to practice
birth control, although Irish family sizes remained high compared to other
European societies (Guinnane, 1997).

The shift from a demographic pattern of high fertility and high mortality, to
one of low fertility and low mortality is now a global phenomenon. Almost all
societies have begun the process of demographic transition. Mortality rates fell
much more rapidly in developing countries in the twentieth century than in
nineteenth-century Europe because of modern medical interventions, including vaccinations against common childhood diseases. As a result, the global
human population has continued to grow rapidly. Nevertheless, it is likely that
in the future the human species as a whole will be confronted with new challenges associated with global ageing – problems already being encountered by
those societies that entered the demographic transition in the nineteth and
early twentieth centuries.

We will return to demographic trends and their consequences for family life
throughout this book. Here, let's consider how demographers have explained
the adoption of birth control by growing numbers of couples in Europe and
North America during the nineteenth century. Most explanations centre on
the idea that this shift in behaviour was linked to the modernization of society.
In the decades after the Second World War, sociologists developed **modernization theory** to explain the rise of wealthy, industrial societies and to contrast
them with poorer societies – both in the present and the past – that were
thought to be more 'traditional'. Modernization was described as a set of fundamental, interdependent changes in the economy, the political system, social
institutions and social values.

According to 'classic demographic transition theory', or the **adaptation
view**, the trend towards smaller family sizes was mainly due to economic modernization. The changes brought about by industrialization and urbanization
initially produced a decline in mortality that 'set the stage' for fertility decline
by increasing the survival rates of children while simultaneously increasing
the costs of raising them (Mason, 2001). In other words, parents' confidence
that children would survive into adulthood increased. At the same time, in
contrast to agricultural societies where women's work and childcare could

---

Panel 1.4   Looking at the data: Irish family size and contraception

There is evidence that at least some people in Ireland were reducing their fertility long before modern methods of contraception were available and at a time when family planning was frowned on by both church and state (Guinnane, 1997). How did this come about? Kate Fisher (2000: 314) found that, in England and Wales, people did not actively plan their families, but instead adopted a 'vague and indecisive' approach to contraception that was nevertheless 'efficient enough to significantly reduce the frequency with which pregnancy occurred'. Is this also what happened in Ireland? Consider the following extracts from the LHSC interviews. What do they tell us about people's attitudes and practices around family planning?

Interviewer: And did you always plan to have a big family?
Rosemary: No, as a matter of fact I said to my husband 'Do you know this amazes me, your mammy had three from her first husband then she had three from her second husband. Why have I got so many [laughs]?' He said 'That's what it's all about'. He never wore a condom, no. He said it was against his religion, because we were both good Catholics. But to tell you the truth, I wouldn't be without any of them. No I wouldn't. I have eight sons and I have two daughters. (Rosemary, b. 1927, LHSC)

Ben: Well I have to say, I was never interested in children, the having of them, do you know. And like if I had had a choice I would have been a one child father, if that. I don't know where that comes from. But that is not to say that I don't love all the six that we have and they are wonderful, all of them, and the grandchildren are a treat to us. [...]
Interviewer: You said 'if you had a choice', does that mean that ...?
Ben: I wouldn't have had children, you know. And I don't know what it is, I think there is an innate bachelor in me, I don't know. I really love them and I have given them everything. [...]
Interviewer: So was it [your wife] who wanted a big family?
Ben: No, they happened! There was nothing done for 'safe period'* people. And every pregnancy you could say was unexpected, but that was the norm. It became a kind of a mini crisis. (Ben, b. 1926, LHSC)

* The 'safe period' method refers to the practice of limiting sexual intercourse to the period of the menstrual cycle when a woman is less likely to be ovulating, and therefore less likely to become pregnant during unprotected sex.

be carried on together around the home, in industrializing societies caring for children impacted on adults' – especially women's – capacity to earn wages. Legislation restricting the hours that children could work, and requiring them to spend more years in education, also meant that children's economic contribution to the family declined. Under these circumstances, parents chose to invest their resources in a smaller number of economically 'worthless' but emotionally 'priceless' children (Zelizer, 1985).

According to an alternative, **innovation/diffusion** view, modernization affected family sizes primarily through the diffusion of new values emphasizing individualism and self-fulfilment. Perhaps the declining importance of religion meant that people no longer felt it was immoral to try to improve their lot by having fewer children. Or perhaps the growing influence of scientific thinking led to a less fatalistic view of humanity's place in the natural world, so that people increasingly believed that such things as fertility were within their control.

Modernization and the conjugal family

Changing demographic behaviour formed the backdrop to changing family relationships. Writing in 1948, Ernest Burgess argued that American families had undergone a shift from what he described as an **institutional form**, in which the bonds between family members were enforced by law, custom, public opinion and duty, to a **companionship form**, in which family bonds depended on the quality of inter-personal relationships – on feelings of affection and love. Burgess described the change from the institutional to companionship form of the family as one of democratization and growing equality: men's power over women and parents' power over their children was diminished in modern families. He attributed the change to urbanization and changing ideology. In urban environments, he argued, the family ceased to be a unit of production, and new opportunities for separate recreational activities opened up for younger people. Both trends tended to reduce the power of fathers over their wives and children. Burgess also attributed the democratization of the American family to the distinctive emphasis on freedom and the opportunity for self-expression in American society.

Twentieth-century modernization perspectives on social change included a **convergence thesis** as one of their key propositions: all around the world, social institutions, including the family would tend to converge as societies underwent the modernizing processes of industrialization and urbanization. Perhaps one of the best-known statements about the modernization of the family is found in a book first published by sociologist William J. Goode in 1963, entitled *World Revolution in Family Patterns*. Goode argued that the diverse family patterns that existed around the world were being altered by modernization to converge on a conjugal family form. Goode summarized the processes associated with the emergence of the conjugal family as follows:

1. Extended kinship ties decline in importance. The sense of mutual obligation we feel towards family members outside the conjugal unit of parents and children becomes much less pronounced.
2. Residence becomes neolocal. Newly married couples no longer feel constrained to live near either the husband's or wife's parents.
3. Choice of mate becomes freer and based on mutual attraction. Arranged marriages become less common.
4. The kinship system becomes undifferentiated. Increasingly, ancestors from both one's father's and one's mother's line are recognized as kin.
5. The small conjugal unit becomes the main source of emotional sustenance. People become less likely to turn to extended family members for emotional support.
6. There is a growing emphasis on individual fulfilment within families. The quality of family life is increasingly evaluated according to how well it meets the emotional and expressive requirements of its members.

Why should we expect modernization to have these consequences for families? As we have seen, structural-functionalist theorists seek to explain social institutions with reference to the functions they perform for the maintenance and reproduction of society as a whole. In his analysis, Goode (1963) emphasized how the conjugal family provided a better fit for modern, open societies, because it facilitated both spatial and social mobility. In industrial societies people must be able to set up house where job opportunities arise. Similarly, in societies where social positions are attained through merit – for example, through the attainment of formal educational qualifications – individuals must be in a position to avail of opportunities for social mobility, that is, to improve the social position of their families. Both forms of mobility are inhibited where family life entails onerous obligations to extended kin: young married adults would find it difficult to move away from ageing parents, for example. Similarly, obligations to provide financial assistance to brothers and sisters would limit the extent to which parents were able to accumulate savings to pass on to their own children.

In seeking to explain the structure of modern conjugal families, Parsons and Bales (1956) focused on a different set of functions. They observed that while many of the functions formerly performed by the kinship system had been taken over by more specialized institutions in modern societies (such as the state and the education system), the conjugal family unit retained the core functions of stabilizing adult personalities (by which they meant providing a kind of 'refuge' for emotional sustenance, away from the public world of work) and of caring for young children. They argued that children had two distinct sets of needs, requiring the specialization of adult roles. Children have **instrumental needs**, insofar as they require access to the material conditions for survival (money to pay for food, clothing, housing and so on), and **expressive needs**, insofar as they require daily nurturance, love and care in order to

Panel 1.5   Landmark Irish study: *New Dubliners* **by Alexander Humphreys (1966)**

Humphreys' *New Dubliners* was conceived as a sequel to Arensberg and Kimball's *Family and Community in Ireland* (see Panel 1.2, p. 22). Humphreys, a Jesuit priest, was in broad agreement with the Harvard researchers about the role and composition of the rural Irish farming family and community. Ireland's economy was still predominantly based on agriculture when Humphreys undertook his fieldwork between 1949 and 1951. Nevertheless Humphreys showed that in the preceding few decades people from the countryside had been 'thronging into Dublin' (p. 3), as the capital's industrial capacity grew. He felt this merited exploring the transition of these country families from rural to urban life, in other words the urbanization of these families. He chose a sample of twenty-nine Catholic families where at least one of the spouses was a 'New Dubliner' – that is, a first-generation resident of Dublin, born and raised in the capital, whose parents had moved from rural Ireland.

Humphreys found that 'the New Dubliner's family differed significantly from that of the countryman in its internal structure' (p. 33), insofar as the gender division of labour was markedly redrawn in such families. For New Dubliners, in the main, the father worked as the sole breadwinner, principally outside the home for either a corporation or a government agency, whereas in the countryman's family (Humphreys' expression) all family members worked on the farm co-operatively. For New Dubliners, running the private sphere (the home) devolved almost entirely to the mother because of the father's day-time absence, whereas for the countryman such duties were roughly shared, as both father and mother were present in and around the home.

This had profound consequences, Humphreys wrote, for family relationships. 'In the rural fashion' (p. 34) the father was traditionally domineering and authoritarian in relation to both his wife and children. 'Under urban conditions' (p. 35) this was much less the case, as it was the mother who had direct responsibility for domestic affairs; fathers played a less central role in disciplining children because they were away at work, and affectionate father–children bonds strengthened as a result. What's more, husband–wife relations grew more democratic, as fathers and mothers saw themselves more as 'partners' in running the family, whereas the 'rural wife is generally subordinate to her spouse' (p. 34). Yet, because the New Dubliner wife was no longer directly involved in earning money (rural wives sold eggs, vegetables, livestock, alongside their other chores), there was a corresponding loss of status, 'since the primary grounds for status in Dublin, as in all the industrial nations of the west, normally lies in income-producing activity' (p. 34).

The pattern of inheritance also changed with this move to the city. Since most city families did not own productive holdings in the first place, and since children would normally find gainful employment outside the home during their adolescence, the marriage of the oldest or firstborn son, 'so central in the cycle of the rural family, simply ceases to be as crucial a factor in the lives of the New Dubliners' (p. 35).

City life, however, did not only affect the 'inner equilibrium' of the family. It also frayed wider kin and neighbourhood bonds that were so robust in the countryside. Because urban individuals relied primarily on impersonal organizations (corporations, government) for a livelihood, community ties were not so central to career advancement. What's more, values, attitudes and belief systems were also transformed among this new generation of urbanites, who were pointedly more secular, more liberal, more licentious, more aspirational, and more egocentric than their rural forebears.

grow up well. Thus Parsons and Bales identified what later became known as the **breadwinner family** – whereby fathers attended to children's instrumental needs through their work outside the home, and mothers attended to children's expressive needs through their work inside the home – as functional for modern societies.

Challenges to modernization theory: the exceptional 1950s

A common critique levelled at **modernization theory** was that it tended to treat mid-twentieth-century American society as a kind of endpoint of history (Cherlin, 2012). In the post-Second World War climate, the United States was a prosperous global economic and cultural hegemonic power and therefore seemed to represent the epitome of a new highly adaptive and functional social system. As we will see in Chapter 2, continuing patterns of family change have contributed towards undermining the view that mid-twentieth-century American families represented the quintessential modern form. Many of the family patterns that seemed 'normal' to observers in the 1950s and 1960s have since been shown to be aberrant when placed in a longer historical context.

Sociologist Andrew Cherlin (1992) showed that trends in marriage and childbearing took an unusual turn in the 1950s. People began to marry earlier than previously, and to have more children. Subsequently, in the 1970s, trends in American family formation reverted to patterns more similar to those that prevailed before the War. This post-War spike in family formation occurred across the developed world, including in Ireland (Coleman, 1992), leading to the 'baby boom', although in many European societies the surge in births was caused mainly by an increase in the number of people marrying, without an accompanying increase in the average number of births per woman.

Demographic post-War family patterns were intertwined with dramatic social and cultural changes in many western countries. As well as growing economic prosperity and rising wages, suburbanization and mass-produced housing made it possible for more working- and lower-middle-class people to aspire to what had formerly been upper-middle-class ideals of family life (Scanzoni, 2000). However, as Stephanie Coontz (1995) documented, not only were the demographic patterns of the post-War period unusual in a longer historical timeframe – 1950s America did not live up to its own TV-generated image of itself:

> happy-families sitcoms were aimed at young couples who had married in haste, women who had tasted new freedoms in World War II and given up their jobs with regret, and returning veterans whose children often resented their attempts to assert paternal authority. The message was clear: buy these ranch houses, appliances and new child-rearing ideals; relate to your spouse like this; organize your dinner like that – and you too can have harmonious families in which father knows best, mother is never bored and the teenagers are always eager to hear words of parental wisdom. (Coontz, 1995: 7)

Almost as soon as it was invented, cracks began to appear in the western post-War family ideal. In their classic study, Parsons and Bales (1956: 14–15) noted the presence of 'large numbers' of women in the American labour force but, concluded that:

> It seems quite safe in general to say that the adult feminine role has not ceased to be anchored primarily in the internal affairs of the family as wife, mother, and manager of the household, while the role of the adult male is primarily anchored in the occupational world, in his job and through it by his status-giving and income-earning functions for the family. Even if, as seems possible, it should come about that the average married woman had some kind of job, it seems most unlikely that this relative balance would be upset; that either the roles would be reversed, or their qualitative differentiation in these respects completely erased.

As we will see in Chapter 2 and in Chapter 4, since Parsons and Bales published their work, gender roles in families have indeed been transformed with consequences for many other aspects of contemporary family life (although we might agree with them that the different roles have not been 'completely erased'). First, however, we need to consider how social science research in the 1960s and 1970s began to undermine the structural-functionalist consensus, first by casting doubt on the idea that pre-industrial families were more likely to be extended and second by questioning the egalitarianism of companionate, symmetrical gender roles.

The extended family: missing or always there?

When Michael Young and Peter Wilmott (1957) published their study on *Family and Kinship in East London*, they documented a phenomenon that took many people by surprise, namely, the importance of extended kinship in the everyday lives of working-class people in one of the most advanced industrial cities of the world. The authors documented the extent to which family life was centred not so much on the husband–wife dyad as on a triangular relationship between a married daughter, her mother and her husband. Mothers were revealed to be at the heart of local kinship networks that structured everyday life. Married daughters 'dropped in' to their mothers almost daily and depended on them for practical and emotional support. When conjugal families were moved from Bethnal Green to new social housing estates in suburban areas they experienced considerable loneliness and isolation as a result of being separated from the networks of kinship that had sustained them in the East End.

Similarly, in an ethnographic study of poor black families in Chicago, anthropologist Carol Stack (1975) documented how mothers' survival strategies entailed the development of kin-extended networks in order to build up a stable number of people with whom they had reciprocal obligations and on whom they could call in times of difficulty. As in East London, she found these kinship networks to be female-centred. Stack's study formed part of a new wave of ethnographic research arguing that the family practices of poor black Americans represented adaptations to socio-economic disadvantage rather than a culturally distinctive way of life (Furstenberg, 2007: 440–441). In Ireland, Damian Hannan and Louise Katsiaouni (1977) found that farm couples who expressed the most 'modern' family values were those with the strongest and most extensive local kinship networks (Hannan and Katsiaouni's study is described in Panel 5.1, p. 133).

All of these studies were important because they highlighted the extent to which extended kinship relations continued to be at the heart of family life in modern urban environments and were consistent with modern value systems. At around the same time, historical demographers began to question the importance of extended family households in historic rural contexts.

As we saw earlier, Frédéric Le Play argued that a stem-family system existed in western agrarian societies before industrialization. Recall that, under this system, a designated heir brought a wife into his parents' household on marriage. This means that, in any given society with a stem-family system, one would expect to find a certain proportion of households comprising both an older and a younger married couple. However, beginning in the 1960s, evidence began to accumulate that from as early as the sixteenth century, at least in north-west Europe, nuclear-family households predominated. Detailed analyses of historic census data suggested that there were insufficient numbers of extended family to support the contention that a stem-family system was in place.

This evidence led historical demographers to argue that before industrialization north-west Europe had its own distinctive family system. In an influential article, John Hajnal (1982) contrasted this 'simple' household formation system with a complex form that prevailed in east Europe and Asia. In western Europe couples married and commenced childbearing relatively late. After marriage, a couple expected to be in charge of their own household. During the period between reaching adulthood and marriage, many young adults spent a period of time in service. This might allow them to accumulate savings that would help them establish their own home. It also ensured that a pool of young workers was available to meet the additional demand for labour that households might need at different stages of the family life-cycle – for example when children were too young to work and occupied much of a mother's time. By contrast, in the complex family systems of east Europe and Asia, women tended to marry and begin childbearing at a much younger age. Newly married couples started out their life together in households where an older married couple remained in charge. Over time, households with several married couples might split to form two or more separate households.

There are similarities between Hajnal's depiction and that of the nineteenth-century scholar, Frédéric Le Play, described earlier. However, there are also some important differences. First, Hajnal argued that west European stem-family households were really just a special form of the simple household system because they arose as part of an arrangement for the retirement of the household head. Thus the system did not necessarily entail a newly married couple living under the authority of an older couple. Second, Hajnal highlighted some important demographic implications of his western European system. In particular, the institution of life-cycle service operated as a means to regulate fertility (in the absence of birth control) by delaying marriage. This meant that regions where this **European marriage pattern** was in place were able to adapt flexibly to changes in economic circumstances by facilitating or limiting household formation and were always likely to contain comparatively large proportions of unmarried people.

The contentious argument that simple or conjugal families have always been at the heart of north-west European households has been the subject of an ongoing, specialist literature. Recent comparative-historical research drawing on large census micro-data samples casts doubt on the claim for a distinctive north-west European pattern, at least with respect to household structure (Ruggles, 2009: 2011). The quantitative research tradition on historic families is also problematic because of its reliance on census and census-type sources which do not reveal much about extended family ties *between* households (Plakans, 1977; Tadmor, 2010). Nevertheless, historical demographic research made an important contribution by highlighting the extent to which social science perspectives on the 'modern' family depended on relatively unexamined assumptions about the form and composition of 'traditional' families.

Panel 1.6   Discussion: was there a stem-family system in rural Ireland?

Because of the detailed ethnographic description of stem-family processes described in Arensberg and Kimball's classic study, there is an extensive literature on whether or not the stem-family system was ever the norm in rural Ireland. The question is also important for understanding Irish demography. As we will discuss in more detail in Chapter 2, early twentieth-century Ireland was characterized by very late ages at marriage and high proportions of never-married people, together with high rates of emigration. This meant that, despite very large family sizes (that is, a high rate of marital fertility), overall the birth rate (that is, the ratio of births to the population as a whole) was low. This has been attributed to the persistence of an extreme form of the European marriage pattern to a much later date in Ireland than elsewhere in west Europe.

Analyses of data samples from early twentieth-century censuses have provided mixed evidence (Carney, 1980; Fitzpatrick et al., 1983; Birdwell-Pheasant, 1992; Corrigan, 1993; Guinnane, 1997) for and against the stem-family. In the only statistically representative sample for Ireland as a whole, Corrigan found that less than 2 per cent of rural households were 'multiple family households' – that is, containing more than one married couple. On the other hand the proportions of 'extended family households' containing relatives other than members of the conjugal family unit were relatively high. Guinnane (1997: 146) concluded that: 'The rural Irish household at the turn of the twentieth century does not seem to fit cleanly into either the stem-family or the nuclear-family model'. More recently, however, Shimizu's (2014) analysis of population data from the 1901 and 1911 censuses has lent support to Hannan's (1972) argument that the west of Ireland represented a distinctive sociocultural zone where the stem-family system described by Arensberg and Kimball persisted well into the twentieth century.

The Irish case illustrates two problems with the historic households approach to understanding family systems. First, the likelihood of finding multiple-family households in an area at any given time depends on demographic factors that are somewhat independent of how people managed the processes of marriage and inheritance. When marriages occur at late ages, and the proportions of older people in a population are high, the numbers of multiple-family households will be comparatively low (Ruggles, 2009). At any given time, peoples' preference for a stem-family system of inheritance will not necessarily give rise to many households with two married couples residing together. Second, the focus on households ignores the extent to which family dynamics, including everyday forms of social support and inheritance practices, were embedded in kinship circles that incorporated multiple households (Gray, 2014).

Questions of power: feminism and household economics

During the 1970s, structural-functionalism was increasingly challenged by new voices arguing that families were sites of conflict and inequality, as well as adaptation. **Liberal feminist** critics argued that gender roles within families were not given in nature; rather they were perpetuated through a process of **socialization**. They also emphasized the extent to which gender roles were not just different, but unequal: the unpaid work of meeting the expressive needs of families within the home was of lower status within society – that is, less highly valued – than working for pay to meet the family's instrumental needs.

In seeking to explain how gender inequality was created and reproduced within families, some feminist scholars turned to Marxist theory. **Radical feminists** developed an analogy between gender and social class, arguing that families were organized around the domination and exploitation of women's sexuality and reproductive capacities. **Marxist** and **dual-systems** theorists sought to understand families as sites where the processes giving rise to class and gender inequality intersected. They argued that the unpaid work carried out by women within the home acted as a kind of subsidy to capitalist employers and the state, making it possible to maximize profits by keeping down wages while also perpetuating inequalities between women and men (Tong, 2014). We provide a more detailed account of some of the issues addressed by feminist theorists in Chapter 4. Here we emphasize how the growing influence of Marxist and feminist ideas affected wider understandings of family change.

In one of the most influential analyses, social historians Louise Tilly and Joan Scott (1987 [1978]) developed a new understanding of industrialization and family change through a gender lens. As we have seen, both nineteenth- and twentieth-century theorists recognized that there was a relationship between family forms and changing ways of making a living. Tilly and Scott showed that these changes were intertwined with a transformation in the gender division of labour within households and the wider economy. Drawing on concepts developed by the Russian economist A.V. Chayanov, and focusing on the experiences of families in France and Britain, they argued that during industrialization, family household economies evolved through three different phases:

1. In agrarian societies household production was based on a **family economy**. All members of the household, both family members and servants, worked together to ensure the survival of the household as a unit of production and consumption. In such households there was no meaningful distinction between productive and reproductive labour. Work was differentiated by gender and age, and women's tasks tended to be consistent with caring for young children. Nevertheless, the importance of women's work for the survival of the family and household was recognized.

2. During the first phase of industrialization (from around the end of the eighteenth century through most of the nineteenth), places of produc-

tion were gradually separated from the home, as more people began to work in urban factories and workshops under the supervision of employers. Families adapted to these new circumstances by applying existing practices and norms in the creation of a **family wage economy**. Just as in the family economy all household members pooled their labour to ensure their survival, in the family wage economy they pooled their wages. As much as they possibly could, men, women and children contributed wages to the household pot, for the benefit of the family as a whole. However, meeting the requirements of reproduction – that is, giving birth, caring for infants and young children, and looking after the daily well-being of family members – was much more challenging under this regime, and if they could, women dropped in and out of the labour force according to the requirements of the family life-cycle.

3. In the third phase of industrialization, from the end of the nineteenth century through the middle of the twentieth century men's wages began to rise, and growing numbers of women began to take on the specialized role of homemaker in what Tilly and Scott described as the **family-consumer economy**. In such families women contributed to the household economy not by earning an income, but by managing the household income to ensure the well-being of all its members. The reasons for this change are complex. They included a shift towards 'heavier' forms of industrial manufacture, such as machine production, the introduction of new legislation that aimed to protect women and children by limiting their participation in the workplace and, not least, the growing power of trade unions who demanded a 'family wage' for male workers.

As we will see in the next chapter, it is possible to argue that the family-consumer household economy has been transformed once again into a **dual-earner economy**.

Tilly and Scott's analysis was important for a number of reasons. First, it placed gender relationships at the heart of understanding family change. Secondly, it emphasized the importance of agency on the part of family members in bringing about change through adaptive **practices**. Thirdly, in tandem with other historically informed analyses, it raised questions about the idea of progress that tended to be assumed in mid-twentieth-century modernization perspectives. As we saw earlier, nineteenth-century theorists were sceptical that modern family forms were better than those that had gone before, but mid-twentieth-century theorists tended to suggest the extent to which modern family forms were freer and more democratic than those of the past.

Later analyses like that of Tilly and Scott raised questions about whether or not modern family forms were necessarily better from a gender perspective. Subsequent research has shown that it is important not to romanticize past households. There is evidence that even though women provided a vital contribution to the prosperity and survival of households under the family economy, their labour was under-valued and they had fewer entitlements to consumption than men (Ogilvie, 2004; J. Gray, 2005). Nevertheless, Tilly and Scott's pioneering work drew attention to the significance of household divisions of labour for understanding families.

Not all scholarship within the **household economics** tradition is inspired by Marxist concepts. In his *A Treatise on the Family*, economist Gary Becker (1991 [1981]) argued that many aspects of family change could be understood as outcomes of rational decision-making in response to changing economic circumstances. **For an application of Becker's ideas to Ireland, see the discussion of Finola Kennedy's work in Chapter 2.** Critics of Becker argued that his approach failed to recognize the importance of cultural norms and practices, and of unequal power relationships, in understanding family dynamics. An alternative model of household practices based on the concept of 'bargaining', rather than rational choice, was developed by Amartya Sen (1990). He argued that households should be understood as sites of 'cooperative conflict'. Different members of the household have more or less power when it comes to household decision-making, because they have different 'bargaining strengths' based on three different sets of perceptions: (1) how well they would fare if the household were to break down; (2) their perceived contribution to the well-being of the domestic group; (3) the extent to which household members perceive their self-interest in terms of individual well-being. (Sen suggested that in traditional societies many people – especially women – find the idea of personal welfare unintelligible and understand their interests only in terms of the well-being of the family unit.) Crucially Sen's model emphasizes the role of perception in the 'cooperative conflicts' that govern family behaviour; people's judgements about the relative bargaining strength of different household members may not always be accurate, and may depend on wider cultural norms and expectations. In this way, households' responses to changing economic and social circumstances tend to reproduce social inequalities. We return to these themes in considerably more detail in Chapter 4 of this book.

Summary and conclusion

We began this chapter with two stories of family life in twentieth-century Ireland. Seamus's story at the start of this chapter matches, in many respects, the corporate, multi-generational model of family relationships that scholars at the middle of the last century described as 'traditional'. By contrast, John's family story exemplifies the 'modern' family of structural-functionalist theory, with its focus on the independence of the married couple and on promoting the well-being of their children.

This chapter has introduced how nineteenth- and twentieth-century theorists sought to explain the changes they witnessed in family life through the development of **ideal types** that corresponded to stages of socio-economic development. Along the way, we have encountered a wide range of concepts and arguments that remain central to family sociology. These include:

1   How demography shapes the potential for family forms and patterns, as well has being an outcome of family behaviour
2. The importance of variation and change in ways of making a living for understanding family systems
3. The related question of how values and perceptions are intertwined with economics in family life

Throughout this book we will return to these themes as we explore the transformation of Irish families from the perspective of different life stages.

This chapter has also introduced many of the debates and cleavages that continue to concern social scientists, policy makers and members of the public as they try to make sense of contemporary family change:

1. Are certain features of family life fundamental to human well-being?
2. Is family change progressive or harmful for individuals and societies?
3. Are families the basis of social cohesion or of inequality and conflict?

We cannot pretend to answer these 'big' questions but we will return to them in the concluding chapter of the book.

Finally, our first chapter has introduced some of the landmark studies that have framed the scholarship on family change in Ireland. In particular, we saw how Arensberg and Kimball's classic ethnographic study not only provided a benchmark against which subsequent Irish family change has been evaluated; it also ensured that Ireland was identified as an extreme and persistent example of a traditional pattern of family life thought to have been widespread in western Europe before industrialization. However, we also noted evidence that, at least amongst some social groups, the demographic transition began in Ireland long before Arensberg and Kimball's study was carried out. We also saw how later research documented the emergence of modernizing trends in Ireland between the 1950s and the 1970s, similar to those occurring in other western countries.

As is the case with all ideal types neither Seamus's nor John's stories conform perfectly to the traditional or modern family depicted in sociological theory. For example Seamus met his future wife at a dance rather than through an arranged marriage. John married somewhat later than was typical for his peers, and had fewer children. In the Ireland that Seamus and John lived through, families varied in their size and shape. However, as we will see in the next chapter, more recent patterns of family change have given rise to greater diversity of family forms both within and between societies. The emergence of these trends increasingly challenged the nineteenth- and mid-twentieth-century idea that specific family forms 'fit' with different stages of societal development.

Key concepts and ideas in Chapter 1

- Kinship systems
- Rules of filiation
- Patrilineal, matrilineal and unilineal descent systems
- Elementary and complex marriage systems
- Patriarchal family system
- Unstable family system
- Stem-family system
- Households and domestic groups
- Evolutionary theories about family
- The theory of demographic transition
- Structural-functionalist theories about family
- Feminist theories about family
- Extended families

2

Beyond the modern family: re-visioning family change

In Chapter 1 we traced the development of the idea of the 'modern family' from its origins in nineteenth-century evolutionary thought to the structural-functionalist perspectives that dominated thinking about family change through the first half of the twentieth century. We saw how this way of thinking about families began to be challenged from the 1960s onwards: first, as a result of empirical scholarship that challenged key assumptions about the contours of family life in the present and in the past; second, because of the growing influence of conflict perspectives that identified families as institutions where patterns of power and inequality were generated and reproduced. In the later decades of the twentieth century, the emergence of new family patterns struck a fatal blow to the structural-functionalist consensus. Consider the following family vignettes:

> Donal was born in 1970. The son of a professional, he grew up on a suburban housing estate. On finishing school he pursued a career in the IT sector, eventually setting up his own business. Donal remembers having the 'craic' as a young man in his twenties, part of a network of about 'twenty guys ... we did everything together'. He had had 'maybe two long-term girlfriends' when he met his future wife at a company event. They lived together for a year and then married and bought a house together when Donal was in his late twenties. About two years later when his wife became pregnant they moved to a larger house. At that time their lifestyle changed: 'I was fed up going to the pub ... It was time to get on and move to the next step'. They have four young children, all of whom are minded in a local crèche while Donal and his wife are at work. Nevertheless, Donal takes an active part in the daily round of childcare: '[Y]ou have to be there changing nappies, telling them to pick up their spilled cornflakes, don't turn on that telly, put your coat on, have you brushed your teeth, feed the rabbits all the rest of it so there's a whole pile of work that is never ending'. (Donal, b. 1970, LHSC)

Ruth was born in the 1970s to working-class parents who lived in social housing. As a teenager, when she started going steady with her boyfriend she went to her GP to ask about contraception but 'by the time I got the pill I was already pregnant, the damage had been done'. Because of her own experience, Ruth's mother discouraged her from getting married. At first Ruth lived at home with her baby, but then moved into separate housing with her partner, the baby's father. Their relationship was tumultuous because 'he was wild and wanted to be out with the boys drinking … Throwing him out, taking him back, throwing him out, taking him back, the usual'. However, following the birth of their second child Ruth's partner began to settle down. They married in the mid-1990s and now have a good relationship. Ruth has worked throughout her life in a series of part-time jobs. (Ruth, b. 1970s, LHSC)

Nine-year-old Damien's mother broke up with his father when he was about three. They moved to her parents' house where Damien developed a very close relationship with his grandmother. Damien and his mother have since moved in with her new partner who has an older son of his own. Damien's mother thinks he is 'getting used to it' although he still likes to spend time with his grandmother. She herself works full time. (Damien, age 9, GUI)

Donal's, Ruth's and Damien's stories illustrate some of the ways in which Irish family lives began to change and diverge, especially from the 1980s onwards. In this chapter we trace the changing patterns of family formation that led to growing diversity in family life experiences and discuss how social scientists have developed new ideas to make sense of these changes. We also caution that some of the diversity becomes more apparent than real when the intersection between individual life paths and longer-term demographic trends is taken into account. Nevertheless, as we will see, since the 1990s innovative ways of thinking about families have emerged that allow social scientists to 'see' family life in interesting new ways. These new perspectives provide the background to Part II of our book.

A second demographic transition?

In 1986, 68 per cent of all family units in private households in Ireland comprised a married couple with children of any age. In 1996, 61 per cent were in this category, but the proportion declined steadily in each census thereafter. It stood at 49 per cent in 2006 and, most recently, in 2011, at 47 per cent. At first glance, we might think this was evidence for the decline of the 'modern' family in recent decades. However, in a detailed analysis of family forms in the 2006 census, Lunn and Fahey (2011: 7) showed that two-thirds of families with children (66.5 per cent) were headed by a married couple who were both in their first marriage. This might seem to suggest that the modern family is in reasonably good health. How do we make sense of these apparently conflicting numbers?

Cross-sectional data can be a misleading indicator of family trends because they are affected by a range of factors including: the proportions of people in different age groups in the population; the ages at which people leave home, establish their own households and start their own families; how long people live and whether or not they are likely to live independently in older age. Just as we saw with respect to studies about the stem-family in early twentieth-century Ireland, it is important to understand data about family structure and household composition in the context of demographic change and, as we will see in more detail below, changes in the structure of the **life-course** – how people's lives evolve over time. As Ruth's and Damien's stories illustrate, many of the people living in families and households that do not conform to the 'modern' family form in any given year, may transition into that type of family in the future, or indeed may have lived in such a family in the past.

Nevertheless, taking those factors into account, Lunn and Fahey's (2011: 7) analysis *does* indicate patterns of family and household formation that were quite different from those that prevailed in 1986 – just not quite on the scale that some of the more dramatic statements about the decline of the family might lead us to expect. Within the one-third of family households different from the 'modern' conjugal type, the next largest group comprised families headed by lone mothers who had been previously married (12.3 per cent), followed by lone mothers who had never been married (9.4 per cent) and then cohabiting couples (5.9 per cent). Such households would have been exceptional in Ireland when Seamus and John, whose stories we examined in Chapter 1, were starting their families.

Figure 2.1 provides an overview of family household composition in Ireland, Denmark and Portugal in 2009, based on the European Survey on Income and

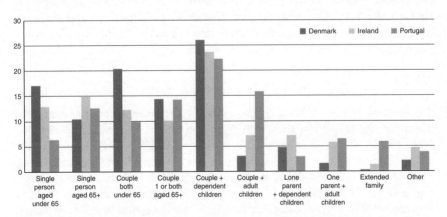

Figure 2.1 Household composition (%) in Denmark, Ireland and Portugal, 2009

Source: Eurostat 2013, Table A1, p. 33

Living Conditions (EU-SILC). It shows some interesting differences between the three countries. Denmark has comparatively high proportions of households comprising single people and couples under the age of 65 without children. Portugal, by contrast, has a comparatively high proportion of households comprising couples living together with adult children. Ireland has comparatively greater proportions of older people living alone and of lone parents with dependent children. Some of these variations can be explained by differences in the structure of the populations of the three countries, but some are also due to different patterns of family-household formation. Later in this chapter we will discuss social science arguments that seek to explain diversity in family patterns across different European countries.

The trends in household composition sketched above appear to cast doubt on the theoretical assumptions underpinning the structural-functionalist perspective on the modern family, in particular the assumption of **convergence** (Cherlin, 2012). Remember that according to modernization theory the conjugal family is best adapted to urban industrial conditions such that family systems should converge on this form – become more alike – as societies industrialize. However there appears instead to have been a **convergence to diversity** (Boh, 1989) in family forms both within and between countries in the developed world.

In order to understand this growing diversity we have to look more closely at three interdependent historical processes:

1. The continuing decline in fertility and increase in longevity
2. The 'unbundling' of life transitions associated with family and household formation
3. The transformation of gender roles

Because each of these changes is discussed in depth, according to different life stages, in Part II of this book, here we provide just a summary overview as an introduction to the challenges faced by family sociology in the later decades of the twentieth century.

Continuing the demographic transition

Classic demographic transition theory posited that once societies had gone 'through' the transition they would emerge into a new period of stability, when low fertility rates were balanced by low mortality rates. However, by the 1980s, demographers were beginning to worry that in some countries fertility rates were falling well below the average number of children per woman required to replace the population (2.1). On average, across the member countries of the Organization for Economic Co-operation and Development, the **period total fertility rate**, or **TFR**, plummeted from 2.88 in 1960 to 1.59 in 1998 (Castles, 2002: 24). In Ireland the TFR dropped from 3.73 in 1960 to 1.93 in 1998. From the 1990s onwards, this rather bleak picture was moderated somewhat, first by evidence that part of the decline could be explained by women postponing childbirth to later ages, and second by signs that the decline was slowing or even reversing in some countries (Myrskylä et al., 2009).

The TFR is an estimate of annual rates of fertility, calculated as 'the average number of births a woman would have by the end of her reproductive years, if fertility levels at each age during her childbearing period remained constant at the levels prevailing at a given time'. Thus if women start to delay having children, the TFR will tend to underestimate the average number of children they will have by the end of their childbearing years. In Ireland, the TFR grew to 2.1 in 2008. This has been attributed to an increase in the number of women in their childbearing years in the population (itself a result of a mini 'baby boom' in the 1970s), and 'catch-up' fertility on the part of older women who might not have had one or an additional child were it not for the economic boom (Lunn et al., 2010). This pattern of improved fertility also occurred in other northern European countries, leading to a notable gap between north-western and northern European countries compared to countries of the South and East (Reher, 2007).

Despite the evidence that fertility decline may be reduced or reversed under some circumstances (Myrskylä et al., 2009), many demographers continue to believe that there is a global momentum towards population decline (Reher, 2007). Together with continuing improvements in healthy old-age life expectancy, this phenomenon has led to population ageing, as the proportions of older people increase relative to those of younger people. Vern Bengtson (2001) drew attention to the consequences of these changes for family life. Increasingly, he argued, vertical family relationships (between, for example, great-grandparents, grandparents, parents and children) will become more important in family life than horizontal relationships (such as those between siblings). This has been described as the emergence of the **beanpole family** (Harper, 2003).

Unbundling family life transitions

In Chapter 1 we described how Arensberg and Kimball (2001 [1940]) depicted marriage as a 'crisis' that had to be carefully managed in order to ensure the integrity and continuity of the farm family household. This was because, under the European Marriage Pattern described by Hajnal (1982), marriage marked the shift to a new stage in a person's life, when he or she took on the responsibilities of being in charge of a household and starting a family. Until comparatively recently, this closely sequenced and ordered set of transitions – marriage, setting up house, childbearing – continued to be followed in both rural and urban settings (Hannan and Ó Riain, 1993). Over time, however, the sequence and timing of these transitions has become 'unbundled' (Elliot, 1996; Harper, 2003; Plane et al., 2005):

Panel 2.1   Looking at the data: emigration and family disruption

In recent scholarship there has been considerable attention to how globalization – the increasing inter-connectedness of social relation-ships across the world – has created the phenomenon of transnational families (Parreñas, 2005; Ryan, 2007; King-O'Riain, 2014). Scholars have been especially interested in the consequences for families when mothers emigrate, often to find work in the care sectors of receiving countries. In a study of Filipino nurses living in Ireland, Humphries et al. (2009) found that separation from family members led to consider-able social strain: 'the focus was on maintaining the remittance flow to them and on holiday entitlements that would allow family unity, even for a brief period'. In Ireland a pattern in which fathers emigrate to find work re-emerged in the current recession (see e.g. O'Shaughnessy, *Irish Independent* 10 October 2014). Bernard's (b. 1951) story shows that this is not a new experience.

Bernard worked in the construction sector in the UK as an unmar-ried man in his early twenties but when he married he returned to Ireland to raise his family. In the 1980s, due to the downturn in the economy, his business ran into trouble, He went back to London for four years, commuting home to his wife and children every third week. Bernard missed out on family life with his children during their teenage years, and felt that his absence might have affected their educational aspirations:

> in the late 1980s I went back to England and started working off again because the kids were coming to college age and I said I wasn't going to be caught not being able to provide for them. So I went over and I was doing very well beyond, working all the hours God sent you, and [the local] airport had opened so I could pre book, £46 and I'd come home every three weeks. And then for the summer I used to bring them over and rent a house beyond ... and have them for three months beyond and we did that for four years ... It was difficult for their mother it was easier for me ... I thought [my son] had a place got in college [...], wouldn't take it, he wanted to go into [the local] factory that had started in town here and he was doing Saturday and part-time work and that's my biggest regret of all, because I thought I would've forced him to it. (Bernard, b. 1951, LHSC)

---

1. Sex has become separated from marriage as more people become sexually active at earlier ages and outside committed relationships.
2. Setting up house has become separated from marriage as people establish cohabiting or 'living apart together' (LAT) relationships.

3. Parenthood has been separated from marriage as women give birth outside marriage.
4. Marriage is no longer necessarily a lifetime relationship. People may move in and out of marriages across their lives (Elliot, 1996).

In sum, marriage has lost its place as the decisive moment of family and household-formation: it has been 'de-institutionalized' (Cherlin, 2004). **For more on this, see Chapter 4.** One consequence of this may be that people move through an increasing variety of family and household arrangements across their lives although, as we will see throughout this book, it is important not to overstate this phenomenon. Many people continue to follow quite predictable life paths in contemporary societies (Gray, 2010), while historically the greater risk of death at all ages led to considerable family disruption (Uhlenberg, 1980).

While the changes described above have occurred to some extent across all developed countries, there are variations in their timing and scale. In the Irish case, some have occurred late and have been compressed into a shorter period of time. For example, births outside marriage started from a comparatively low proportion in Ireland in 1980 (5 per cent) but had converged with the European average by the mid-1990s. Similarly, the proportion of people in cohabiting relationships has increased steadily in Ireland since the mid-1990s. Halpin and O'Donoghue (2004) showed that 11.1 per cent of people aged 25–34 were in a cohabiting relationship in Ireland in 2001, compared to 21.6 per cent in England. Analysis of the 2006 census showed that 22 per cent of those aged 28 were cohabiting in that year (Lunn et al., 2010: 16). This suggests that rates of cohabitation in Ireland lie below those in the Nordic countries, where a third or more of people aged 26–35 years are in cohabiting relationships, but above those in the southern European countries where 15 per cent or fewer people are in this category (see Kasearu and Kutsar, 2011). By contrast, despite being a late entrant (in 1997) to the group of countries that liberalized divorce laws from the 1970s onwards, Irish divorce rates have not shown any sign of matching those of the northern countries, but instead remain similar to those of the 'low divorce' countries of southern Europe (Lunn et al., 2010: 44).

The transformation of gender roles

As we saw in Chapter 1, amongst mid-twentieth-century social scientists the **breadwinner family** with its characteristic gender division of labour was taken for granted as the normal state of affairs. The mass entry of women – especially mothers – into the labour force is perhaps the most striking aspect of how the modern family has been transformed. This change in gender roles has been accompanied by a transformation in attitudes in favour of partners' sharing income-earning and homemaking responsibilities. Here again, the speed of change has varied across countries, and different patterns

---

Panel 2.2   Landmark Irish study: *Family Figures* by Pete Lunn, Tony Fahey and Carmel Hannan (2010)

Lunn, Fahey and Hannan's 2010 report for the Family Support Agency is a landmark in Irish family studies because it represents the first example of research using census microdata made available under a new policy on access to data initiated by the Central Statistics Office. The report shows that while there have been significant changes in the make-up and composition of Irish families, much stability and continuity are also evident across the period of 1986–2006 examined here.

The well-trodden path for the majority of people from singlehood, to marriage, to parenthood remained – much like earlier decades – the dominant family type during the period. Yet, notably there was a significant decline in the three-generation family of earlier decades, as well as a fall-off in households composed of unmarried adult siblings. Alternatives to the norm of the **nuclear family** rose substantially during the period also: for example, a steep rise was recorded in the numbers of same-sex couples, those forming second partnerships, lone parents (of which 91 per cent were headed by females), and most significantly, unmarried cohabiting couples. Divorce figures also rose rapidly in the 1990s following the introduction of divorce legislation in 1997.

One major change in family structures was the timing of **life transitions** into marriage and parenthood. In the main, adults from all social classes delayed the age at which they formed lasting unions when compared with their 1970s and 1980s forebears. Delayed fertility was another headline trend to emerge from the study, whereby the majority of women postponed childbirth beyond the age of thirty, at which point there is a sharp increase in fertility rates. Social background and fertility also showed strong overlaps; in 2006 over half of thirty-two-year-old women graduates were childless while less than one quarter of those with secondary-level qualifications were childless.

Distinct patterns of family formation were also evident around ethnicity, nationality, and religion. One standout statistic was the contrast between Muslims and those of no faith. Of all the different sections of society, and of all the different confessional groupings, Muslims were the most likely to marry and the least likely to cohabit; while for those of no faith, the reverse situation was the case. The lone parent group was overwhelmingly made up of women from lower socio-economic backgrounds. Various cohort effects were also evident; those most at risk of marital breakdown were couples in their forties in 2006; cohabiting among couples after the age of twenty-five rose sharply; fertility rates surged among higher educated women after age thirty.

Overall, younger couples showed a different path to family formation than their parents' generation, with far higher incidences of cohabitation and lower fertility rates. Yet, here *Family Figures* sounds a note of caution in over-interpreting these trends: it could not be assumed that cohabitation and lower fertility rates among younger couples would continue throughout their lives, or whether marriage and childrearing were merely being delayed. As such, it begs the question: Is cohabiting an end in itself, or merely a prelude to marriage? This question was further discussed in research by Margret Fine-Davis in 2011 (see Panel 4.3, p. 109).

can be detected (Aboim, 2010). In this respect also Ireland was a late starter; women's participation in paid employment grew rather slowly in the 1980s, but then very rapidly from the early 1990s onwards, so that by 2004 a majority of mothers were in the labour force (McGinnity and Russell, 2007). Compared to some other European countries, the proportion of women who withdraw from the labour force when they have young children remains comparatively high in Ireland. In 2013, for example, 51.7 per cent of women with a child aged 4–5 years were in the labour force, compared to 76.2 per cent of men in that category, and 85.6 per cent of women without children (CSO, 2014d). Nevertheless, by the beginning of the twenty-first century, the male breadwinner norm had clearly been replaced in Ireland by a dual-earner norm (McGinnity and Russell, 2007).

Explaining the second demographic transition: from the decline of the family to post-modernism

The transformations in family patterns that occurred from the second half of the twentieth century onwards were, to some extent, inexplicable within the principal theoretical frameworks that had guided understandings of family change since the nineteenth century (see Chapter 1). Both structural-functionalist and conflict perspectives tended to assume – in their different ways – that a particular institutional form of the family 'fit' with a given stage of societal development. Thus, at first, social scientists focused on why the family appeared to be 'breaking down'.

Some explanations centred on the contradictory effects of growing individualism and democratisation in family life (in fact, this had been anticipated by Goode (1963) in his ground-breaking work (Cherlin, 2012). Demographer Dirk Van de Kaa (1987) argued that, whereas the 'first' demographic transition was governed by parents' altruistic desire to improve the life chances of a smaller number of offspring, the 'second' demographic transition was motivated by a growing desire for 'self-fulfilment' on the part of adults, a change he described as a movement from the 'king-child' to the 'king-pair with child'

Panel 2.3   Landmark Irish study: *Cottage to Crèche* **by Finola Kennedy (2001)**

Economist Finola Kennedy's study, *Cottage to Crèche*, is notable for being the first comprehensive, book-length study of family change in twentieth-century Ireland and builds on an earlier report produced for the Economic and Social Research Institute in 1989. Kennedy charts the path of family change in Ireland over the twentieth century, addressing the interplay between economic developments, changes to government policies and legislation, and changing values in Irish society, but with a particular emphasis on how economic effects moulded the modern Irish family. The core argument of the book is that changes in family patterns over the course of the century were driven by people's adaptation to changing economic factors, which in turn tended to over-ride the forces of religion and tradition once they had attained sufficient strength. Kennedy's argument was influenced by Gary Becker's perspective on the family (which we discussed in Chapter 1).

Changing family patterns, which started in earnest during the third quarter of the twentieth century, are interpreted in the context of a kaleidoscope of factors that intensified in the latter half of the twentieth century, including: economic restructuring following Ireland's accession to the European Economic Community in 1973 and the resulting decline of the small farming family; the rise of women's organizations; greater access to mass media; and a proliferation of information outside the realm of Church teaching that 'helped create a mood for change' (p. 103). All of these factors acted as 'catalysts for change' in attitudes to family roles, particularly attitudes about motherhood and the role of women outside of the home. But economic opportunities, in the form of jobs, free post-primary education and changing employment law, which facilitated the participation of married women in the paid workforce, were key to the emergence of the dual-earner household so commonplace today.

Kennedy documents changes in government policy and law in great detail, which appear reactive to the profound changes already underway within the Irish family. A chapter of the book charts landmark policy changes, including changes to the laws on marriage, separation and divorce, ownership, inheritance and illegitimacy, and the extension of social welfare in the form of children's allowance payments, lone parent payments and other social supports. While the study presents data from library and archival documents, statistics and published reports, an interesting dimension is the inclusion of recollections from senior government figures, including former Taoisigh and senior civil servants, who were involved in the development of policies that have been significant in the story of the modern Irish family.

A central assertion in *Cottage to Crèche* is that, rather than being a special case, Ireland followed a path similar to other European countries. However, Kennedy doesn't underestimate the importance of the culture-specific context when examining family change, so that 'Ireland marched to the same drum, but at her own pace and in her own style' (p. 7).

(see also Lesthaeghe, 2010). Sociologist Andrew Cherlin (1990) argued that the transformation should be understood as a consequence of both economic and cultural change, emphasizing in particular the growing labour market participation of women.

Changes in the structure of western economies led to a growth of female-typed occupations and new labour market opportunities for women. This meant that women had more to lose if they continued to follow the pattern established in the post-War period; instead, it was in their interests to postpone marriage and have fewer children. They were also less likely to remain in unsatisfactory marriages – more likely to get divorced – because the possibility of economic independence outside marriage had improved (see also Becker, 1991 [1981]). More recent research has suggested that the relationship between married women's labour force participation and fertility may be more complex than this broad sketch allows. We will discuss this further below.

Some scholars interpreted family change specifically in terms of the decline of the family as an **institution** and worried that the societal functions of the conjugal family were no longer adequately being met. David Popenoe (1993: 539) has been perhaps the most forceful proponent of this view, arguing that 'the family is by far the best institution to carry out [the functions of child-drearing and the provision of affection and companionship], and insofar as these functions are shifted to other institutions, they will not be carried out as well'. Concern about the consequences of family change for children remains an active issue in sociological research and public discourse; we discuss this further in Chapter 3.

In opposition to the thesis of dysfunction and decline, other scholars argued forcefully in favour of the emancipatory features of new family patterns. According to Judith Stacey (1990: 18), American families of the 1990s represented an aspect of **post-modernism**; they were not a new stage in the evolution of the family, but rather 'the stage in that history when belief in a logical progression of stages breaks down'. In other words, Stacey sought to challenge the whole corpus of scholarship that family sociology had inherited from the nineteenth century, in particular the idea that each stage in the evolution of society had a corresponding family 'ideal-type'. In her ethnographic research in Silicon Valley, California, she revealed how working-class women created and re-constructed sequences of 'new' family relationships in order to meet the challenges of living in a post-industrial environment. The post-modern family, she argued, was not a single functional type, but rather a diversity and fluidity of forms as people moved in and out of different family settings, developing complex kin networks over the course of their lives.

European scholars sought to explain family change as an aspect of 'late modernity'. Anthony Giddens (1991 [1981]) argued that, in an increasingly globalized world, social relationships had become dis-embedded from local contexts, leading to the erosion of tradition as a guide to life. Personal life had become a reflexive, 'open project' and people sought out 'pure' relationships that endured only as long as they met the needs of the individual. Elisabeth Beck-Gernsheim (1998) elaborated these ideas further, arguing that we had entered the era of the 'post-familial family'. As a result of globalization and individualization families had become centred on the challenges of 'staging' family life, including: managing the tempos and places of parents' and children's everyday schedules; constructing multi-cultural marriages in an increasingly inter-connected world; developing elective family relationships following divorce. In all these decisions and negotiations, Beck-Gernsheim argued, people could no longer rely on 'well-functioning rules and models' (p. 59), as they had done in the past. Instead, family life had become 'an acrobatics of balancing and co-ordinating' (p. 67).

Jeffrey Weeks et al. (2001) argued that non-heterosexual people were innovators in the development of 'families of choice', which were nevertheless part of the wider societal changes described by Beck-Gernsheim and others. As egalitarianism increasingly became the measure by which people chose and judged personal relationships, LGBT (lesbian, gay, bisexual, transgender) people claimed the language of family as their own, contributing to the development of a new understanding of 'family' that was broader than before but still 'kin-like' in terms of its meanings and commitments. **For more on LGBT families see Chapter 4.**

All of these arguments shared the central idea that family relationships had become fluid, autonomously chosen and constructed, no longer trammelled by the 'taken-for-granted' rules and conventions that were assumed to have governed family life in the past. Families sometimes seem strangely dissociated from their social environments in this literature, which did not go uncriticized. In a scathing critique of Stacey's work, historian Christopher Lasch (1997: 153–160) argued that it was based on a 'false and ideological' interpretation of history – one that failed to recognize that the 'isolated nuclear family' was attainable by working-class women for only a brief period, 'just as it was becoming unfashionable'. Rather than pioneers of new, post-modern forms of family living, Lasch claimed, Stacey had simply encountered working-class women doing as they always had done: striving against the odds to hold their families together in times of economic hardship; contributing to their families' economic survival; becoming disillusioned with men and struggling with expectations of wifely submission; and seeking emotional and material support from friends, extended family members and religion.

In an influential critique, Carol Smart and Beccy Shipman (2004: 492) questioned how individualisation had become the core 'metaphor through which sociological analysis of family life' was being pursued. They argued that in this scholarship there was a tendency to conflate individualization as a socio-historical process with **individualism** as personal motivation, with the result that people were sometimes represented as making easy, selfish choices, and abandoning any commitment to care about others. Instead, they argued, a sociological understanding of choice should recognize that choices are always both contextual – that is, exercised within socially constructed (and constrained) options – and relational, in the sense that they take account of the interests and needs of others. Drawing on a qualitative study of kinship amongst Pakistani, Indian and Irish ethnic communities in Yorkshire, they showed how tradition continued to be a basis for family life while also being subject to negotiation and realignment from one generation to another. Similarly, Ryan-Flood (2014) documented the considerable emotional labour expended by Irish LGBT people towards 'families we keep' rather than 'families we choose', that is, towards maintaining bonds with families of origin.

Comparative perspectives: family systems and the state

While the post-modernist and globalization scholarship attempted to explain new family patterns in the context of the long sweep of social change, a different literature emerged to address questions about cross-national diversity in family patterns. This literature adopted a 'middle range' comparative-historical approach that aimed first to identify clusters or typologies of countries according to their distinctive family patterns and second to trace the historical factors that gave rise to them. There are two broad traditions within this literature.

The first tradition is linked to a highly influential study by David Reher (1998) that identified what he argued were persistent contrasts between the weak family ties that characterized family systems in northern European countries and the strong family ties of southern European family systems. He identified two key dimensions of this difference: (1) patterns of leaving home and independent household formation; (2) forms of intergenerational solidarity.

Historically, in the weak family systems of northern Europe, young adults left their parental households before marriage, under the system of life-cycle service that we described in Chapter 1. By contrast, traditionally in southern Europe, young adults left their natal households permanently only when they married. Reher argued that contemporary evidence on late ages at leaving home in the Mediterranean countries was consistent with this enduring historical pattern: people continue to wait until they are married to leave home, but age at marriage has increased. This might explain the high proportion of households with adult children in Portugal, shown in Figure 2.1 above. **See Chapter 3 for further discussion of this topic.**

Similarly, Reher drew a contrast between attitudes and practices relating to care of the elderly in northern and southern Europe. Historically, in the Mediterranean countries, care of the elderly fell exclusively on the family, reinforced by strong norms of **intergenerational solidarity**. In the north, by contrast, smaller proportions of older people appear to have co-resided with their children in the past, and non-family sources of support for the elderly, such as the English poor laws, appeared much earlier. Reher argued that these differences persisted in the present, in patterns of intergenerational co-residence and in norms and attitudes. **See Chapter 6 for more on this in the Irish context.** Reher (1998: 221) concluded that the transformations associated with the second demographic transition would lead to:

> convergence in the external indicators of family life, but this convergence will not undermine the deep disparities that have always characterized the family in the different regions and cultures of Europe. ... No matter how nearly universal the factors of modernization may be, once they enter into contact with different historical, cultural, geographical or social realities, the end result will necessarily be different in each context.

A second tradition in comparative-historical scholarship focused on the relationship between different **welfare-state** 'regimes' and divergent family patterns across countries. This research was inspired by Gøsta Esping-Andersen's (1990) distinction amongst the 'three worlds' of welfare capitalism. Esping-Andersen's concern was not, initially, with family outcomes, but rather with identifying and explaining different social policy configurations across countries, based on the ways in which they intervened in, or 'decommodified', the relationship between capital and labour. In the **liberal welfare regime** social policy is oriented primarily towards supporting the market. Social welfare transfers in this regime are targeted towards marginalized and stigmatized groups. The **social democratic welfare regime**, by contrast, is oriented towards de-emphasizing the market and reducing the inequalities arising under capitalism. Countries in this category have universal welfare schemes but in order to pay for them they promote universal adult participation in the labour market. The **conservative welfare regime** intervenes in the market to preserve existing status inequalities such as those based on institutions like the family. When Esping-Andersen devised his typology, the United States represented the archetype of the liberal regime, Sweden that of the social democratic regime and West Germany that of the conservative regime. Scholars working in this tradition added the idea of a 'fourth world' of welfare capitalism to encompass the Mediterranean states, which were characterized by underdeveloped social welfare systems with few rights to welfare or employment.

Esping-Andersen's categorization was soon criticized for being 'gender blind' (Lewis, 1992); it failed to take account of the divergent and unequal consequences of different policy regimes for family life because it focused only on how states intervened in market relationships and neglected the implications for unpaid work and caring (Daly and Lewis, 2000). An alternative, feminist scholarship sought to develop new typologies of welfare regimes by addressing the extent to which social policies 'defamilialized' care, or focused on how divergent welfare regimes emerged in the context of different 'gender contracts' rooted in culturally divergent ideas about gender roles (Duncan, 1995; Pfau-Effinger, 1998; Aboim, 2010). As Saxonberg (2013: 27) noted in a recent review, 'it proved much easier for feminist scholars to criticize [Esping-Andersen's] typology than to agree on an alternative'. Nevertheless, this way of thinking about the relationships amongst social policy, gender and family outcomes has been enormously fruitful for scholarship on divergent family patterns in the decades since the publication of Esping-Andersen's work.

Attempts to modify or improve Esping-Andersen's model have resulted in a multiplication of typologies, partly because of the incorporation of new dimensions such as defamilialization, but also because individual countries and regions rarely conform precisely to type in every respect. In a review of social policy on the family in Ireland, Fahey (1998) identified a transition from **patriarchal familism** to **egalitarian individualism** in the context of an overall societal shift away from rural, family-based production systems to urban, wage-based systems of production. The key features of each paradigm are summarized in Figure 2.2.

These changes are notable insofar as they emphasize increasing individual rights, rather than adding claims on the state for support relating to care. In general, Ireland appears to 'fit' best within Esping-Andersen's Liberal welfare-regime category (Payne and McCashin, 2005). In her ground-breaking gender

Patriarchal familism	Egalitarian individualism
• Individual welfare deemed to depend on inclusion in a cohesive family unit	• Individual welfare defined as principal measure of quality in family life
• Well-defined, differentiated, complementary and hierarchical family roles	• Expectation that family organization should meet requirements of individual welfare rather than vice versa
• Legal status of persons defined by reference to family status rather than broader principles of citizenship or community	• Regards large proportion of individual rights as undifferentiated – not dependent on family status or role
• Reflected in clauses relating to the family in the Irish Constitution	• Reflected in legislation on gender

Figure 2.2 Changing Irish family policy paradigms
Source: Fahey, 1998

**Panel 2.4   Discussion: are Irish family trends exceptional
or converging?**

Until the 1980s, it was possible to make a good case that Irish family
trends were exceptional amongst developed countries. As we saw in
Chapter 1, in the early decades of the century Ireland seemed to be a
bastion of pre-modern demographic and household-formation patterns,
with comparatively very late age at marriage and high levels of marital
fertility. While noting that Irish fertility had declined slowly during the
first three quarters of the twentieth century, and that the Irish had 'given
up their unique pattern of very late marriage during the 1950s', D. S.
Coleman was moved to write in 1992 that: 'Irish exceptionalism cannot
be matched on any comparable demographic scale by any subdivision of
a larger western European country except Northern Ireland' (Coleman,
1992: 57).

From the 1980s onwards, some features of Irish family life converged
rapidly with those of other European countries: the **TFR** declined and
the rate of births outside marriage converged on the European average
(Fahey et al., 2000). On the other hand female labour force participation remained low by European standards until the 1990s. Despite
the legal introduction of divorce in 1997, rates of marital dissolution
remain comparatively low (Fahey, 2012). On the other hand, there
has been a steady increase in cohabitation since the mid-1990s, and
there is evidence of a significant 'modernization' of attitudes relating to
non-traditional forms of family formation and gender roles (Fine-Davis,
2011; O'Sullivan, 2012). But Irish fertility rates remain among the
highest in Europe.

Assessing the evidence Seward et al. (2005: 422) concluded that:

> Irish families were less exceptional than earlier portrayals insinuated.
> Yet at certain times the combination of family patterns was exceptional.
> Overall, Irish family patterns do appear to be converging with those in other
> industrialized nations and, in a few instances, at an unparalleled pace.

As we explain elsewhere in this chapter, whether we focus on what
makes Ireland different or the same as other countries, depends in part
on the temporal scale we adopt.

---

analysis of welfare regimes, Lewis (1992) placed Ireland firmly within the
'breadwinner' category of states that failed to support adult female participation in the labour force. In a more recent study, Korpi et al. (2013) classified
countries according to three dimensions of the organization of care: the extent

to which they support or assume traditional family arrangements; the extent to which they transfer care arrangements to the public sphere; the extent to which they promote redistribution of care within the family. In this analysis, Ireland fits within a cluster of countries with low scores on all three dimensions. These countries do not intervene to support care across any of the three dimensions but have what may be described as a market-oriented approach. **See Chapter 5 for more on this.**

Family configurations, practices and displays

The debates surrounding post-modernism and individualization that we discussed above, highlighted the inadequacy of theoretical traditions focused on identifying the 'rules' governing normative models of families and households. However, in attempting to develop alternative 'grand theories' of family change in the contemporary era, the post-modern and individualization theses resorted to sweeping generalizations that were easily shown to be inconsistent with empirical evidence. This has inspired a new wave of empirical research on the contours of family relationships, meanings and practices in lived experience.

Just as the extended family was 'rediscovered' by researchers in the 1970s, contemporary sociologists have returned to questions about the networks of kin and friends that make up **family configurations** (Widmer and Jallinoja, 2008) and **personal communities** (Pahl and Spencer, 2004). This empirical focus has enabled them to see the contours and boundaries of families from the 'bottom up'; that is, from the perspectives of peoples' lived understandings and practices. In contrast to the depictions of some authors writing on individualization, these scholars recognize that networks of family relationships are patterned, and embedded in wider social and economic structures, but they understand those regularities as the outcomes of processes that are continuously enacted and negotiated.

This concern with how family networks are enacted leads to a focus on diversity of outcomes. Ray Pahl and Liz Spencer (2004) questioned the assumption of a directional change between 'families of fate' and 'families of choice', arguing instead that there was a complex blurring of the boundaries between 'familial' and 'non-familial' relationships in many people's personal communities. Nevertheless, they showed how it was possible to identify patterns in these configurations. In a theme that is echoed frequently across the literature (for example see Jamieson et al., 2006), they questioned the 'soggy notion of traditional' so often invoked in sociology, emphasizing that we cannot assume that the suffusion of friendship and kinship in contemporary families is necessarily new. Writing from a historian's perspective, Naomi Tadmor (2010: 15) drew attention to the importance of 'enmeshed patterns of kinship and connectedness' in early modern England, and their similarities

---

Panel 2.5   Looking at the data: new Irish families

The number of people who are 'non-Irish nationals' has more than doubled in Ireland since 2002 (CSO, 2012). Lunn et al. (2009) identified some distinctive characteristics of these new Irish families as recorded in the census: immigrants were more likely to be married, but also more likely to be divorced, and levels of fertility are higher amongst some groups. It is important to remember that new Irish families come from many different places around the world; the largest group of non-Irish nationals is from the UK, but there have also been increases in the numbers of people from central and eastern Europe, Africa and Asia. As we have seen there are many aspects of family life that census data do not capture. Here we give just one example.

> Jamie was born in Africa and has been living in Ireland with her mother and two sisters for several years. Her father, who is still living in Africa, and Jamie's maternal grandmother, had visited them in Ireland once. When Jamie spoke about seeing her cousins once or twice every week Jamie's mother explained that her daughter was not referring to blood relatives, but rather to children with whom she felt close.

> If you say 'aunty' or 'uncle' in [African Country] anybody is their aunty. I don't have a sister, I only have brothers and they are in Africa. Any elderly person would be 'mummy', so that is just how we say it in our country. If [Jamie] sees another child, if you were asking who it is, she would say it is 'my cousin' or she can say it is 'my sister' even if it isn't her sister, depending on how close they are. (Jamie's mother, GUI)

Jamie's story illustrates how the suffusion of family and friends discussed by Pahl and Spencer (2004) does not map onto notions of tradition and modernity.

---

to the configurations of kin and friends that make up contemporary family networks.

As well as looking at the changing configurations of social ties that make up family relationships, contemporary scholarship has shifted the focus of research away from questions about the putatively shared values and attitudes that govern family life to questions about the construction of meaning in the everyday practices of 'doing family' over time. This change in focus is related, in part, to the emergence of major new sources of **qualitative** and qualitative **longitudinal data** that enable researchers to capture family life as process (Neale and Flowerdew, 2003; Holland, 2011; Neale et al., 2012;

Holland and Edwards, 2014). This approach has allowed researchers to under-stand how people construct morally inflected understandings of 'good' family roles and practices (Shirani et al., 2012) and how variations in moral identities and rationalities emerge amongst different social groups and in different social and historical contexts (Duncan et al., 2003).

In their analyses of family life as process, researchers often draw on the concepts of **doing** (Morgan, 2011) and **displaying** (Finch, 2007) family. People 'do family' in everyday practices oriented towards others who are identified as family members: 'In this way ... family practices are reflective practices; in being enacted they simultaneously construct, reproduce family boundaries, family relationships and possibly more discursive notions of the family in general' (Morgan, 2011: 163).

The concept of 'display' relates to the ways in which family practices are embedded in wider systems of meaning: it refers to how people 'convey to each other and to relevant audiences that certain of their actions do consti-tute 'doing family things' and thereby confirm that these relationships are 'family' relationships' (Finch, 2007: 67). Both concepts derive from the micro-sociological tradition of symbolic interactionism, especially the dramaturgical perspective of Erving Goffmann (1959). In this tradition, social identities are understood as accomplishments: as outcomes of what people do, rather than of the structures of the institutions in which they take place (Morgan, 2011: 162). Morgan's conceptualization of family practices was also informed by Bourdieu's (1977) distinction between theory and practice, between formal 'rules' and practical relationships, and by the concept of 'habitus' that aims to capture the 'taken-for-granted' forms of behaviour that are maintained in everyday actions (Morgan, 2011: 24–27).

Finally, the **life course** perspective has been essential to recent scholar-ship on family process. This way of thinking about social change has been applied in both quantitative and qualitative research and has become increas-ingly salient amongst scholars trying to understand contemporary family patterns. It brings together four interdependent ideas (Elder, 1994) that help us to understand the relationship between biography and history (Mills, 1959).

1. It draws our attention to the fact that *when* people are born affects the constraints and options available to them across their lives. This is partly because people are born in particular **historical periods** of course, but also because within the same periods their experiences vary according to their age. For example, on average, the economic crisis that began in 2008 affected the **cohort** of people who were born in 1975 – in the middle part of their lives when many had already established families and working careers – quite differently from those who were born in 1990 and who found themselves trying to start out in life during a recession. The life course perspective also recognizes the developmental nature of lives; our

experiences at a particular age in a given historical period may have consequences for how our lives evolve over time.

2. The life course perspective takes account of the social construction of different **life stages**. Both custom and official rules and regulations create expectations about the 'normal' transitions and stages people expect to go through at different times in their lives. Of course real lives – and expectations – are practically accomplished in the ways we have described above, and so customs and expectations are subject to change and variation. Nevertheless, 'untimely' transitions that violate official or customary expectations can have consequences for individual lives.

3. The principle of **linked lives** emphasizes how individual lives are embedded in sets of social relationships – especially those of family and kin – that travel with us through the life course.

4. A key principle of the life course perspective that aligns it with research on family practices is that of **human agency**. Scholars working within the life course tradition recognize the extent to which people act and make choices with reference to their understandings of what is possible and likely.

Summary and conclusion

We began this chapter with an overview of the changes in family life that led to the displacement of the kinds of 'grand theories' that dominated sociological perspectives on family change from the origins of the discipline in the nineteenth century until the latter decades of the twentieth century. We saw how the phenomenon of 'convergence to diversity' of family patterns in western countries initially led scholars to hypothesize a new stage in the evolution of the family, but that this has been superseded by a body of scholarship focusing on detailed examinations of how the contours of family life are enacted through practices and displays in changing historical circumstances across the life course. The different strands of this new family scholarship share a number of features in common:

1. They adopt an **inductive** approach to identifying the meanings of 'family' and the contours of families as these are enacted and displayed in everyday life and across lives over time. They do not attempt to specify the essential characteristics of 'the family' as an institution.

2. They 'take history seriously' in the sense that they recognize that 'when things happen within a sequence has consequences for how they happen' (Tilly, 1984: 14). They are also open to the possibility of both continuity and change within family life patterns across time and treat this as an empirical question. This is in contrast to approaches that begin with the assumption of theoretically sharp (but historically ill-defined) distinctions

between, for example, 'tradition' and 'modernity', or 'modernity' and 'post-modernity'.

3. They favour conceptual 'toolkits' for understanding complex patterns of variation and diversity in the lived experience of family life, and the processes that give rise to them, over theories oriented towards developing generalizations about families and social change.

There are considerable strengths to these approaches to understanding family, and our book has been inspired by the opportunity they present to think about Irish families differently. However, one weakness may lie in their capacity to connect rich understandings of the fluid practices and contours of everyday life with broader understandings of longer term social change (Irwin, 2009) and to account for the significance of habitual and institutional aspects of family behaviour in determining social outcomes. Duncan (2011) has proposed a model of family change as **bricolage** that aims to understand 'how people adapt and re-serve tradition in reacting to new circumstances, how this may – or may not – secure legitimation, how meanings leak from older to newer traditions and, not least, in what ways these processes and their outcomes are socially uneven and unequal'. This analytical approach has promise for explaining how family practices and displays across the life course can give rise to complex patterns of continuity and change in family patterns.

Nevertheless, theoretical approaches to family change should be evaluated differently according to the temporal scale at which they are applied (see Mason, 1997 who made this argument about fertility transitions). Some of the generalizations that nineteenth- and twentieth-century evolutionary theorists developed may hold true when considered in the long sweep of modernity. It remains to be seen where contemporary patterns of family life will fit within these grander time scales when they come to be re-evaluated by future scholars. The comparative welfare-regimes approach helps us to understand cross-national variations in family patterns on an intermediate temporal scale. Finally, the family practices approach applies at the relatively short temporal scale of individual human lives.

Using qualitative longitudinal data, as we have done, to make sense of changes in the textures and rhythms of family life across generations or cohorts, requires attention to how they fit within the patterns of social development that apply on longer temporal scales. For that reason, in each of the chapters that follow, we interpret our qualitative data in the context of the broader questions and concerns that have guided sociologists in their analyses of family change, focusing specifically on continuities and changes in demographic trends, household economies and ways of making a living, values and attitudes, and configurations of family, kin and community.

Key concepts and ideas in Chapter 2

- Bricolage
- Comparative welfare-state regimes
- Family configurations
- Family displays
- Family life transitions
- Family practices
- Gender roles
- Individualization
- Life course
- Post-modern families
- Second demographic transition
- Strong and weak family systems
- Temporal scales

Part II

Changing families across the life course

3.1 Group of little girls in front of the tower blocks, Ballymun, Dublin, 1969.
The Wiltshire Collection, courtesy of the National Library of Ireland

3

Changing childhoods

When Claire and her brothers and sisters arrived home from school in the 1930s:

> we had to do the homework and when we went to the national school we'd always have work to do when we came home from school outside. When the potatoes had been dug and that we often had the job of picking potatoes, well the big ones might be gone but you might have to pick the small ones and it would be cold weather at that time, the potatoes were dug later than they are now. We'd all have to do that because they could have had four or five men digging all day, there was no machines then, so that when we came from school that would be the first thing that we'd do. (Claire, b. 1931, LHSC)

In contrast to the work she had to do at home, Claire loved the freedom of going to and from school: 'Great fun, off on the bike in the morning, meet a few others down the road and we'd all go in and out together'. Today, when nine-year-old Heidi finishes school:

> I do my homework, I go to after school because my Mum and Dad are in work until half five and I come here and eat my dinner and then I normally get changed then I play on my Nintendo and before that I have my dinner and before you came I was reading my school book. I go on my bike.
> *Interviewer*: And do you go on the road or around here?
> *Heidi*: No it is too busy because it is a main road. I just go around the house.

Heidi also participates in scheduled after-school activities:

> I like swimming and football and Jazz Ballet. I like Speech and Drama but not the most.
> [...]
> *Interviewer*: How do you get there?

Heidi: In my after school and there is a hall and just run around there and I just go across there and then you are into Jazz Ballet. And Football my Mum or Dad collects me and brings me. Speech and Drama my dad is going to work on Saturdays and my mum brings me down and I walk back up. (Heidi, age 9, GUI)

Claire's and Heidi's narratives starkly illustrate how Irish children's lives have changed. In the past, children were expected to help their parents with work around the house as soon as they were physically able to do so, leaving them with little opportunity for recreational time. Many were employed outside the home as domestic servants, farm hands, messengers and factory workers. In 1936 more than 12,000 Irish girls aged fourteen to seventeen were in domestic service, about 11 per cent of all girls in that age category (Census of Ireland, 1940). Having left school at the age of fourteen Kathleen (b. 1924, LHSC) was 'out the door slaving for other people and it was, literally, slaving'. Her father drove her down 'in the ass and cart' to her first job which was 'the same as the next one, scrubbing floors and washing delph and ironing and cleaning and scrubbing down on your bended knees'. By contrast, many contemporary children like Heidi live leisure-centred lives that are, nevertheless, highly scheduled, spatially restricted, and subject to adult supervision.

In less than a hundred years the lives of Irish children – and our expectations about what childhood should be like – have been transformed. This chapter traces the long-term shifts in the social meanings and experiences of childhood that have accompanied children's changing roles in Irish families, and more broadly, in Irish society. Memories of childhood from the LHSC participants allow us to trace these changes from the early part of the last century and to make comparisons with the contemporary childhoods described by the nine-year-old GUI participants, through a sociological lens.

Children have always been central to social scientists' understanding of the family as a social institution. Early in the last century, anthropologist Bronislaw Malinowski placed the social identity and nurture of children at the heart of his argument that the family is a universal social institution (see Collier et al., 1992). Writing in 1981, sociologist Andrew Cherlin (1992 [1981]) noted that, while twentieth-century families had shed many of the characteristics once thought essential for functional family life, caring for children remained one function met almost exclusively within families. More recently, some social scientists seemed to suggest that children have become an 'optional extra' in intimate adult relationships even as states begin to alter the definition of families by enshrining the idea of children's rights. **This is discussed in more detail in Chapter 3.**

In this chapter we see also how social scientists' approach to studying children in families has changed, from a focus on **socialization** at the middle of the twentieth century to an emphasis on understanding children's **agency** in family practices and displays at the beginning of the twenty-first century. We trace changes in the construction of children's place in families as a public

issue – from anxiety about their moral welfare to concerns about the consequences of changing family patterns for children's socio-economic well-being
– and assess the evidence relating to contemporary issues. We begin with what
is perhaps the most significant long-term change for children across the globe:
the continuing decline in risk of dying before your life has really begun.

The demography of childhood

As we saw in Chapter 1, the first phase of the demographic transition in
Europe was driven by significant decreases in infant and child mortality. At
the beginning of the last century, more than 90 of every 1000 babies born
alive in Ireland, died before their first birthday (Kennedy 2001: 51). This compared quite well to other European countries. In Denmark, for example, more
than 100 in every 1000 infants died during their first year at that time. In
the course of the twentieth century, however, Ireland was slower to improve
its record of infant mortality, only beginning to 'catch up' in the 1980s (see
Figure 3.1).

Today, infant mortality in Ireland is comparable to that of most countries in
the rich world. By contrast, in many countries in the developing world, rates of
infant mortality are as high as those in Ireland more than one hundred years

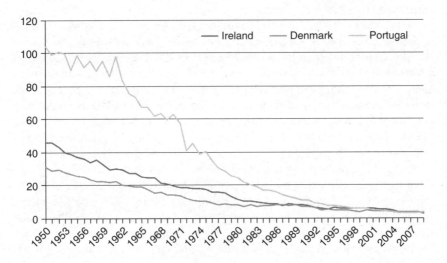

Figure 3.1 Infant mortality in Ireland, Denmark and Portugal, 1950–2010

Source: Human Mortality Database, University of California, Berkeley (USA) and Max Planck
Institute for Demographic Research (Germany). Available at www.mortality.org and
www.humanmortality.de (data downloaded 10 October 2013)

ago. In Nigeria, for example, an estimated 79 out of every 1000 infants died during their first year in 2011 (CME Info, 2015). Compared to the present, young children's risk of dying in the past was also high. At the middle of the last century, one child in every sixteen died before his or her first birthday. Infectious diseases, such as pneumonia, tuberculosis, measles and whooping cough were significant causes of death, as was diarrhoea (Heanue, 2000: 36).

Did the risk of losing an infant or child to disease affect parents' feelings for their children? Controversially, authors such as Lawrence Stone (1977) and Nancy Scheper-Hughes (1992) argued that high rates of infant mortality may cause parents to invest less emotion, especially in new-borns. John's (b. 1946, LHSC) memory of his grandmother included a perception that she 'seemed able to handle grief very well'. Despite the death of her husband, son and grandchild in quick succession, 'there was no huge grief', which John attributed to, 'more death in them days, bigger families'.

However, other scholars (Pollock, 1983) argued against the view that, because death was more frequent, parents experienced less grief. Mary (b. 1929, LHSC) described how a neighbouring family experienced the tragic death of their four-year-old son in a household accident while both parents were out saving turf on a nearby bog: 'She was bad, they were blaming themselves ... they had family after, but it was a terror'. This tragedy was shortly followed by the death of their twelve-year-old son to tuberculosis, and Mary's mother supported her neighbour during this bleak period by helping out with domestic work: 'My mother used to go running down to her, she'd bring clothes down to her'.

Mary's account also helps us to understand the economic context within which childrearing took place in the past, which we will return to below. But John's account highlights other aspects of the demographic regime that affected the experience of growing up in families in the past, namely, the high rates of fertility that gave rise to larger families and long, overlapping generations. Because John's mother came from a large family, and his grandmother continued to have children over an extended period of her adult life, John was able to remember the loss of one of his own aunts or uncles when they themselves were young children.

As the shape of the population has changed from a pyramid family structure towards a **beanpole structure** (see Chapter 2), children's experiences of spending time with a large group of siblings has also changed. Older respondents recalled that the large numbers of brothers and sisters in their families made them 'self-contained' during childhood – they did not need (or sometimes weren't allowed) to seek out playmates from other families: 'I often say it is a good thing we are a big family, if we weren't we probably would have turned out queer ... so we stayed on our own ... and played our own games' (Delores, b. 1934, LHSC). By contrast, many parents of the GUI children alluded to the importance of getting their children involved in local clubs, training sessions and summer camps as a means of socialising with other children.

Panel 3.1   Looking at the data: coping with the loss of stillborn babies

In a study of Irish 'cillíní' – unconsecrated burial grounds where, under Canon Law, unbaptized infants were interred from the seventeenth century until as recently as the 1960s – Eileen Murphy (2011) demonstrated that parents made considerable efforts to replicate funerary practices for baptized people, suggesting that privately they mourned their loss. Some of the older LHSC participants recalled the rituals around burying a stillborn baby that were common in the early decades of the century. For example, 'you had to take a man who was not a member of the family with you, and you took it up and you buried it at night in a corner of the graveyard that wasn't concentrated' (Eileen, b. 1928, LHSC). Eileen was a young girl when her mother delivered a stillborn son at home, and she overheard her father making the preparations for the burial that night, 'I was the eldest and I always had my ear open if there was people in the house. My father was looking for a shoe box to put the baby in'.

Lillian (b. 1932, LHSC) delivered twin boys at home, one of whom was stillborn, and that night her husband and the gravedigger buried the corpse in 'a special part of the cemetery, it was just a hole in the ground, there was no mark or anything'. Lillian was never sure of the exact location of her child's grave and 'the awful thing about it was [my son] wanted to know there a few years ago where his twin was buried'. During her childhood Sarah (b. 1946, LHSC) also witnessed some of the practices around burying stillborn babies in her village, and recalled that 'babies used to be thrown over the walls in orange boxes [as] people didn't have the money, so if a baby was stillborn or died after a couple of hours, that was the only way they could have had of burying it'.

Despite the comparative frequency of miscarriage, stillbirth and child mortality in past generations the LHSC narratives reveal how the death of a child was still a source of misery for parents and a cause for neighbourly sympathy and support. Lillian was not told about her stillborn child until her family believed she was strong enough to accept the news, and she was 'terrible disappointed, I thought God, wouldn't it have been lovely to have twins'.

Demographic evidence on changing population structures has led many scholars to believe that young children today have fewer opportunities to develop relationships with family members in their own generation and more frequent relationships with older family members, including grandparents and, increasingly, great-grandparents (Bengtson, 2001). However, other scholars (Herlofson and Hagestad, 2011) urge caution about this inference. Certainly, qualitative evidence from the GUI study suggests that in 2008 many nine-year-olds continued to have lots of interaction with cousins, as well as with grandparents, as exemplified by Mathew (age 9, GUI) who included in his relationship circle 'all my cousins and I am close to them and I get on with them and that'. In an earlier study on suburban living during the 'Celtic Tiger' period, Corcoran, Gray and Peillon (2010) also found that most school-aged children in the greater Dublin area had regular contact with circles of extended kin. This may be because Irish families remained comparatively large until more recently than in other European countries, but it may also reflect a greater emphasis on extended family relationships in Irish culture (Quail et al., 2011).

Grandparents were very important in the lives of the nine-year-olds who participated in the GUI study – but this was also true amongst some of the oldest respondents in LHSC (Gray et al., 2013). Nevertheless, because of chang-ing demographic patterns, more children in the present are likely to experience a relationship with more of their grandparents over a longer period of their childhoods than was true in the past. Furthermore, fewer grandchildren are competing for their grandparents' attention, and many of today's grandpar-ents come from a cohort of people who married and had children at earlier ages than those in earlier and subsequent birth cohorts, so that they themselves are comparatively young grandparents (A. Gray, 2005). **The changing texture of grandparent–grandchild relationships is discussed in Chapter 6.**

Zelizer (1985) described how changing demographic structures have been accompanied by shifts in children's roles within families. For example, in the early part of the twentieth century, poor mothers resorted to 'baby-farmers' to take infants off their hands for money. By contrast, by the end of the century, middle-class adults were prepared to pay poor women to act as surrogate mothers so that they could have a 'priceless' child of their own. While the LHSC narratives do not contain any reference to baby-farming, it is clear that many parents with very large families coped by having other relatives – including grandparents – take young children in on a temporary or semi-permanent basis (Gray, 2014). The practice of raising siblings in separate households often led to strained relationships within families as the fostered child became increasingly distant from their parents and siblings as they settled into a new life elsewhere. Children who were sent to live with unmarried relatives were often considered lucky by their younger siblings, as these relatives 'were able to give [them] things that [they] couldn't have at home' (Deirdre, b. 1930, LHSC).

Before moving on to discuss explanations for the changing experiences of children in families, one more aspect of the demography of childhood must be explored, namely, the growing likelihood that children will spend at least some of their childhoods in single-parent families and/or step-families as a result of increasing rates of births outside marriage and of separation and divorce. Demographers have drawn attention to the fact that changing family patterns mean children are today more likely to experience a sequence of different kinds of family living arrangements across their childhoods. For example, Frank's (age 9, GUI) parents split up when he was very young and when his father remarried, Frank gained four step-siblings from his step-mother's previous marriage, plus two more half-siblings from this new relationship. Frank normally lives in a quiet home with his mother and older brother, but when he visits his father, 'he is one of a multitude' and his mother observed that, 'when he is talking about his family he just talks about it as a one unit, he doesn't talk about it as two separate things' (Frank's mother, GUI).

Nevertheless, it is important not to exaggerate the significance of this pattern. First, as Andersson (2002) showed, it remains the case that most children in Europe spend their whole childhoods living with two married parents. Furthermore, it must also be remembered that, in the past, children experienced disruptions in their family living arrangements for other reasons. We have already mentioned the practice of sending infants to live with other family members in order to relieve the strain of large families on young parents. In remote rural areas, older children were sometimes sent to live with other relatives in order to facilitate school attendance. For the five years of his secondary education, Francis (b. 1952, LHSC) spent the school term living with his father's siblings, an unmarried aunt and uncle who were still living on the family farm. As he explained, 'We lived where we lived, at that time there was no free transport or no school transport, so it was either a boarding school or nothing ... so there was a compromise worked out'. In exchange for this accommodation Francis assisted his uncle with farm work. However, it was 'a fierce lonely, isolated existence; my uncle and aunt would be very conservative people, probably at that time in their fifties'.

In homes where a parent was suddenly deceased, especially where the mother had died, it was common for a family of young children to be divided up amongst their relatives and raised apart from each other for the remainder of their childhood. Uhlenberg (1980) calculated that, in the United States, children were as likely to lose a parent to death early in the twentieth century as they were to lose a parent to divorce at the end of the century. As we will see in Chapter 5, Ireland has comparatively low rates of divorce compared with the United States and northern European countries. In the GUI study, just 4 per cent of the children interviewed at age nine had moved from a two-parent to a one-parent family for any reason when they were interviewed at age thirteen: 79 per cent of children continued to live in a two-parent family across that period (*Growing Up in Ireland*, 2012).

While there is ample evidence that Irish children have experienced family disruption and separation from their parents for multiple reasons over an extended period of time, it is important to remember that different forms of family disruption may have different consequences for children in varying social and historical contexts. We discuss the research on this issue in detail below. First, we turn to explanations of children's changing family experiences, beginning with changing sentiments about childhood.

Panel 3.2   Landmark Irish study: *Growing Up in Ireland*

Growing Up in Ireland is the first government-sponsored national longitudinal study of children's lives in Ireland. Starting in 2007, GUI's aim is to follow the lives of two different groups of children – 8,500 nine-year-olds, and 11,000 nine-month-olds – and see how they are developing in their current social, cultural and economic environment. Needless to say, no study of this size or scale has ever been conducted with Irish children before.

As a **longitudinal study**, GUI will help us understand how children develop over time – it is more than a static snapshot. Its research design is geared towards eliciting what factors contribute to happy and unhappy childhoods, what factors towards typical and atypical child development. Also –and this is crucial – it seeks to understand what children themselves think of their own lives, what it means to be a child growing up in today's Ireland. To this end, GUI involves interviewing not only adult parents, but also their children. The information gathered will help contribute towards government policy formation regarding the lives of children and their families both now and into the future.

GUI contains both a quantitative and qualitative stream. For the latter stream, 120 families from each of the infant and nine-year-old cohorts were chosen, with more in-depth information about their views, experiences and aspirations around family life gathered through semi-structured interviews with parents and children (in the case of the child cohort). This book draws extensively on the qualitative interviews with nine-year-olds and their parents.

Clearly, the economic downturn of the last few years has impacted on the extent to which government can invest resources in services like children's health and education. Therefore, getting a grasp on how children and families cope in straitened times – how they collapse, struggle or remain resilient – is even more important now than it is during periods of economic expansion, when monies are more freely available to spend on child-related facilities. Targeting what little resources are available at the most vital areas is paramount. GUI can help identify what these areas might be. You can learn more about GUI at www.growingup.ie.

The invention of Irish childhoods

In his classic study, Philippe Ariès (1962) argued that childhood as a distinct phase of life is in many ways an 'invention' of modernity. The idea that children have unique characteristics and requirements that mark them off from the world of adults would have seemed absurd to mediaeval parents, according to Ariès. Right up until the beginning of the twentieth century, children in some social groups were introduced to their future adult role at a young age, when boys, in particular, moved from the world of women to that of men. In his study of the rural community of Iniskillane in the west of Ireland in the late 1960s, Brody (1986 [1973]: 110) described the transition of the young teenage son into the working world of his father;

> A son came under his father's full control only after confirmation [about thirteen years of age]. Before that his life did not go much beyond home and schooling, in both of which he was his mother's responsibility. The more intimate relationship, formed as it was before the boy was thirteen, was thus with the mother ... Once at work on the farm, however, sons began to spend the greater part of every day in the father's company, working under his direction.

Building on Ariès' work, a number of scholars attempted to delineate stages in the history of western childhoods (Sommerville, 1982; Cunningham, 1995; Heywood, 2001). Many, including Ariès himself, identified the seventeenth century as a key turning point, when puritan thinkers introduced the idea that parents had a responsibility for developing the moral capacities of their children. By the eighteenth century enlightenment thinkers, notably including Jean-Jacques Rousseau, had begun to develop the notion that the kind of adult a child would become was influenced by his or her education – and by the experiences he or she had during childhood.

The nineteenth century saw the emergence of a romantic vision of childhood in western culture in which children came to occupy a distinctive symbolic position – representing, for example, the natural 'innocence' of a pre-industrial past in harmony with nature. Condon (2000) showed how children were mobilized to invoke competing symbols of the nation during Ireland's struggle for independence from Britain at the start of the twentieth century. Queen Victoria's review of Irish children in the Phoenix Park in Dublin during her visit in 1900 served to reinforce her image as the 'most motherly of queens'. In the same year Irish nationalists organized a rival 'patriotic children's treat' in Clonturk Park in Dublin, where the children in attendance were interpreted as symbols of loyalty to a different queen, Cathleen Ní Houlihan, the mythical emblem of Irish nationalism: 'With the shining gold of their hair, and the sapphire gleam of their eyes, and their rosy lips they made a long bright garland for our Queen, Ireland, to wear, and whose richness and beauty all the world might envy' (Maud Gonne writing in the United Irishman, quoted in Condon, 2000: 174).

Social historians have documented the practical consequences of changing ideas about childhood in children's everyday lives (Stone, 1977; Cunningham, 1995). Some of the changes included a decline in the practices of swaddling infants and the promotion of breastfeeding, production of books and toys designed for children's amusement rather than just their instruction and a reduction in the use of corporal punishment. It's clear, however, that changing sentiments towards childhood in the emergent middle-class were not followed speedily by changing experiences for all children. Corporal punishment, for example, was not completely banned in Irish schools until 1982, although there is evidence that public opinion had begun to turn against the practice from the mid-1950s onwards (Maguire and Cinnéide, 2005). Childhood memories from the LHSC participants born before the 1950s include many memories of corporal punishment of children by adults, which ranged from a 'clip round the ear' to a beating. In such situations, obedience was maintained through an implicit threat of violence so that 'children at that time were afraid of their fathers and their mothers a bit' (Seamus, b. 1916, LHSC).

However, many of the oldest participants interpreted such punishments as reasonable and bearable, and LHSC participants, born right up to the middle decades of the twentieth century, often recount physical chastisement by their parents with humour. Pauleen (b. 1952, LHSC) remembered her mother's threat; 'if you don't stop I'll bash your heads together [...] eventually she got the two of us and she went *chonk*'. Amongst those born from the 1960s onwards, however, there is a notable reduction in accounts of corporal punishment by parents, and even where the threat of being 'smacked' or 'hit' existed, it was rarely followed through on, so that 'it was twice a year maybe like it wasn't like every week' (Niamh, b. 1960s, LHSC). By the early twentieth century, public opinion on corporal punishment of children had become so unfavourable that in 2013, a study by the Irish Society for the Prevention of Cruelty to Children found that 62 per cent of adults believed slapping a child was already illegal in Ireland, and 57 per cent supported making it illegal (Flaherty, 2014). This negative view of corporal punishment is also evident in the GUI interviews; few of the GUI parents spoke of using any form of corporal punishment when disciplining their children, while the nine-year-old participants identified 'whacking their child' (Maura, age 9, GUI) or 'smacking [their child] for no reason' (Colm, age 9, GUI) as the actions of 'a bad parent'.

During the early decades of the twentieth century, in addition to physical punishment within the home, children were likely to experience, or witness, corporal punishment in school on a daily basis. Even when unfairly dished out, most children understood that 'there was no point in complaining' to parents (Laura, b. 1928, LHSC) as 'you might get a cuff around the ear and be told that you must have deserved it' (Patrick, b. 1934, LHSC). However, it is also evident from the accounts of older participants, that many parents were aware of brutal and unwarranted assaults on their children, yet were reluctant to intervene 'because they felt if [they] done anything about it that you would be selected [by the teacher], perhaps even more so' (David, b. 1945, LHSC).

As in many other areas of children's lives, the experience of corporal punishment was differentiated by social class so that not all children experienced beatings to the same degree or severity. None knew this more than children of the poorer classes who were aware that: 'if the child came from a family of substance the child was pampered and promoted' (Bernard, b. 1951, LHSC). Children soon learned that classmates from the wealthy, professional classes would be 'the pets, they were never slapped [... while] the poorer you were the better chance you had of being slaughtered, that was par for the course, you accepted that' (Patrick, b. 1934, LHSC). In primary school Bernard shared a desk with the son of a local judge: 'I was literally pulled and dragged and he got the time and he never got a slap ever in his life, and you could say that about the sergeant's son and so on and so forth'.

Poverty also exposed children to the risk of being removed from their families to the harsher environment of an industrial school. The *Commission to Inquire into Child Abuse*, which was established in May 2000, arose from controversy surrounding the abuse of children in the care of residential institutions, including industrial schools. Since the 1930s these were operated by Catholic religious orders, funded by the Irish state, and overseen by the Department of Education. A series of media broadcasts during the 1990s brought to light the extent of the abuse, most famously Mary Raftery's *States of Fear* (1999) for RTÉ television, leading to a state apology to victims of the abuse by the then Taoiseach on the 11 May 1999 and the subsequent establishment of the commission.

In May 2009 the report from the *Commission to Inquire into Child Abuse*, commonly referred to as '*the Ryan Report*', was published. It includes testimonies from former 'inmates' of industrial and reformatory schools. Established in Ireland in the mid-1800s, industrial schools were specifically for children that were neglected, orphaned or abandoned, while reformatory schools were for those convicted of offences. During the period covered by the Ryan Report, there were sixty certified industrial or reformatory schools in Ireland and, according to the report, the majority of children were committed to industrial schools because of poverty. In the 1940s, the Department of Education estimated that about a third of children in industrial schools were there simply because their parents were unable to support them (Raftery and O'Sullivan, cited in Ferguson, 2007: 127–128).

The next most common reason for committal, accounting for 10 per cent of the children, was conviction for an offence or non-attendance at school (Ferguson, 2007: 126). The LHSC narratives reveal that children were fully aware of the consequence if caught missing from school. James (b. 1924, LHSC) was from an agricultural area in the south-west of Ireland and contributed to his family's income throughout his childhood and adolescence by working as a farm labourer. He recounted the weekly visits of the Gardaí to his school to check attendance records. As he recalled; ''Twas wicked [at] that time. I did know one boy who went there alright ... the Christian brothers used to beat the devil out of him'. In addition to those children that were committed directly from home due to poverty or misdemeanour, many 'illegitimate' children that had spent their infancy in state care, including Magdalen laundries and 'Mother and Baby Homes', were transferred on to industrial schools as young as eight years of age. Anne-Marie (b. 1966) described the long term damage caused to her father by his upbringing as a 'ward of the state' in the 1940s and 1950s: 'My dad had been institutionalized. Because he is very humble, he'd always sit like this [demonstrates how] and never looks people directly in the eye, no confrontation at all. That has actually been a major influence on all our lives'.

As the social structure of Ireland changed, and the country became more prosperous and urbanized, from the 1960s onwards, changing sentiments towards children diffused throughout the population, in a process of **informalization of relationships** between parents and their children. Traditional, authoritarian models of parenting started to give way to more democratic approaches. Like in other western countries, Irish parents were increasingly influenced by the advice of 'experts' on how to raise children. In Ireland these included 'a young devout, Catholic mother', Angela Mcnamara (Ryan, 2012), whose problem page in *The Sunday Press* newspaper attracted many letters from conservative Irish Catholics between 1963 until 1980. Paul Ryan's (2012: 122) analysis of the letters sent to Angela Mcnamara during this period revealed that from the 1960s, 'Parenting itself emerged as a skill to be learned rather than an intuitive practice'. Ryan's analysis showed that parents, especially mothers, were 'distressed and anxious at the new challenges that their children would face, and their own incompetence' in navigating their children through a very different upbringing to their own (Ryan, 2012: 122).

This changing orientation towards childhood was reflected in a shift in parents' aspirations and values for their children. Over the course of the twentieth century, parents' values for their children changed away from an emphasis on conformity and obedience towards a focus on autonomy and independence (Alwin, 1996). In Ireland, from the 1980s onwards, data from the European Values Survey shows that parents increasingly valued independence and imagination more, and religion less (Gray and Geraghty, 2013). Some of the GUI parents appeared caught in the transition between their own childhood education in good behaviour, whereby 'your neighbour was always Mrs. This or Mrs. That' (Sebastian's mother, GUI) and the contemporary trend for the autonomous child who is 'afraid of nothing and [...] can stand up for anything that he believes in' (Sebastian's father, GUI). This **ambivalence** is exacerbated by their worries that in contemporary society there is no consequence for bad behaviour, unlike past generations where, 'you got a clout around the ear if you were ever out of kilter' (Sebastian's father, GUI). The qualitative interviews shed additional light on the context and meaning of these changing values for parents. Whereas the oldest participants hoped that their children would have an adequate standard of living and retain their religious faith and identity, participants born after 1945 articulated a striking new emphasis on happiness and the capacity to shape one's own life as key aspirations for their children. Contemporary parents' aspirations for their children were tempered by increased anxiety about the world they would grow up in, as evident in the GUI parent narratives.

These more recent trends in values and aspirations for children may reflect what Christopher Jenks (1996) described as the emergence of a **nostalgic construction of childhood** in late modernity – a sense that past childhoods were better than those of today. But what are the consequences of these new constructions for children's experience of family life? In her now classic study of *Unequal Childhoods* Annette Lareau (2003) documented the phenomenon of **concerted cultivation** – the ways in which middle-class parents invest time in extra-curricular, structured activities for their children in the company of adults which contrast with working-class parents approach in which children spend unstructured after-school time in the company of peers. Lareau suggested that middle-class parents were thereby providing their children with a better preparation for middle-class jobs, a hypothesis that has since been supported by quantitative research in the United States (Cheadle and Amato, 2011) and Ireland (McCoy et al., 2012).

Lareau's research complements earlier research by Melvin Kohn (1977), which showed that class differences in parents' values for their children reflected parents' different experiences of the workplace. Whereas middle-class occupations require employees to exhibit innovation and independence of thought, working-class jobs impose conformity and obedience on employees. Thus changes over time and continuing class-differences in parental values and child-rearing practices reflect changes in the structure of opportunity within Irish society while also contributing to the reproduction of social inequalities. In GUI, parents described signing their children up for activities they felt would help them 'to do well', and persuading a child to keep up an activity long after his or her interest in it had faded.

However, while the practice of concerted cultivation may be good preparation for the labour market, there are other costs for children. Weininger and Lareau (2009) observed that middle-class parents' attempts to promote self-direction in their children paradoxically entailed subtle forms of control, whereas working-class parents, who placed greater value on obedience to authority, adopted a parenting style that granted children more everyday autonomy. When asked about their weekly activities, many GUI children listed off a packed schedule of formal evening classes, training sessions and tournaments, leaving very little time for unstructured, spontaneous play. For example, Billy's (age 9, GUI) week was structured around regular tennis lessons on Mondays, music practice on Tuesdays, piano lessons on Wednesdays, drama lessons on Thursdays, and hurling and tennis training on Saturdays. Weary of the pressure to keep her children 'occupied for every minute of every day', Billy's mother confided, 'I think they should learn how to do nothing, not even a ... actually do nothing' (Billy's mother, GUI). As with many of the children in GUI, Billy was persuaded by his parents to take up these activities, rather than necessarily choosing them for himself.

> **Panel 3.3   Landmark Irish study:** *Irish Children and Teenagers in a*
> *Changing World* **by Pat O'Connor (2008)**
>
> As we saw in Chapter 2, one explanation for contemporary patterns of
> family change centres on the idea that we live in a world characterised
> by rising levels of **individualism** and narcissism. What this means is that
> people, generally, are becoming more and more disengaged from – more
> and more disenchanted by – traditional roles ascribed to them by state,
> creed, class, caste or family. Rather than looking towards these time-
> honoured structures, institutions and communities for answers to life's
> many conundrums, people look inwards instead seeking biographical
> solutions to what may well be structural problems, inequalities or imbal-
> ances. Sociologists call this process the 'reflexive project of the self' (**see
> Chapter 2 for a discussion of this theoretical tradition**).
>
> Pat O'Connor's *Irish Children and Teenagers in a Changing World* pro-
> vides much compelling evidence in its attempt to measure the **indi-
> vidualization** thesis in relation to young people growing up in today's
> Ireland. Analysing over 33,000 documents written by Irish children
> (aged 10–12) and teenagers (aged 14–17) in response to a school exer-
> cise to 'describe themselves and the Ireland they inhabit', O'Connor's
> book examines the impact, for better or for worse, of rapid social change,
> de-traditionalization and accelerating globalization on their young lives.
>
> And the results – interestingly – are largely ambiguous. O'Connor
> found that young people do display many of the signature traits of
> advanced individualism, including transnational media consumption,
> participation in global youth culture, perpetually scripting a story of the
> self – a script that is forever and constantly edited, updated and revised.
> Yet, at the same time, more traditional influences like family, community
> and local neighbourhood participation remained very much to the fore
> in guiding their lives, in informing their decision-making, self-perception
> and future aspirations.
>
> The narrative excerpts from the written texts presented throughout
> the different chapters of the book are illuminating insights into Irish chil-
> dren's lives and thought processes. They are also vivid reminders that our
> ever mixed-up, messy reality is more complex than the sociological theory
> of late-modernity, accompanied by a rising tide of individualism, suggests.

Children in the household economy

In pre-industrial societies where labour-pooling households predominated,
children contributed to the **household economy** as soon as they were physically able to do so. **Labour-pooling in the household is discussed in Chapter 1.**

Jane Humphries (2003, 2010) has shown how demand for children's labour increased during the early stages of the process of industrialization. Before the introduction of the factory system, families increased the amount of labour dedicated to producing commodities for sale in the marketplace in what Jan De Vries (1994) described as the 'industrious revolution'. Women's and children's work became increasingly important during this period. In Ireland, many households in the north and north-west of the country devoted more labour time to linen spinning and weaving from the middle of the eighteenth century onwards (Collins, 1982; J. Gray, 2005). The linen yarn and cloth they produced was exported principally to the industrializing cities of Great Britain and to the British colonies in North America and the Caribbean.

With the development of linen-spinning and weaving factories in and around Belfast, household manufacture of linen slowly declined during the nineteenth century. Children now became an important source of labour for the spinning mills, while their small wages often made a vital contribution to the survival of their family-households, which increasingly depended on pooling wage income (rather than labour in production) for their survival. **This is discussed in more detail in Chapter 1.** As new laws were introduced regulating child-labour and making attendance at school compulsory, employers and parents worried about the effects of losing children's contributions in the home and workplace. At the beginning of the twentieth century, from the age of twelve onwards, children worked as 'half-timers', alternately attending school and working in the mill; at thirteen they could legally leave school and work full-time. In her wonderful oral history of the Ulster linen industry, Betty Messenger (1980) documented the importance to impoverished families of getting their children into the mill as soon as possible, sometimes even before the legal age had been reached (Messenger, 1980: 81).

Industrialization was not confined to Northern Ireland before the 1950s. Deirdre (b. 1930, LHSC) grew up in the South-West of Ireland, and at sixteen started working with the 'dangerous machines' at her local woollen mill; 'they called it a mule, it worked in and out and if you stood in the wrong place, I witnessed a girl getting her leg caught in it ... you had to be very careful'. Usually the lion's share of earnings was handed over to parents as a contribution to total household income. Of the 12s and 6d earned by Deirdre each week, 10s were given to her mother. Many older LHSC participants described leaving education after primary school to take up paid employment in unskilled labour; girls typically worked in shops, factories and in domestic service, while boys worked on farms, building sites and fishing boats. For many, turning fourteen was a release from what they perceived to be a futile education, and they could 'get out and get at it' (Bernard, b. 1946, LHSC).

Agriculture remained the principal way of making a living throughout most of Ireland up to the 1960s (Hannan and Commins, 1992). On the family farm, children worked from as young as eight, doing 'every odd job' (Enda, b. 1950, LHSC) including milking cows, feeding animals, bringing in hay, fetching fuel for the fire or water from the well, and assisting with sowing and tilling crops. To accommodate their obligatory attendance at primary school, children's labour mostly took place before and after school hours and at the weekend. From the age of eight Mark (b. 1933, LHSC) worked alongside his siblings: 'we all helped when we came home from school in the evenings, and before we went to school we'd get cows in, milk them, get them out to pasture'. In rural communities, during crucial agricultural periods, such as when crops were being harvested, children were expected to be absent from school for a number of weeks to assist on the farm. While both boys and girls helped out with heavy work in the fields, particularly during sowing and harvesting, daily housework was exclusively the domain of female family members. Girls were expected to assist their mothers with 'baking and cooking and tidying and cleaning and washing and everything' (Enda, b. 1950, LHSC) while the boys 'were outside helping Daddy' (Delores, b. 1934, LHSC). This identification of domestic labour as female work served to establish a gender hierarchy within the home, which placed girls in the service of male family members. Girls, especially, were also expected to help with caring for younger siblings in large families: 'In them days the oldest ones would mind the younger ones that was the way' (Liam, b. 1934, LHSC).

Despite the ubiquitousness of childhood memories of hard work on the farm, some scholars query whether children's labour really was essential to the success of farm enterprises in Ireland during the early decades of the twentieth century. Fahey (1992) argued that children and their families fell foul of the law requiring school attendance more because of the harsh conditions at school, and the difficulty getting there for some rural children, than because their labour was required at home. For example, James (b. 1924, LHSC) spent all of his childhood summers 'tilling beat and turnips and maize and all that craic' for pay, and he lamented the nine years that he 'wasted' making the daily round trip of six miles on foot to his local school: 'when I think about those wasted years [laughs], we had half the day to learn Irish and 'twas useless'. Nevertheless, it is clear that contemporaries believed that poor farm families would suffer hardship if they could not draw on their children's labour, such as the *Inter-Departmental Committee on Raising the School-leaving Age* which reported in 1935:

> It seems to us almost inevitable that if juveniles were compelled to go to school instead of to work there would be a demand for maintenance allowances for the disemployed juveniles – a demand which the state would find difficult in refusing. The cost of a scheme of maintenance allowances would be prohibitive. (quoted in Kennedy, 2001: 129)

As we saw in Chapter 1, scholars writing about the European marriage pattern emphasized the importance of life-cycle service in the west. Households that centred on comparatively small family units addressed shortages in their

---

Panel 3.4   Looking at the data: children's work in the farm household, 1920s–1950s

During the first half of the twentieth century, children routinely helped out with heavy agricultural work. However, children's work was differentiated by gender and age. Here is Kathleen's (b. 1924, LHSC) account of girls' work within the family home in the 1920s and 1930s:

> The girls had to do all, the boys were gods. [...] And on Saturday night we were given the polish and we had to polish the lads' boots, the two lads would be [there] and we working here. We had our own to do, Daddy's, Mammy's and our own three to do and the two of [the boys] to do as well. And they'd be [shouting], 'Mammy they're not getting in between the nails on the boots, they are not getting out the dirt! They are only half doing them!' (Kathleen, b. 1924, LHSC)

David (b. 1945, LHSC) gave a detailed description of the way in which his tasks on the family farm had changed as he grew older and more able-bodied:

> Helping would be gauged in such a way of what you were capable of doing but I remember feeding little calves [at the age of eight] and you'd have so many calves to feed, I remember doing that, there were cubicles and you'd just go in with the bucket and feed them. As I got older, and was more able to work, you would be expected to have hay in the manger for horses and cows and that sort of thing and things like bedding, and you'd spread it out for calves and that sort of thing. And then as you'd develop further on you'd be out in the field gathering potatoes, and at that stage youd be tying corn in sheaves and making hay and going to the bog and making turf. At that stage you'd be eleven or twelve or thirteen. (David, b. 1945, LHSC)

---

labour supply based on the family life-cycle or gender composition of their families, by bringing in children and young adults from other households as servants. We already saw how Kathleen left her family to enter domestic service in the late 1930s as soon as she finished primary school, and how Francis assisted his uncle on the farm when he went to live with him while attending secondary school. It is worth noting that right up through the 1940s (Breen, 1983), hiring fairs for servants continued in many parts of Ireland.

As the twentieth century progressed, expectations about children's contribution to the household economy changed in Ireland. Children were required to attend school up to fourteen years of age, and in 1972 this was extended to fifteen years (Kennedy, 2001). As we will see in the next chapter, increasing proportions of young people are remaining in education, or are participating intermittently in the labour market, well into their adult years. Nevertheless, it would be a mistake to think that children make no contribution to their family economies in the twenty-first century, although this topic is relatively neglected in the literature. School-aged children engage in a wide range of formal and informal paid work. During the 'Celtic Tiger' period the proportion of Leaving Certificate students engaged in part-time work grew from 51 per cent in 1991 to 61 per cent in 2002 (McCoy and Smyth, 2007). Children and young people are active in a range of informal jobs outside the home, such as delivering newspapers and babysitting (Leonard, 2005). Although the majority of the nine-year-old GUI children did not work outside of the home, some of the children were industrious about earning their pocket money, such as Robert (age 9, GUI) who 'started up a grass cutting business' in his neighbourhood, and Damien (age 9, GUI) who worked in his father's shop vacuuming and answering phones in exchange for his 'wages'.

Madeleine Leonard (2009) found that Irish children aged 14–15 years reported participation rates of between 60 and 80 per cent for routine household tasks such as cleaning floors, setting tables and washing dishes. Similarly, the GUI children regularly assisted parents with light domestic tasks, although they were not obliged to help out, or persist with any particular task if they became bored with it. Chores were noticeably frivolous in comparison to the chores of older LHSC participants at around the same age, and were often listed alongside recreational activities carried out with parents, such as watching a particular TV show, going to the cinema, or playing a ball game.

In Leonard's 2009 study, 80 per cent of boys and 85 per cent of girls thought that children should do household chores for a range of reasons – including preparing themselves for the future, instilling responsibility and helping their parents. However, housework was also a source of tension between parents and children: 14 per cent of the young people in Leonard's study felt that children should not have to do housework, or that their participation should be limited. An earlier UK study of 15–16 year olds and their families found that parents often complained about the housework that young people did not do (Brannen, 1995: 325). The normative shifts described above have given rise to ambivalence on parents' part about how much they can expect children to help around the house:

> Parents, depending on their cultural values, are caught in a number of dilemmas: the wish to encourage their young people's independence and not to be overly directive; the desire to regulate and 'keep an eye' on them; together with their own requirements for help in running the household; especially in the context of a dual-earner lifestyle. (Brannen, 1995: 335)

The GUI parents described similar dilemmas trying to encourage their younger children to help around the house. They were caught between a belief that

learning to share in the work was an important part of children's moral development and a desire not to 'burden' them too much. Parents described making
sometimes half-hearted efforts to encourage children to work by drawing up
rotas, trying to make the work seem like fun or threatening to withdraw pocket
money. Jonathon's (age 9, GUI) mother expressed the **ambivalence** of contemporary parents:

> we'd do a little bit of cooking together ... he'd do little jobs for me. He probably
> isn't doing as much as he probably should be doing, but he'd do the watering
> for me outside, he'd do the washing up the odd time. But you'd have to tell him,
> I suppose ... we should be giving him more to do at their age as opposed to what
> they actually do do. They're probably getting away with more than we would
> have got away with, our generation, we would have had a certain amount of
> jobs. I suppose my biggest thing would be that I would like them to get a good
> education and I don't mind if all they do is the homework and I don't mind if they
> put the effort in to the homework cos I can do the other jobs in my own time.
> (Jonathon's mother, GUI)

In the long transition to modernity, children's labour has been transformed
from an essential contribution to the survival of the family household – and a
net marginal contribution to economic growth and development – to an aspect
of socialization and moral development rooted to some extent in memories of
the practices of the past. While hard-pressed contemporary parents desire help
around the house, they wish to protect childhood as a 'special' time, free of
the burdens of adulthood. But also (and perhaps paradoxically) these parents
perceived contemporary children to have a greater obligation to work hard at
their schoolwork, in order to secure their own futures in a world where the
balance of **intergenerational flows** between children and adults has changed
direction.

Children, families and communities

As discussed in Part I of this book, the care and socialization of children was
at the heart of the structural-functionalist perspective that dominated social
science thinking about families at the middle of the last century. However,
despite their centrality to the model, children were seen only as passive recipi-
ents of adult care. Similarly, perspectives centring on household economies
and family systems, including **Marxist-Feminist** perspectives, recognized that
children contributed to family survival, but tended not to examine their role as
active agents in **family adaptive practices**. In more recent scholarship, the new
emphasis on family practices and configurations beyond the nuclear family
has dovetailed with the emergence of a new sociology of childhood, which has
opened a fresh window on family life through its insistence that children are

actors in their own right with capacities to construct and shape their social world (Morrow, 1996; Valentine, 1996).

We saw, in the section above, how young people negotiate and push back against their parents' demands with respect to housework, and how tensions between children and their parents on the issue are framed within changing norms and expectations about childhood. Yet even in the authoritarian family environments of the early twentieth century, children found ways to resist adult expectations about work at home and at school. Children in rural areas 'lingered' on the way home from school in order to expand the brief time when they were together with their peers, away from the supervision and discipline of teachers and parents. In spite of the long journey to school 'across the fields', that often led to sore feet and a day spent in wet clothes, many LHSC participants had fond memories of it, including Delores (b. 1934, LHSC), who recalled the joy of walking barefoot in the summer and sliding on the ice in the winter; 'all the things that we weren't supposed to do, you know, that would hold us up coming home from school'.

The LHSC interviews show how children growing up during the 1940s and 1950s played an active role in creating, reproducing, and sometimes subverting, the community ties that bound families and households together, while also reinforcing local status hierarchies. During their daily circulations from home to school, children regularly dropped in on neighbours and extended family members, thereby constructing and reinforcing community and family ties in ways not entirely controlled by adults (Gray, 2014). Brenda's (b. 1934, LHSC) experience demonstrates how children's practices could impact on community relationships:

> I remember one time my pals ... used to come to my house and I went off to their house, and stayed a bit longer than what I was told and they came back with me and there was a terrific present, my Daddy got a rod and beat me for ten minutes and they went home crying to their mother saying that I was beat so much. And their mother wasn't pleased because I was in a good house and playing with her children and she was offended that I should be beat after leaving her home because she wouldn't do that to her children. (Brenda, b. 1934, LHSC)

Brenda's friends' mother was offended because Brenda's father's treatment of his daughter seemed to reflect negatively on her own family's status.

While many children continued to have work obligations that constrained their opportunities to socialize with peers right through the 1950s, from the 1960s onwards new sentiments towards childhood combined with a changing socio-economic structure to create greater opportunities for carefree socialization with peers. This pattern was especially marked in new urban residential areas where families were all at similar stages of the family life-course, so that there were 'always plenty of people to play with' (Rachel, b. 1972, LHSC).

New scholarship on children emphasizes how they are active agents in creating and maintaining **social capital** (Morrow, 1999). Madeleine Leonard (2005: 619) described how children in deprived communities in Belfast and Dublin were 'resourceful and active in developing networks with each other and with adults within and outside the family' by doing favours, through voluntary activities and by participating in paid employment. Corcoran et al., (2010) found that children were the 'glue' that created ties amongst families in new suburban communities during the 'Celtic Tiger'. Parents frequently observed the sentiment that 'kids help you settle in more' by creating opportunities for social interaction and incentives for neighbourly co-operation.

At the same time, Corcoran et al. (2010) found that in these new suburban communities children struggled to create and retain spaces for childhood activities away from adult supervision in the context of ongoing suburban development and new fears about the perceived risks that children face in public places. Similarly, some GUI parents spoke of their 'massive worries' (Damien's parents, GUI) about the risks to their child of injury or attack. They were caught between conflicting desires to protect their children and to allow them to ramble freely around the neighbourhood, as they had done during their own childhoods. For example, to enable Damien (age 9, GUI) to 'go back and forth' to his friend Cian who lived in the neighbourhood, both mothers kept each other updated by phone on the boys' location: 'Cian's mom would ring us and vice versa, like Cian will come and play on the green and I'd let her know that he's here and when he's leaving, so we know at what stage they'll be [home]'. This co-operative solution between the mothers created an impression of unsupervised play while also providing the parents with peace of mind. However, it was dependent on the children remaining in the visible environment of 'the green' in the centre of their housing estate.

In Corcoran et al. (2010), while adults often expressed a preference for suburbs as 'safe' places in which to raise children, children themselves regretted the loss of green spaces in which to play. The comments from a child living in Mullingar reveal the encroachment of development on open spaces and changing adult attitudes to childhood, and how these interact with class differences to limit children's opportunities for unstructured social activity.

> Unless you have a big garden, and you can play soccer or something, there's not much else to do unless you join a club. Like, there's no fields that you can go to that are set up just for a game of football, if you're not with a club. So you can only do that [play football informally] if you have a big garden (focus group with school children, Mullingar, quoted in Corcoran et al., 2010: 164).

According to some scholars, changing social constructions of childhood have been accompanied by the increased segregation and 'domestication' of children within controlled environments (Zinnecker, 1995; Holloway and Valentine, 2000; Karsten, 2001). Paradoxically, our contemporary emphasis on childhood as a special time of life, with distinctive needs and requirements, which

**Panel 3.5   Landmark Irish study: *Childhood and Migration in Europe*
by Caitríona Ní Laoire, Fina Carpena-Méndez, Naomi Tyrrell and Allen
White (2011)**

If it is broadly accurate to claim that children's voices have long been
silenced in most sociological studies of the family, then it is likely that
migrant children's voices in immigrant-receiving countries have been
even more muted. Recognizing this, a group of migration researchers at
University College Cork thought a study of the worlds of child migrants
to Ireland was long overdue. Their results, *Childhood and Migration in
Europe*, provide a fascinating insight into the lives of children who were
born outside of Ireland, then moved there with their parents in their
early childhoods.

Of the existing research on child migrants, argue Ní Laoire et al., much
of it focuses on their vulnerabilities, their near-total dependence on adult
decision-making. And much of it has been on those in extremely at risk
situations – children who have been illegally trafficked or separated
from their parents, child refugees and asylum seekers. This has resulted
in a body of work that almost entirely overlooks children's agency and
subjectivities, examining instead their reliance on state immigration
regimes, welfare and social care agencies.

Childhood and Migration in Europe differs to the extent that it focuses
on the lives of migrant children themselves, looking at how they understand, experience and interpret their own situations, from their own
perspective. Also, another distinguishing feature is that it focuses on
children who are not necessarily victims of forced migration: migrant
children from Latin America, central and east Europe, Africa, and the
offspring of returned Irish migrants make up the four child groups
studied.

How each group integrates into Irish society – in schools, play-
grounds, their local communities – forms the central research theme in
each chapter. The ties they maintain with family and friends in the countries where they were born emerge as another important aspect in these
children's lives. As does the children's sense of identity and belonging in
a context where most are framed by the broader Irish society as being
'different' from the mainstream population – either because of their skin
colour, accent, language ability, or religion. Negotiating their childhood
in such situations, and making the pathway to early adulthood, often
proves challenging, though rarely insurmountable. In essence, this
study showcases migrant children's ingenuity, resilience and creativity
as they grow up in a country that is still predominantly white, Catholic
and Irish.

has led to the creation of 'child-centred' places, may also contribute to the segregation of children from wider community and cross-generational family ties. Geraghty et al. (2014), describe how, while today, as much as in the past, children spend time in the company of grandparents, now they are more likely to experience that care within the confines of a domestic setting, whereas in the past, grandparents provided a bridge to a wider, intergenerational world. **Grandparents' care of grandchildren is discussed further in Chapter 6.**

By contrast, in contemporary middle-class Irish families, creating child-centred community networks is often a parent-driven activity requiring working parents, such as Audrina's mother, 'to be involved, to bring them there and bring them home and just put in the time with them'. Nevertheless, these practices serve to develop social ties amongst families, so that 'you get to know the other people'. There is also considerable evidence of continuity in the extent to which Irish children are embedded in extended family networks. For example, Freddy 'has cousins up the road ... as far as he is concerned they're brothers and sisters' (Freddy's parent, GUI). Ní Laoire (2014) described the importance of extended family – and especially cousins – in the family lives of children who are members of return-migrant Irish families. Extended kinship ties provide 'social support, a sense of belonging, cultural capital and access to other networks' (Ní Laoire, 2014: 155).

Changing childhoods as a public issue

In 2012 Ireland voted in favour of a constitutional referendum to replace Article 42.5 of the 1937 Constitution of Ireland with the new Article 42A. This change brought into being an explicit, constitutional recognition of the rights of the child, independently and in addition to the 'inalienable and imprescriptible' rights of the family unit (as defined in the pre-existing Article 41 on the family). For example, the new article includes the provision for legislation that enables a child to be adopted, regardless of the marital status of their biological parents; that children of a particular age and maturity can have a say in court decisions on their own welfare along with an explicit reference to the child's best interests in all court decisions on protection, adoption, guardianship, custody and access. The new article also contains a redefinition of failure in parental duties; gone is failure for 'physical and moral reasons' (Article 42.5) and in its place failure that affects the 'safety and welfare' of the child (Article 42A).

The new article, in affirming the principle that a child's best interests should be the paramount consideration in decisions about his or her future, and by providing for children's own views to be taken into account, was a significant milestone in the Irish state's recognition of the changing status of children within families and society. It reflects the continuing shift in emphasis described in Chapter 2, away from the protection of the family from state interference that characterized the **patriarchal familism** of the first half of the twentieth century, in favour of the **liberal individualism** that seeks to protect the rights of individuals within families (Fahey, 1998).

Yet concerns that some families could not provide adequate care for their children are not new. More than 130,000 children spent time in industrial schools in Ireland between 1869 and 1969 (Ferguson, 2007: 125). Inspectors from the National Society for the Prevention of Cruelty to Children (a branch of which was first established in Ireland in 1889), played a leading part in the removal of children from their homes. According to Ferguson (2007: 131–132), the 'neglect' that prompted intervention in most cases was framed in the context of a romanticized Victorian notion of childhood 'innocence'. Within this worldview, concern for children centred on how neglect might expose them to moral corruption; children were seen 'as future threats to social order as much as victims' (Ferguson, 2007: 132). As in other countries, the perceived moral risk was highly gendered, depending, as it did, on notions of appropriate gender roles and sexuality. In Ireland, there was an added emphasis on enforcing moral purity as a way of establishing a distinctive national identity in the context of independence (Ferguson, 2007: 135).

Ferguson (2007: 133) argued that, 'It is impossible to exaggerate the symbolic power that these [industrial school] children and their families had in the social order'. We have already seen how early twentieth-century Irish nationalists invoked a romanticized image of children in promoting their vision of an independent nation (Condon, 2000). In an Ireland where a property-holding class of patriarchal farm families was at the heart of the project of state-formation, children from families characterized by poverty and neglect – often in urban areas – represented a moral threat to shared understandings of social order.

Skehill (2003) identified the 1970s through the 1990s as a transitional period during which child protection increasingly became the preserve of professional social workers in the context of the 'moralization and normalization of the unmarried mother' (although, as Fahey et al. (2012) show, children living in large family households comprised a greater proportion of vulnerable children at the middle of the century than did children living in one-parent households). As Ireland has moved into a policy regime characterized by 'liberal individualism', changing family patterns have given rise to new public concerns about the consequences of those changes for children.

Within this shift, social science research has come to occupy a central role in public debate, and to be mobilized by advocates of different positions in a pattern that can sometimes take the form of 'going to extremes', presenting research findings in ways that do not do justice to the complexity of the phenomena or the limitations of what social science can achieve (Cherlin, 1999). If concerns about children in families were articulated within an overtly moralistic framework during the first half of the twentieth century, in contemporary Ireland social science research is sometimes inappropriately invoked as objective evidence that removes the requirement for moral judgement. Here, we illustrate this point with reference to the sociological literature on three topics: the increased likelihood that a child will spend at least part of his or her childhood living in a one-parent family, with cohabiting parents or in a step-family; the effects on children of mothers' employment; and the putative decline of the family meal.

The GUI study found that eight out of ten nine-year-olds were living with two married parents in 2008. Just over 18 per cent were living in one-parent families; of these, about half were living with parents who had never married, and half with adults who were parenting alone as a result of separation, divorce or widowhood (Hannan et al., 2013: 12–13). Just 3.1 per cent of nine-year-olds were living in families headed by cohabiting biological or adoptive parents and a further 3.3 per cent were living with step-parents (half of whom were cohabiting) (Fahey et al., 2012: 19). Ireland is somewhat unusual compared to other rich countries insofar as children are more likely to live in one-parent families because their parents never married than because their parents had divorced (Fahey et al., 2012: vii). **We examine the demographic trends and sociological factors giving rise to these changes in patterns of family-formation in Chapters 4 and 5.** Here we review the evidence that spending time in childhood in the absence of a biological father – either in a one-parent or step-parent household – is detrimental to children's life chances.

There is considerable international evidence that growing up apart from a biological father is associated with a wide range of negative outcomes for children. These include poorer performance in education and lower earnings in adulthood, greater risks of psychological and behavioural problems, and earlier adult life transitions including first sexual intercourse, becoming a parent and leaving home (Amato, 2005; McLanahan and Percheski, 2008). **Family life transitions in early adulthood is discussed in Chapter 4.** However, these findings are subject to **selection bias**: children living apart from a biological father are different (on average) from children living with both biological parents in lots of other ways. Most significantly, they are more likely to be living in economically disadvantaged circumstances. Even before they were born, their parents may have had social or psychological characteristics that made them more likely to have children outside a stable relationship, or less likely to remain married. In the case of children who live apart from their fathers as a result of separation or divorce, family troubles before their parents separated may explain some of the negative outcomes observed by researchers (Cherlin, 1999).

Social scientists are faced with considerable difficulty in trying to disentangle the effects of family structure, if any, from these other factors. Many studies have concluded that, once the whole range of potential causes are taken into account, living apart from a biological father has a small independent effect on child outcomes and child well-being. In Ireland, researchers have found that educational attainment is the outcome most affected by growing up in a non-traditional family, once adjustments for selection bias are made. However, as

Hannan et al. (2014: xii) point out, we don't know whether or not this effect is due to additional, unknown factors not examined by the researchers. Family structure might be a mediating factor in the pathway leading from pre-existing difficulties to poor child outcomes. For example, women with lower levels of educational attainment are more likely to become never-married lone parents (Hannan et al., 2014: 62). In Chapter 4, we show how qualitative data can shed light on the pathways linking lower levels of education to early childbearing outside marriage (c.f. Hannan et al., 2014: 65).

Two teams of researchers working on the quantitative GUI data (Fahey et al., 2012; Hannan et al., 2013) have concluded that there is insufficient evidence that growing up apart from a biological father is in itself a substantial cause of poor child outcomes. According to Fahey et al. (2012: ix): 'Once resource differences are controlled for, family type is not a strong predictor [of child well-being]'. Hannan et al. (2013) used a sophisticated statistical technique (propensity score matching) to adjust for selection bias and concluded that:

> when faced with similarly adverse conditions growing up, children from one-parent families and cohabiting families fare similarly in most regards to children from families of married parents. However, some differences do remain, especially in terms of maths scores and school attendance among children from never-married one-parent families. This is most likely the result of bias caused by factors not taken into account in the analysis. (Hannan et al., 2013: xii)

When faced with cautious and qualified findings like this, students, policy makers and members of the public often express frustration. The conclusions do not provide us with clear guidelines about what to do, and researchers make conflicting or ambivalent policy proposals.

Internationally, some researchers conclude that programmes to reduce the number of children who grow up in non-traditional families should be implemented, even though the share of children whose life chances would be improved might be relatively small (Amato, 2005; Marquardt et al., 2012), but others argue that policies to ameliorate the deficit in resources faced by single parents would be more effective (Cohen, 2015). In Ireland, the Iona Institute (2010) draws on international research about the consequences of non-traditional patterns of family formation to argue in favour of policies oriented towards the promotion of marriage. **Some of the challenges faced by pro-marriage programmes are discussed in Chapter 4.** Both Fahey et al. (2012) and Hannan et al. (2013), argue in favour of policies oriented towards alleviating the contextual factors giving rise to poor child outcomes across all family types, and against policies that focus on 'the residential status of their parents' (Hannan et al., 2013: 61).

Ultimately, the policies adopted will be based on value judgements informed by social science research. Research evidence has an important part to play in

---

Panel 3.6   Landmark Irish studies: evidence-based interventions in child and family well-being

In recent years research evidence has played an increasingly central role in the design and roll-out of community based programmes to bring about better outcomes for children, young people and families, particularly those living in disadvantaged areas. These early intervention and prevention programmes are usually delivered in the form of community based support services, such as school-based programmes, mentoring, family therapy and antenatal classes, to name but a few. In addition to service provision, these initiatives usually carry out an evaluation of the effectiveness of their services at specific intervals and feed the findings from each evaluation back into further service development.

In Ireland, the Area-Based Childhood (ABC) Programme, co-funded by the Irish Government and Atlantic Philanthropies, aims to break the cycle of child poverty by funding a range of collaborative services in disadvantaged areas. Each stage of the design, planning and evaluation of the ABC Programme is overseen by the Centre for Effective Services (CES), an organization that links innovative design that is emerging from international research with the work of policy makers, service providers, community workers and expert groups. The ABC Programme continues to build on the experience of the initial projects that were rolled out in Tallaght, Ballymun and Darndale. By 2015 a further nine had entered the design stage of the programme. More information on the ABC Programme can be found at www.dcya.gov.ie.

Archways is a national organization established in 2006 'to promote and research evidence based programmes for children and young people'. The organization works in collaboration with local and national agencies to bring initiatives with a strong international research evidence base into local Irish communities. One example is The Mentoring for Achievement Programme (MAP), which is a primary school-based, early intervention programme for students that have been identified by school personnel as being at risk of academic failure and early school leaving. The MAP intervention incorporates learning theory into practices that assist young people at risk of academic failure to realise their full potential. The full list of programmes that are operated by Archways can be found at www.archways.ie.

---

ensuring that the judgements we make are informed by sound evidence, but it does not provide an escape route from difficult moral and political debates (Cherlin, 1999). Sometimes, instead of providing complex or ambivalent findings, social science research debunks conventional wisdom in ways that we may find uncomfortable. This is the case with research on the consequences for children of working mothers. The proportion of married women in paid employment increased in Ireland from the mid-1980s onwards, but really accelerated during the 'Celtic Tiger' boom. Between 1998 and 2007 the proportion of women with school-aged children in the labour force increased from 52 per cent to 65 per cent (Russell et al., 2009: 18). Inevitably, this rapid change in household gender roles led to concerns about the consequences for children. How could they hope to fare as well without the care of a mother working full-time in the home? In fact, the research evidence on this is counter-intuitive for many people. According to an authoritative review of research from the first decade of this century: 'The vast majority of studies of maternal employment showed either no or small effects on child outcomes ... [and] ... positive effects were increasingly reported for young children in low-income families' (Bianchi and Milkie, 2010: 710). **Changing household gender roles are discussed in more depth in Chapter 5.**

In a similar vein the media regularly run stories about how the decline of the 'family meal' in contemporary life is leading to all variety of health, behavioural and social problems. A recent article in the *Irish Times* (Gilham 2012) entitled, 'Serving up a little family stability' cited research that supported the adage that the 'family that eats together, stays together'. The 'family meal' – a meal at a set time, with a set menu, with all family members present round the same table – is said to be in decline across all contemporary developed nations as meal times become increasingly individualized, so that family members dine separately, eat their own favoured foods, and eat at times and locations of their own choosing. However social science research refutes the popular idea that the 'family meal' is in decline by debunking the portrayal of the regularly practiced, stable shared meal of the past as historical fiction, so that much of the contemporary concern about the decline of the family meal is actually a misreading of the past (Jackson et al., 2009; Murcott, 1983).

In his examination of narratives from the LHSC archive, Ralph (2013) found a similar misreading of twentieth-century Irish eating habits. Contrary to popular belief, accounts of family meals in the past also display temporal fragmentation in family eating practices, whereby 'domestic commitments and the exigencies of different family members' working circumstances contribut[ed] to more fragmented family eating practices'. For example Peter (b. 1928, LHSC) recalled, 'We wouldn't have been all there at the same time ... it would have been a very rushed time. There wouldn't have been much time for socialising, you came in, sat down, got your dinner and took off again'.

Some of the LHSC participants described a rather undemocratic, authoritarian hierarchy at the dinner table where members had their own demarcated seat at the table, where the food was distributed in order of rank, and where children were expected to 'keep silent if an older person was speaking' (Mark, b. 1933, LHSC). Finally, large family size often prevented all members from dining simultaneously, and instead in such households food was doled out through multiple sittings at the dinner table, for example, 'There was a time in our house when we had relays nearly. The smaller ones were fed either first or last depending on what things were on or how busy and what was done. They were fed last or first so it would depend on what went on' (Daniel, b. 1947, LHSC).

In fact, the most significant change in contemporary family mealtimes that was evident across the narratives from both LHSC and GUI is the way in which people use food to give expression to the significant relationships in their lives. In other words, more than ever contemporary families 'display' family through food and food practices, such as the communal consumption of food in public spaces on special occasions such as birthdays, weddings and anniversaries.

Summary and conclusion

This chapter has examined the changing significance and experiences of children and childhood in Irish families. We saw how changes in the demographic context affected children's lives by reducing the size of sibling sets and increasing the salience of relationships with members of ascendant generations. These demographic changes were also closely intertwined with a transformation in the social construction and meanings of childhood which affected the quality of relationships between parents and children. Where once children's contribution to the household economy through labour was a taken-for-granted part of their daily lives, today children are carriers of their family's aspirations for socio-economic mobility through education and cultural attainment. Middle-class parents, in particular, have taken on the responsibility of co-ordinating children's friendship and community lives.

Our analysis also revealed ample evidence of children's agency in pushing back against parents' expectations and creating their own social and familial worlds, both in the present and in the past. Furthermore, class differences mediated Irish childhoods – and public discourses about the consequences for children of 'failing' families – in different ways across all historical periods. In the next chapter, we consider changing family life from the perspective of a 'new' life stage: early adulthood.

Key concepts and ideas in Chapter 3

- Children's labour contribution
- Romantic vision of childhood
- Informalization of relationships
- Children's agency in family practices
- Nostalgic construction of childhood
- Concerted cultivation
- Domesticization within controlled environments
- Debunking conventional wisdom

4.1 Irish Shell staff dance at the Shelbourne Hotel, Dublin, 22 November 1958. © Irish Photo Archive / © Lensmen Photographic Archive, www. irishphotoarchive.ie

4

Early adulthood and family formation

No place like mammy's home. (Holmquist – *Irish Times* 16 October 2010)

In 2010, a Eurostat report showing that almost half of all European adults aged eighteen to thirty-four years were still living with at least one of their parents led to consternation – and some amusement – in media reports in Ireland (Holmquist, 2010). Census 2011 revealed that just over a third of young Irish adults in this age group were still living with a parent or parents (CSO Statbank CD217). However, media attention has subsequently moved on to concern about high levels of emigration amongst young Irish adults. Estimates from the Central Statistics Office showed that in 2013 net outward migration (that is, the surplus of people leaving Ireland compared to those entering the country) was almost 22,000 in the age group fifteen to twenty-four years (CSO, 2013).

Both trends are linked to the increasing difficulty experienced by young adults in establishing themselves in **independent households**. While the Great Recession has exacerbated this difficulty due to high levels of unemployment and of precarious employment amongst young adults, a trend towards extending the life stage of early adulthood has been evolving in Ireland since the mid-1980s and from an earlier date in other countries. This chapter describes how delayed adult life transitions are linked to changing family patterns, including the **unbundling** of marriage, parenthood and household formation. As the norms that formerly confined sexual activity, cohabitation and parenthood to within marriage have broken down, multiple pathways to family formation have emerged.

According to American sociologist Andrew Cherlin (2004), these patterns are associated with the **de-institutionalization of marriage** – that is, with a weakening of the social norms that define people's behaviour in family and personal life. In Ireland, recent legislative changes introducing **civil partnership** represent an acknowledgement by the state of the altered status of marriage. However, debates about the May 2015 referendum to introduce same-sex marriage revealed that marriage continues to have considerable

95

significance as a **cultural ideal** and as an institution governing relationships between parents and children. We explore these issues in the final section of this chapter. First, however, we examine the changing demographic trends associated with the emergence of early adulthood as a new family life stage.

Demography: extending early adulthood

In recent years, a number of scholars have drawn our attention to changes in the **timing and sequencing of the transitions** associated with family formation in contemporary western societies Furstenberg et al., 2004; Billari, and Liefbroer, 2010; Furstenberg, 2010; Settersten, 2012). Whereas in the 1950s and 1960s, young adults left home, entered employment, married and started a family in a tightly ordered sequence of events within a comparatively short period of time, today these transitions have become separated and prolonged, and their sequencing has become more variable. In Ireland, these changes began a little later than in other countries, but they can still be seen quite clearly in Figure 4.1. People born in the 1940s, who reached adulthood in the late 1950s and 1960s, were likely to marry and have children at a younger age than those in later cohorts. Furthermore, the age gaps between leaving home, marriage and first birth were narrower for those born in this decade. Within individual lives each transition tended to follow on quickly from another. By contrast, for people born in the 1970s who reached adulthood in the late 1980s and 1990s, the period in their lives between reaching **formal adulthood** and forming their own families was much more extended, and this pattern looks set to continue, as people remain longer in education and postpone marriage and first births to later ages.

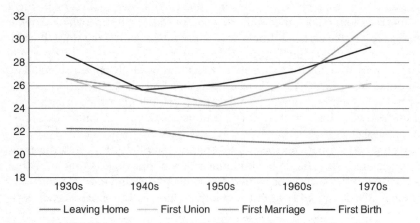

Figure 4.1 Median age at early family life transitions by birth cohort

Source: ESS Round 3: European Social Survey Round 3 Data (2006)

Figure 4.1 also shows that amongst those born in the 1970s a gap had opened up between the median age at 'first union' and that at first marriage. This is because, in this cohort, the proportion of people who cohabited before they married had increased significantly: in the European Social Survey more than 60 per cent of Irish women in this age group reported that they had lived with a partner before marriage. As we saw in Chapter 2, rates of cohabitation increased rapidly in Ireland from the 1990s onwards (Halpin and O'Donoghue, 2004). In contrast to some European countries where cohabitation has emerged as a lifelong alternative to marriage (Kiernan, 2002), in Ireland cohabitation is still principally a transient life stage, and most Irish people move on to marriage, especially once children come along (Halpin and O'Donoghue, 2004; Lunn et al., 2010: 18). This suggests that cohabitation has not really replaced marriage as an institution in Ireland. According to Lunn and Fahey (2011: 36):

> [It] is perhaps not appropriate to think of the dramatic increase in cohabitation as a change in preferences regarding the status of couples. It is arguably more accurate to characterize the development as the change from a situation where marriage was the norm for couples who lived together, to one where marriage is the norm for couples who have children together.

However, it is important not to assume that this situation will continue, given the scale of increase in cohabitation and the emergence of a minority group of older (more than 35 years) cohabitants with children (Lunn et al., 2010: 16–17). Growing proportions of couples may choose to remain unmarried as they go through their lives together, whether or not they have children.

It is also striking that the median age at first birth amongst those born in the 1970s is younger than the median age at first marriage. This is explained by the fact that growing proportions of women are giving birth outside marriage – either within a cohabiting relationship or as single parents. The European Social Survey (see Figure 4.1) data show that, amongst Irish women who were born in the 1970s and had given birth, more than half had their first child before marriage – one of the highest percentages in Europe. Ireland witnessed a dramatic increase in the proportion of births occurring outside marriage during the 1980s and 1990s, from about 3 per cent in 1980 to just over 30 per cent at the beginning of the twenty-first century, when rates appeared to stabilize. More recently, however, the proportion of births outside marriage (or civil partnership) increased again to 35 per cent in 2012 (CSO, 2014c: 31).

While the initial change in the 1980s was precipitous, qualitative life history data hint that in previous decades, some births outside marriage may well have been hidden from the statistics. LHSC participants described how, in the past, such births were concealed within families by assigning the children of unmarried mothers to married relatives; Elizabeth (b. 1970, LHSC) remembered regular visits to an aunt: 'we never knew until later that she was actually our granny; we always thought she was our mother's sister'. In addition, a number of participants recounted stories of 'shotgun weddings' in which expecting couples married hastily in secret before the birth of their child. Rosemary (b. 1927, LHSC) explained that her brother 'was married behind the Pro-Cathedral because [his girlfriend] was seven months pregnant'.

Some of the increase in births outside marriage revealed in official data may be attributable to changes in both cultural norms and in legislation since the 1980s that meant it was no longer necessary to conceal non-marital births. We discuss those changes in more detail in the next section. It is important to remember that most women who have children outside marriage are in stable or cohabiting relationships, and subsequently do marry. While unmarried mothers tend to be younger, the age difference between them and married mothers has lessened over the years (Fahey and Field, 2008: 35). Few births outside marriage are to teenagers: of the 24,393 non-marital births registered in Ireland in 2013, just 1,218 (about 5 per cent) were to women aged less than twenty years (CSO, 2014c: 39, Table 2.4).

The 'unbundling' of early family life transitions that led to the postponement of marriage and childbirth has also been associated with a significant reduction in age at first sexual intercourse. Most women born in the 1940s had their first sexual intercourse after the age of twenty-two, while the median age for women born in the 1970s was four years younger (Fahey and Layte, 2007: 161). As we explore in more detail later in the chapter, amongst the oldest LHSC participants (those born in the 1950s or earlier), sexual activity was inhibited by fear of pregnancy outside marriage. For many of the LHSC participants that reached adulthood in the late 1980s and 1990s, by contrast, moving out of the family home was a key event in the commencement of sexual activity. Many of these participants moved away from home for the first time around the age of eighteen, to pursue higher education or job opportunities, although prior to this sex 'wasn't even on the radar' (Anne-Marie, b. 1966, LHSC). The lack of private space, and in some cases limited contact with the opposite sex, were major factors in delaying sexual activity until late adolescence for these participants, as Chris (b. 1965, LHSC) explained: 'First of all we didn't have cars and we had no place to go, and I suppose when I think about it really, there weren't all that many girls our age around here'.

In summary, then, we can understand much of the recent transformation in patterns of family formation as changes in the timing and sequencing of transitions during early adulthood. The separation of sex from marriage and childbearing, and of marriage from cohabitation and family formation, has occurred in the context of a prolongation of the phase of life between formal adulthood and establishing a family of one's own. Before the 1980s, for most young adults in Ireland, the sequencing of these transitions was tightly ordered and highly sanctioned (as we will see in the next section), and thus recent changes represent a significant transformation in family practices.

Panel 4.1   Landmark Irish study: *Pathways to Adulthood in Ireland* by Damian F. Hannan and Seán Ó Riain (1993)

In 1987 Damian Hannan and Seán Ó Riain conducted a study into transition patterns amongst a large sample of young adults that had completed their secondary education in 1981/1982. According to Hannan and Ó Riain, as the individual moves from full dependence on their family of origin to complete economic independence and the establishment of their own household, they move through a sequence of interrelated 'statuses', namely, employment, new household formation, marriage and parenthood. A central aim of the research was to discover whether a single, 'normal' pattern (both in the statistical and normative sense) of transitioning through these statuses could be identified in the 1980s.

A national sample of adults aged between twenty and twenty-three participated in a survey interview which examined their progression to independent adulthood over the preceding five to six years since completing their secondary education. The research revealed that progression to adulthood was just as structured for young adults in 1987 as it had been for their own parents, so that 'a "normal" or majority pattern of integration into adult life [existed] for over ninety per cent of young people, at least up to age twenty-two' (p. 223). The study found that the period of transition from school to marriage averaged about nine years for men and six years for women. They also found a close association between marriage and establishing a separate household – a pattern that, as we have seen, began to unravel in the 1990s. The dominant pattern in 1987 was therefore still very traditional. Young adults progressed through the steps of getting a job, getting an independent residence, then marriage, and then family formation, and the attainment of each status operated as a prerequisite to moving on to the next. While the majority of interview respondents had managed 'successful' transitions, Hannan and Ó Riain found that deviations from the normal pattern, such as early marriage or pregnancy outside of marriage, were rare, tended to be reactionary rather than chosen – such outcomes were often the result of the 'persistent failure to find a normatively approved pathway' (p. xvi) – and were often distressing for the individual.

Accounting for 'success' or 'failure' in transition, Hannan and Ó Riain found that educational achievement was the biggest determining factor in achieving successful transitions. 'Failure in education almost guarantees failure in employment' and due to the interrelated and sequential nature of transitioning, further negative consequences could follow. Unemployment had very serious stress and personally disabling effects on the well-being of young adults, and these effects could be modulated by young adult's economic and social supports, along with personal attributes such as their attitude and self-conception and their sense of control over their lives.

However, the timing of the transitions associated with family formation fluctuated to a greater extent during the twentieth century. For those born before the 1940s, these transitions were often prolonged and uncertain so that young people who completed their education at fourteen might have waited many years before they were in a position to establish their own families and households. Many of those without an inheritance emigrated in search of work, and in some cases, managed to return with a dowry that allowed them to marry (Arensberg and Kimball, 2001 [1940]: 110). Furthermore, the proportion of the population who remained single throughout their lives was very high in the early decades of the twenty century: in the 1930s 27 per cent of those aged fifty to fifty-four years had never married, and the average age at marriage was thirty-three for men and twenty-eight for women (Fahey and Layte, 2007: 167). It was not until the 1960s and 1970s that the timing of early family life transitions became more tightly bundled. Because average age at marriage has increased again, the percentage of people who remain single in their late twenties is actually higher today than in the early part of the twentieth century. However, the percentage of people in this age group who are alone is lower, because of the prevalence of cohabitation (Lunn and Fahey, 2011: 17).

It is also important to recognize that, while the unbundling of transitions described above has led to greater variation in the pathways to family formation followed by young adults, the variation is not random or unpredictable. One of the leading scholars in the field has suggested that we can identify four 'packages' of closely configured transitions in contemporary westerns societies: (1) early and orderly; (2) early and disorderly; (3) late and disorderly; and (4) late and orderly (Furstenberg, 2013: 35). Transitions are 'orderly' insofar as they are consistent with social norms and institutional constraints surrounding the timing and sequencing of life events (Elder, 1994). The packages of transitions described by Furstenberg are at least partly determined by the social circumstances in which people find themselves when they set out on their journeys to adult life.

Thus Lunn and Fahey (2011: 24–36) found that Irish people with middling levels of educational attainment were most likely to be cohabiting or married in their late twenties or thirties; postponement of partnership was more typical of those at both the higher and lower ends of the range of educational attainment. On the other hand, working-class men, and people with low levels of education, were over-represented amongst those who married at comparatively young ages. Similarly, women with low levels of education are more likely to become lone parents in their twenties (Lunn and Fahey, 2011: 80–83).

Different packages of family life transitions also have longer term consequences across the lives of individuals and those of their children. As we saw in Chapter 3, lone parenthood, in particular, acts as a mediating factor that tends to reproduce patterns of inequality over time (McLanahan and Percheski,

---

Panel 4.2   Looking at the data: contrasting generational transitions to an independent household

Ben (b. 1926, LHSC) left school at fourteen to train as a technician for two years, before starting his career at the age of seventeen. Ben's transition to adulthood during his early twenties was both orderly and tightly sequenced. Within five years he completed his training, met his future wife, secured a permanent job, married and established an independent household with his wife and first born child. Once Ben had obtained a permanent job, the new-found financial security enabled him and his fiancée to marry quickly and establish a home independently of any financial support from their parents. Ben described how they eloped:

> [My fiancée] and I said one day, goddamit we are not going to wait anymore. So what we did was, I was living in my aunt's house at the time, [my fiancée] came in on a Friday night, I put her up in the hotel and I came back to my digs in my aunt's. And the next morning I got up and collected my brother, he was going to be my best man, and a friend of ours and his girlfriend. And all five of us went in the taxi to [the town nearby] and got married. (Ben, b. 1926, LHSC)

Donal (b. 1970, LHSC) completed his Leaving Certificate examination (final exam) at seventeen during a period of economic stagnation, and was thwarted from his career of choice as there were 'no jobs available at that time and there was no apprenticeships'. After a short period of unemployment, he commenced a degree in IT engineering, on the advice of a relative; 'he told me computers were the next thing, they were coming in, so I said right, we'll have a look at this computer thing and we'll see what the story is'. Donal's transition to adulthood was elongated due to a longer period spent in education and temporary work. Also the sequence of his transition was more typical of his birth cohort:

> *Donal*: We got engaged over Christmas and then we got married the following Christmas.
> *Interviewer*: And did you live together before you got married?
> *Donal*: Yeah, [my wife] had a house and I moved in, so we moved in together [and] a year after I moved in we bought the house and then got married in the Christmas. (Donal, b. 1970, LHSC)

2008). Thus while some scholars have viewed the emergence of variable paths to family formation as an aspect of growing individualization, the evidence suggests that not all pathways are equally available – or desirable – to everyone, and that different packages of transitions are linked to the reproduction of privilege and disadvantage. In order to make sense of why patterns of family formation have changed, and the factors giving rise to different pathways, we need to investigate changes in values and the socio-economic contexts within which young adults forge their life choices.

Reconstructing partnership, de-centring marriage

The extension of early adulthood and the changing significance of marriage in western societies can be understood to have taken place in two stages (Cherlin, 2004). During the first stage, marriage was transformed from a **patriarchal** institution to a **companionate relationship**. In western pre-industrial societies, as we saw in Chapter 1, marriage was central to the process whereby each new generation acquired access to the resources necessary for survival – whether that took the form of land, or recognition as full members of a trade. For this reason, young adults from landless households, or those headed by unskilled fathers, were less likely to marry, or married later than those who could hope to inherit the means to support a family. As the social and economic structures of western societies were transformed, creating new possibilities for earning a living through wage labour, husbands and wives were increasingly 'supposed to be each other's companions – friends, lovers – to an extent not imaginable by the spouses in the institutional marriages of the previous era' (Cherlin, 2004: 851).

During the second stage, gender roles became 'more flexible and open to negotiation' as increasing proportions of women remained in the workforce after children came along. According to Cherlin this has been accompanied by the rise of **individualized marriage**, in which relationships are evaluated according to how well they meet each partner's 'sense of self and the expression of their feelings' (Cherlin, 2004: 852). **See Chapter 2 for a discussion of critiques of the theory of individualization.** We will discuss how changing household economies gave rise to changes in marriage and household formation in more detail below. In this section we explore the implications of those changes for people's experiences of courtship, sexuality and marriage.

The transformation of courtship

In early twentieth-century rural Ireland, marriages were frequently arranged, as Arensberg and Kimball (2001 [1940: 105) famously described in their account of 'the match'. **See Chapter 1 for more on this.** Arranged marriages were no longer widespread when most of the oldest LHSC participants were finding their partners in the 1940s and 1950. However, Joan (b. 1916, LHSC) was old enough to remember the practice of 'made-marriages' amongst the farming community in her local area in the Mid-West of Ireland, which remained prevalent there until the 1950s and 1960s. As she recalled, when a man was about to inherit the farm, a friend of the family was dispatched to propose a marriage to the father of a suitable local girl:

> People would never have met or wouldn't know anything about each other. We'll say a man ... had inherited a farm or the parents were giving him over the farm and he'd have to get a fortune from the woman that he'd marry, she'd have to have some money and then that would be suggested by some friend. (Joan, b. 1916, LHSC)

Joan did not have an arranged marriage. However, as a young woman, she was the object of negotiations between her father and various 'match-makers' in the area on behalf of newly eligible local bachelors. As she recounted:

> a lot of people would have come to my father saying that they had a man with money for his daughter. I met one man on his way here, and he told me his business, why he was coming, so I think he went away with a bug in his ear anyway! [Laughter] He said, 'She's alright, she is a great worker, but she is very wicked' ... I wasn't going to be bought or sold. (Joan, b. 1916, LHSC)

Did the instrumental nature of arranged marriages mean that no love was involved? Scholars disagree on whether or not the idea of romantic love between husband and wife is a modern invention (MacFarlane, 1986). However, Arensberg and Kimball (2001 [1940]: 108) emphasized that the young couple's wishes were taken into account – if a prospective partner 'didn't suit', the match would not go ahead. John's (b. 1946, LHSC) grand-mother met her future husband just once before they married through an arranged match, and he recalled that theirs 'seemed to be a loving relation-ship from what I know'. John remembered his own mother arranging the last match in his home community, a Gaeltacht (Irish speaking) area in the west of Ireland when he was around nine or ten years old and that 'certain things were taken into account' by the matchmaker, such as the extent to which the couple were similar in their background and age. John did however witness some 'terrible matches when old fellows married young girls'.

As the century progressed, young people increasingly met their future part-ners at social events, especially at dances, céilís and card drives. Joan remem-bered going to a 'tournament' before they were outlawed by the Public Dance Halls Act of 1935: 'all the fellows would come and they would play cards and there would be so many girls in the house it would be filled, and there'd be music'. In rural areas, open air dances, known as 'platforms' or 'decks', were held during the dry summer months, and involved the entire community, young and old, married and single: 'there would be an area set out ... in a field adjacent to a crossroads or a flat area, and these [timber frames] were set out in the summer time and there'd be dances on those, and that was the main form of entertainment' (David, b. 1945, LHSC).

Platform dances provided an opportunity for young, rural people to meet with their peers, and to make subtle advances towards the opposite sex, as recounted by Seamus (b. 1916, LHSC), 'you'd see such a one going out, she let her man down, and another one would have brought out her coat'. Travel to and from the platform dance in large groups afforded young adults in rural Ireland a space to socialize, free from the usual limits of parental observation. Seamus gleefully recalled the banter and teasing amongst the group as they travelled home together by bicycle: '"How'd you get on last night?" was the first thing you'd be asked, "I saw you trying the moves on such a one", you know? Ah sure we had a great old time! Twenty or thirty going off on the bikes'. Having access to a bike was vital for the independence of young adults in mid-twentieth-century Ireland but those who were fortunate enough to own a car were much in demand. James (b. 1924, LHSC) managed to procure a 1937 Ford Ten when he was a young man and 'was delighted ... we'd go away to the dancing in the night time. You'd always get plenty, plenty of passengers [laughing]'.

Car ownership had a significant impact on the courtship behaviour of young adults, particularly as custom built dancehalls began to spring up on the outskirts of towns from the mid-1950s. Vincent Power (cited in Ryan, 2012: 45) argued that, in contrast to cohorts before them that were confined to cycling to local dances, young adults in the 1960s 'drove to ballrooms miles away' where they escaped the surveillance of their local communities. These commercial venues had evocative names, such as *Arcadia*, *Fairyland* and *The Crystal Ballroom*, and enticed the young and unattached with the promise of romance and coupling. As a young woman, Lillian (b. 1932, LHSC) attended *The Ritz Ballroom* in Carlow town every week where, 'there was a huge band, a big band and brilliant musicians and they had their own singer, a brilliant singer ... [and we] could dance around the ballroom and talk to our partners'. A 2014 article in the *Irish Times* captured the typically rousing performance at *The Rainbow* 'Ballroom of Romance' in Glenfarne, Co. Leitrim during the 1950s:

> *The Rainbow*'s 'romantic interludes' were famous when the owner, dressed in a tuxedo, white shirt and dickie bow, took over from the band, performing songs such as the Jim Reeves classic *Have You Ever Been Lonely*. (McDonagh, 2014)

During the 1950s and early 1960s, economic growth was stagnant in Ireland and many young people departed for Britain, attracted by better pay and the opportunity for professional training. To cater for this influx of young Irish migrants, 'Irish ballrooms' were established in areas with large ethnic populations, most famously *The Galtymore Ballroom* in Cricklewood and *The Gresham Ballroom* on Holloway Road, both in London. These ballrooms 'served a crucial function in aiding adjustment to life in Britain, often being the place to meet potential spouses [and] catch up on the news from home' (Delaney, 2007: 171).

According to Delaney (2007: 129), the Irish communities were not immune to the social transformations underway in post-War Britain 'concerning sexuality, gender roles, the role of youth, individual rights and freedoms'. This is supported by the narratives of the LHSC participants who lived in Britain at the time. Many remarked on the unprecedented freedom and autonomy they experienced for the first time while in Britain. Bernard (b. 1951, LHSC) was one such migrant who had followed his brother into construction work in London after seeing him 'driving his brand new car, an Anglia, and money to throw around the place'. He recalled that even within the ranks of the Irish Catholic clergy that circulated amongst the young migrants there was an obvious departure from the stricter doctrines on morality and sexuality that they had known in Ireland:

[The local priest] was a young fellow [from Ireland]. He'd often come to *The Galtymore* with us and that, a bit of craic. I couldn't understand how priests always behaved totally different over there, even though they were from here. Far more natural, far more outgoing, have a bit of craic with you. I went into marriage counselling and he told us about contraception, he left it out on the table and [I said] 'Hold on there Father, you're too late' [laughs]. He put all back into the drawer again. (Bernard, b. 1951, LHSC)

Ballrooms remained popular in Ireland into the mid-1960s, when the 'show-bands' mixed traditional genres with contemporary pop music, reflecting a growing international influence on the tastes of young Irish adults. The new affluence of the 1960s created a generation of consumers for venues that catered specifically for the young. More young adults were leaving the family home to work in the cities and towns, to live amongst their peers in flats and dormitories, and to earn their own money (although many LHSC participants describe regularly sending money home to parents, along with the occasional visit). David (b. 1945, LHSC) moved to Dublin in the mid-1960s to work as a public servant and recalled a condensed network of night time venues in Dublin city centre that catered for these professional youths:

[At] Finlater's church on Parnell Square ... On one side of the square you had the *Irish Club* with the Irish dances ... and then there was the *Teachers' Club* ... then on the other side of Parnell Square you had the *National Ballroom* ... there is a gallery there now. And then you come around the other side of it from Findlater's Church right down to the junction of Parnell Street there, you had the *Ierne* there on the left had side. And at the top of O'Connell Street you had the *Hotel St. George*. You had the *Town and Country Club* on the right hand side, it is now the Gate Theatre ... and the *Ambassador Cinema* was just around the corner from that place and then you had O'Connell Street itself with the *Savoy* and all that. (David, b. 1945, LHSC)

The liberalisation of sexuality

Living and socialising with other young people in the urban centres of Ireland and abroad meant greater opportunities for romantic 'dates' and pre-marital sex. This contrasted with the self-conscious courting in local dancehalls that was the experience of older cohorts. In his analysis of letters sent by young adults to Angela McNamara's problem page during the 1960s, Ryan (2012: 44) claims that the 'changing dating scene ... created anxiety and uncertainty among young people as they struggled to observe a range of informal rules that had to be navigated'. This anxiety is also evident in some LHSC narratives; both male and female participants alluded to their discomfort with what they perceived as the loosening of morals, and preferred to stay on the outskirts of such interactions when they encountered them. Anthony (b. 1946, LHSC) moved into a flat with male friends in the mid-1960s and found 'there was quite a lot of sexual activity going on [... but] I was rather scared, so there was something in me that had me running away from that'. Similarly, Sharon (b. 1951, LHSC) 'took a month off sick' to avoid a party in the house that she shared with two female colleagues as 'I knew what would be going on and everything else, I literally went home for the weekend because I just didn't want to be part of it'.

Many of the changes described above can be understood as part of the emergence of adolescence as a distinct life phase, with an associated 'youth culture' (Demos and Demos, 1969). From the beginning of the twentieth century onwards, young adults acquired increasing opportunities to develop their own spaces for leisure away from the supervision of older people. However, in Ireland, through the middle decades of the century, young people – especially young women – continued to be subject to close regulation, and many of the older LHSC participants remembered this with some resentment. In a number of cases, brothers were required to keep an eye on their sisters, a responsibility some of them took very seriously: 'I had brothers and believe you, if I had been seen talking to a fella, they would run me home' (Rosemary, b. 1927, LHSC).

Pre-marital sex was inhibited by fears about pregnancy outside of marriage. But even more significantly, the LHSC narratives show that, in their youth, participants adhered to a stringent set of social norms for courting couples that were couched in Catholic morality. Young people were discouraged from spending time together unseen by their elders, and it was 'just absolutely "verboten"' (Denise, b. 1945, LHSC) for a single woman to be observed courting a young man for fear of appearing sexually loose. Single young women in particular were instructed by their mothers to be 'civil and strange' in the company of all men (Eileen, b. 1928, LHSC) as '[i]t was the task of single women to remain chaste and virginal [and ...] the task of mothers to make sure that they instilled a sense of modesty in their daughters and that they did not lose it' (Inglis, 1998: 27). John (b. 1946, LHSC) attributed the customary self-monitoring amongst the young to the 'huge overbearing presence' of the Catholic Church in everyday life:

> I would say that growing up in the 1950s was very like the Taliban, it was really, really controlled in a subtle way. Like the priest came to school and asked questions, and Confession was almost compulsory [...] And of course the only sin they saw was sex and put their nose into all of this stuff.

According to Inglis (1998: 35–36) during the nineteenth and twentieth centuries in Ireland:

> the whole field of sexuality was constructed and dominated by the Catholic Church ... Talk about sexuality ... was generally confined to the language of the Church and specifically – in terms of when, where and how sexuality was talked about – the confessional ... Beyond the confessional there was silence.

Instruction of the young in the biological facts of life and sexual morality was considered the domain of the private family, with guidance from the Catholic clergy on how to broach the subject; consequently children and young people received no formal sex education. Even after introduction of a state-run programme for sex education in Primary and Secondary schools in 1997, the decision on the content of these school-run programmes was chosen by teachers, parents and school authorities, which often included members of the clergy (Inglis, 1998).

The LHSC narratives show that, for most participants, sex was a topic entirely off-limits for discussion with parents due to awkwardness and embarrassment on both sides. This resulted in generations of young men and women who reached adulthood with 'absolutely no idea' (Denise, b. 1945, LHSC) about sex or conception. John recalled the bravado of young men who bragged about getting hold of condoms from Britain, but 'wouldn't even know how to use them'. Despite their own deficiency in knowledge about the facts of life, older brothers were conscious that younger, more naive sisters could be 'targeted by older fellows' at the dancehall, and so felt obliged to watch out for them (John b. 1946, LHSC).

Employers of single young women also felt responsible for monitoring their behaviour, particularly where such employees had to 'live in' during their apprenticeship. Through the middle of the twentieth century apprentice nurses lived in dormitory accommodation on the site of the hospital in which they were trained, and many found themselves in very restrictive environments, under the watchful eye of a senior nurse called the 'Home Sister'. This affected their sense of independence well into their adult years, particularly when it came to socialising during the evening. Claire (b. 1931, LHSC) remembered life in a nurses' home in the west of Ireland:

these were grown women, they were all over twenty-one or twenty-two and you wouldn't get a key and you had to go to the porter to get in. And of course some of the cute ones used to leave the window open, the bolt off the window and get in the window. This one, the Home Sister there, she got them to nail the windows that they couldn't get in and that was the last straw.

Young women's sexuality was subject to more regulation than that of young men, in part because the consequences of having a child outside marriage were so much greater for them. Many of the older LHSC participants remembered the gossip and commentary that circulated about young women who 'got into trouble', the common euphemism for a pregnancy outside of marriage. Brenda (b. 1934, LHSC) remembered vividly that a young woman who was known to have had a baby outside marriage was ostracized by her peers at the local dancehall: 'It would have been a shame to be seen dancing with her or you'd be cast as like her, do you see'. Sex outside of marriage was considered immoral but the vitriol was directed mainly at unmarried mothers, while young unmarried fathers were sometimes depicted as unwitting victims of female temptation, so that 'the young buck that did it was kind of looked on as "Poor Mike or Johnny wouldn't do that"' (John, b. 1946, LHSC).

It's important to note that while these experiences of highly regulated sexuality and dire consequences of becoming pregnant outside marriage are predominant in the LHSC narratives, they are not universal. Young women from higher-class, professional backgrounds often had more independence, even in mid-twentieth-century Ireland. Clara (b. 1933, LHSC), from a prosperous rural background, described how she was sexually active from her mid-teens and had love affairs with older men. Linda (b. 1950s, LHSC), from an urban professional background, became pregnant outside marriage in her early twenties:

> back in [the late 1960s] it was very hard to be an unmarried mother and actually all these stories that have come out now and all these films, *The Magdalene Sisters* and all these things, they have actually … affected me greatly. Because I realised that there but for the upbringing, for the upper-class upbringing, how shall I put it, or whatever, there but for the grace of God went I.

Linda was able to discuss with her parents the possibility of going to England to give birth to her baby, who would then have been put up for adoption, but subsequently decided to marry the father of her child in a small, discrete ceremony of 'thirty people, including aunts and things like that'.

The rise of cohabitation

The restrictive attitudes to sexuality and partnership described above began to change very rapidly amongst young Irish adults from the mid-1980s onwards.

Panel 4.3   Landmark Irish study: *Attitudes to Family Formation in Ireland* by Margret Fine-Davis (2011)

Funded by the Family Support Agency, Margret Fine-Davis's major study represents a landmark in our understanding of contemporary attitudes to family formation in Ireland in the context of both demographic and social change including: changing gender roles; increased labour force participation by women; falling birth rates; fertility control; the increased likelihood of remaining single; increased cohabitation; postponement of marriage and delayed fertility. The aim of the study was to identify the forces that determine family formation (or lack thereof) in modern Irish society, and secondly to determine the consequences of different family statuses for people's well-being.

Between August and September 2010 face-to-face surveys were conducted amongst a national sample of 1,404 Irish men and women of childbearing age (aged twenty to forty-nine). Respondents were selected using a stratified sample to achieve a diversity of age, socio-economic status, family status (single / cohabiting / married and living with a spouse), and educational and geographic characteristics. Prior to the survey Fine-Davis conducted a qualitative research module with forty-eight adults from which many of the quantitative survey items were developed.

Fine-Davis found that while there was widespread support for women's participation in paid work outside the home, traditional gender roles persisted 'at least in a psychological sense' across both genders, so that half of the sample believed that 'being a wife and mother are the most fulfilling roles any woman could want'. There was evidence of a positive attitude towards egalitarian parenting – the vast majority thought fathers could be as nurturing as mothers, yet this was also inflected with ambivalence as many also felt that mothers make the better carers of children.

There were some interesting findings on attitudes to cohabitation, with 84 per cent believing it was better to live with a partner before marrying them. The findings also suggested that rather than being an alternative to marriage, cohabitation was a step towards this, and 43 per cent of those that were in a cohabiting relationship at the time of the study said that they would definitely marry their partner. The main barrier to marriage was financial – being able to afford a wedding, or a marital home. While marriage remained a status to be aspired to, two thirds believed that having a child was a much greater commitment than getting married. Also, people expected to have fewer children (closer to two) than what they ideally would like to have (closer to three) and many felt financially restricted from pursuing their ideal family size.

> In terms of well-being Fine-Davis found that married people had the highest level of well-being on all indicators, followed by cohabiting people and single people. Single mothers had the lowest life-satisfaction and were the loneliest of all the social groups examined, leading Fine-Davis to conclude that: 'While there is an acceptance of single-parenthood and a belief, especially among women, that one parent can bring up a child as well as two parents, it is clear that this comes at a price in terms of the poorer well-being of this group' (p. 10). Consistent with other research on family forms in Ireland, Fine-Davis found that socio-economic status was an important mediating factor.

In 1991, more than half of the eighteen to thirty-four-year-olds interviewed as part of the International Social Survey Programme agreed that 'it is not wrong at all if a man and a woman have sexual relations before marriage'. By 1998 that proportion had increased to more than 70 per cent (SIMon, 2015). Approval of cohabitation before marriage also became widespread, increasing from 75 per cent agreeing that it was a 'good idea' in 1994, to more than 80 per cent in 2002. In a national survey, 84 per cent of respondents agreed in 2010 that 'It's better to live with someone before you marry them' (Fine-Davis, 2011: 60). Fine-Davis's study also revealed that, while attitudes to cohabitation before marriage are strongly favourable in Ireland today, attitudes towards cohabitation and marriage once children come along are more complex. Thus, for example, 82 per cent of respondents agreed that 'marriage provides security and stability for children', and 67 per cent agreed that 'deciding to have a child together would be a far greater commitment than getting married' (Fine-Davis, 2011: 59–61). These attitudinal findings are consistent with the demographic evidence on cohabitation discussed above: amongst contemporary Irish people having children is usually accompanied by marriage – although not necessarily always preceded by marriage.

In a qualitative study of cohabitation, Ashling Jackson (2011) found that couples took the decision to marry very seriously, and that this transition was accompanied by considerably greater negotiation than the decision to cohabit. Having a child together was an important factor in making the decision to marry, but the quality of the couple's relationship remained a primary concern.

Jackson's findings resonate with accounts of unplanned pregnancies amongst the youngest LHSC participants (people reaching adulthood in the late 1980s and 1990s). For these respondents, it was the ill-timing of pregnancy and birth that created challenges in their life trajectories (Elder, 1994; Gray, 2010), rather than the birth taking place outside marriage per se. When Niamh (b. 1960s, LHSC) found out that she was pregnant during her first year in college her partner wanted them to get married straight away but she was hesitant: 'I was kind of, no we've only just met. Under other circumstances would we be getting married now?' A month before the birth, Niamh moved in with her partner. While she had 'never wanted children before', she was quite optimistic about becoming a mother: 'I kind of looked on it as a second chance because I'd blown it in terms of college and I was given a chance to raise a fantastic child'.

By contrast, Grace (b. 1970s, LHSC) chose not to marry her boyfriend, whom she found 'immature' and continued living with her parents while she got to grips with motherhood. Eventually she established an independent household as a single mother. Ruth (b. 1970s, LHSC), similarly, remained in her parent's home for a year after the birth of her child because, 'I knew at the time I would never have married [my boyfriend] anyway because he wasn't the settling down type then, he was wild and wanted to be out with the boys drinking'. Consequently, years later, when her partner matured, she allowed him to move into the home that she had established with their daughter, and the couple married. The marriage was tempestuous but she felt 'he is a different man to what he was when he was seventeen'.

In each of the three cases, support from parents, especially their mothers, enabled the young women to manage as single mothers. Niamh's mother discouraged her from moving in with her partner as she 'felt we should get to know one another and if it worked out we'd get married and then we'd move in together'. Ruth's mother was herself locked into an unhappy marriage, and strongly objected to her daughter making the same mistake: '"She is marrying no one," my mother said, "she is not going to be like me getting married just because she is pregnant, she is marrying no one."' It is very interesting in this context to note how the mothers of some respondents who had 'ill-timed' pregnancies were reluctant to see their daughters make hasty decisions about partnership. Undoubtedly this was partly due to fears about separation and divorce (a topic we will discuss in Chapter 5), but it was also certainly a rejection of the limitations they had experienced in their own lives. In contrast to the unmarried mothers described above, Doreen (b. 1945, LHSC) had an unplanned pregnancy during the mid-1960s, and encountered conflicting opinions from her parents. While her mother had always been quick to condemn pregnancy outside marriage, her father was ambivalent; a few days before the wedding she was left 'flummoxed' when: 'my father turned round and he said to me, "You don't have to get married, you know" ... I thought to myself, had he said it two months previous, maybe I would have done something different. But, it was too late'.

In summary, dramatic changes in values and attitudes towards sexuality and pregnancy outside marriage, and towards cohabitation and marriage, occurred across the twentieth century. The qualitative life history data reveal that, amongst those born in the 1920s and 1930s, resistance was already emerging to the highly restrictive social environment in which they spent their adolescent and young adult years. By the 1990s the norms and institutions that had governed the restriction of sexuality and childbearing to within marriage had completely broken down. While older respondents expressed concern at the changes they observed in young adults' behaviour, many also articulated a critical view of how they themselves had been treated in their youth so that '[I]t was wrong, it was wrong, in hindsight now, you see that it was wrong' (Deirdre, b. 1930, LHSC).

The rapid changes in values and behaviour that occurred towards the end of the twentieth century have understandably given rise to ambivalence and sometimes conflicting views across the generations. According to one older LHSC participant:

> Drugs and drink and bad living and sex and living with men before it is time for them and before they get married and all this modern way of life that is going on today. I can't stand it. I have no time for it. I don't think it is right. It isn't right, I am sure of it. They see no wrong in it, but I do. I suppose I am as old fashioned as they come but I would prefer to be old fashioned than the way that they are going on today. (Kathleen, b. 1924, LHSC)

Kathleen regretted the loss of 'the mystery of being married, the mystery of going into bed with your husband for the first time ever in your life'.

Contemporary parents of nine-year-olds expressed concern about the early 'sexualisation' of young people so that, 'at fourteen they look like they are in their twenties' (Susan's mother, GUI), with 'the false tan, the make-up, carrying handbags into school' (Sebastian's mother, GUI). Parents felt that once a child had entered their teenage years, 'you've less control over them' (Eoin's mother, GUI). In order to counteract negative peer pressure, parents tried to ensure their child's 'circle of friends [were] good' from an early age (Susan's mother, GUI). The GUI interviews reveal considerable worry amongst parents about the exposure of teenage children to peer pressure to be sexually active. For example Frank's mother (GUI) thought that Frank's teenage brother was 'totally sexualized' and worried about the intensity of his relationship with his younger girlfriend. Whereas GUI parents were primarily concerned with their child's welfare in an increasingly sexualized world, in the past parental concern was focused on protecting the good family name within the community. Even though sexuality was never discussed between parents and their children, it was implicit that young adults should 'never bring trouble' (Irene, b. 1928, LHSC) to their parents' door.

From our twenty-first-century perspective, the regulation of young adults' sexuality in early twentieth-century Ireland seems almost incomprehensible. Yet, as we have seen, the changes giving rise to contemporary family formation patterns occurred extremely rapidly, and within living memory. In the next section, we attempt to make sense of these changes by examining intergenerational family relationships in the context of changing household economies.

Young adults in the household economy

As we saw in Chapter 1, the west European marriage pattern – characterized by late marriage and comparatively high rates of non-marriage – was linked to a system of inheritance in which one heir succeeded to the family farm or business. Rural Ireland in the early part of the twentieth century has been described as an 'extreme' case of this pattern of marriage and inheritance. Considerable intergenerational tension was inherent in the system, which was exacerbated in the Irish case by a father's power to postpone his decision about which of his sons would inherit. In contrast to the custom in other European countries, there does not seem to have been a fixed rule of **primogeniture**, favouring the eldest son (Ó Gráda, 1980). In this context, the father's power over his sons was supported by a status system that explicitly treated young (and not so young) male adults as 'boys' until they took over the farm (Arensberg, 1988 [1937]).

Thus inheritance, which coincided with his marriage, marked a man's entry to full adulthood. For daughters, marriage into another household marked their transition to adult status (although, as Arensberg and Kimball 2001 [1940]) describe, they often remained subject to their husband's mother while she lived). Seamus (b. 1916, LHSC) described how important taking over his father's farm was for his sense of independence:

> *Interviewer*: can you remember what that was like in the beginning, were you nervous about it or how did you feel?
> *Seamus*: Ah no, my age was about thirty at that time. No you wouldn't, you'd be looking forward for to be the boss, you know, with the cattle and all ... And have your bit of independence ... You could make your own judgment on things.

Under this system, young adults – both heirs and non-heirs – might experience an extended period of disempowerment when their lives were constrained by the requirements of the household and the demands of the older generation. As many scholars have noted, the system depended on emigration as a 'safety valve', removing many young men and women not destined to occupy an independent adult status on the land, who might otherwise have become a source of social unrest.

The life history interviews contain a number of stories suggesting that the dominant older generation struggled to keep young adults in a position of dependence over an extended period of time. Sometimes they simply ran away. Joan (b. 1916, LHSC) recounted that: 'one of my uncles, my mother's brother ... put his clothes out through the window, went up the hills, changed his clothes, tucked the old ones under a bush, drove out a few cattle to the fair and sold them and took off and never came back!' Mary's (b. 1929, LHSC) older sister started out in service at the age of fourteen, but then decided 'I am not going to stick at this', and ran off to Northern Ireland on her own on the train: 'Mother didn't know about it of course, she had saved up for this'. Many young adults resented – and resisted – parent's attempts to keep them at home:

> Well I remember when I met my future husband, I just went out with him for one year and I was just twenty-one then. And my parents, because I think they kept me down so much, then I was that age twenty-three coming twenty-four, I wasn't going to listen to them. They didn't want me to get married because they thought I was too young, and I just said, 'Well it is like this, all my days I was kept down and I am getting married now and that is it'. (Brenda, b. 1934, LHSC)

Other respondents resented being 'earmarked' as sources of household labour and carers for their parents. This could lead to tension between siblings. Patricia (b. 1933, LHSC) described how her younger sister was supported by her parents to go on to secondary education, while she was kept at home to work in the house and on the land: 'Everything was for her then that was the way I felt'. The 'traditional' rural system of marriage and inheritance, therefore, was characterized by relationships of power and domination across the generations – relationships that were constantly subject to resistance and contestation. It is important to recognize that this 'traditional' pattern was dynamic and subject to fluctuation and change depending on wider demographic, economic and institutional contexts. Thus scholars have shown how, when other sources of income were available, the balance of power between the generations might be altered. For example, long before the twentieth century, opportunities for earning income through domestic industry increased opportunities for young adults to marry and set up households of their own, and reduced parents' ability to control their children's marriage choices (Miller, 1983; J. Gray, 2005).

The early twentieth-century system of marriage and inheritance in Ireland depended on industrialization elsewhere (Mokyr, 1980) – especially in the United Kingdom – to provide opportunities for marrying and making a living to non-inheriting sons and daughters. The model developed by Arensberg and Kimball (2001 [1940]) to describe the relationship between household economies, marriage and family-formation in Ireland is an 'ideal type'. Not all of its characteristics will necessarily be present in every historical case, although, as we have seen, aspects of their model resonate with many of the life history narratives. However, evidence that **family failure** (that is, inheritance without marriage) appeared earlier in the eastern part of the country where farm sizes and potential earnings from farming were greater, does pose a problem for this way of explaining patterns of family formation in early twentieth-century Ireland (Guinnane, 1997). Why should young adults find it more difficult to marry on prosperous farms in the east than on marginal holdings in the west? According to one explanation, the 'peasant system' associated with the European marriage pattern survived longer in the west because of a distinctive socio-cultural regime that lasted into the 1950s (Hannan, 1972). An alternative explanation proposes that already in the early twentieth century, marriage was not the only route to adult independence: that in effect some people might prefer not to marry, especially once the introduction of the old-age pension in 1909 made it possible to survive into old age without the support of adult children (Guinnane, 1997).

Regardless of which argument is correct, it is clear that, by the 1960s at the latest, the link between marriage and land inheritance was broken by the increasing availability of economic opportunities within Ireland, making it possible for greater numbers of young adults to marry and start a family of their own based on paid employment. The balance of power between the generations – already under considerable strain in earlier decades – shifted in favour of the younger generation. As the century progressed, new economic challenges began to emerge. Today, young adults who no longer depend on property inheritance for their independence must increasingly invest longer periods of time in education and training in order to secure the kind of employment necessary to establish a home and support a family. In the context of limited state support for participation in further education, they may find themselves dependent on their parents for longer than was typical for young adults in the 1960s and 1970s. Furthermore, maintaining a house and family increasingly requires participation in the paid labour force by both adult partners, creating new challenges for starting and raising a family. **The challenges facing dual-earner families are discussed in more detail in Chapter 5.**

The twentieth century was characterized by fluctuation and transformation in the pattern of exchanges of wealth and social support across the generations. At the beginning of the century, within the rural smallholding class that predominated in Ireland, older adults transferred wealth and other assets to the younger generation in exchange for support in their old age. In order to prevent the dispersal of wealth – and to retain power within the household and family for as long as possible – the older generation exerted substantial control over the lives of young adults, who often had to wait for extended periods of time before acquiring the independent adult status that enabled them to establish families of their own.

Because of the cultural and political hegemony of the small landholding class in Ireland during the earliest decades of independence, widely held social values and the policy of the Irish state tended to conform to the perceived requirements of this 'contract' between the generations (Hannan and Commins, 1992; Kennedy, 2001). Nevertheless, in the longer run, state policy interacted with changing social and economic contexts to bring about a radical transformation in the balance of power. We have already seen how the introduction of the old-age pension subtly altered the dynamics of inheritance and marriage. In Chapter 3 we saw how the introduction of compulsory education for schooling impacted on children's place within the household production system. The growth in opportunities for making a living from wage labour from the late 1950s onwards decisively shifted the balance of power in favour of the rising, younger generation. However, as Ireland's economy became increasingly centred on service activities, and young adults required further years of education in order to access the kinds of jobs that would allow them to establish families and maintain households of their own, changing values accompanied changing practices leading to the 'unbundling' of transitions described above. In the process, marriage was displaced from its pivotal position in family formation (although not eliminated as a desirable transition within a more extended process of family formation).

As we saw in Chapter 2, state policy responded, sometimes belatedly, to these changes in family formation practices. Financial support for single mothers was introduced in 1973, on the recommendation of the Commission on the Status of Women that unmarried mothers should be entitled to a welfare payment 'at the same rate and conditions that apply to a deserted wife' (Kennedy, 2001: 219). Following a challenge to Irish law on succession in the mid-1980s, the Status of Children Act, 1987 abolished the concept of illegitimacy: 'The principle underlying this Act is to place children whose parents have not married each other on the same footing, or as nearly as so as possible, as the children of married parents in the areas of guardianship, maintenance and property rights' (Kennedy, 2001: 234). In 2011 the state acknowledged the altered status of marriage with the introduction of civil partnerships. Nevertheless, marriage remained the subject of cultural and political contestation as Ireland held a referendum in 2015 on same-sex marriage. We discuss the implications of this from a sociological perspective below.

The transformation in family formation practices in the context of the extension of early adulthood can be understood as part of a long-term trend towards the **democratization** of family life. It is hard to imagine relations between the generations reverting to a pattern of domination by older adults similar to that which prevailed in the past. Nevertheless, as young adults experience growing difficulty with attaining the credentials and resources necessary to form independent households of their own, and as the unbundling of early family life transitions continues to give rise to 'untimely' transitions, some young adults find themselves dependent on the older generation for extended periods of time in ways that earlier cohorts might not have anticipated, including sharing a household. But there are considerable class differences in how this extension of early adulthood is experienced with consequences for the life chances of the young people involved (Furstenberg, 2013).

One parent in the GUI study reflected on the merits of his adult son continuing to live at home, while acknowledging how this might compromise his son's independence:

> He's nearly qualified now and he's living at home. He doesn't want to move out and I wouldn't want him to move out [...] he's in the process now of trying to build a house. But I mean, what's the point in moving into an apartment unless you owned it, it's a complete and utter waste of money in my opinion you know

[...] People say, 'Would you not kick him out?' I don't want to kick him out, he's here to give me a hand it's great [...] He gets his dinner and he gets his food here and [his mother] does his washing [...] He pays his way but it's not as if he's paying dead money in an apartment or something you know, so I mean being a parent you know it's all an advantage. It's great when you can keep them here, that's one of the best things about being a parent, is having your kids around you the whole time. (John's father, GUI)

This account of delayed transition to full adulthood contrasts vividly with Grace's story (b. 1970s, LHSC). From an urban working-class background, she became pregnant at sixteen, and continued to live in her parents' house for ten years, when she finally succeeded in getting accommodation from the corporation, by which time she had had a second child. For Grace, becoming a parent marked a stage on the road to adulthood, 'the start of an adult barrier thing, like they were not going to treat me like a child anymore'. Nevertheless, living with her parents presented obstacles to full independence:

You see there is my mother, there is my father, there is myself, so it was like there was three parents and I didn't feel it was right, it wasn't fair on the child [...] And then my mother was heartbroken when I moved out because we'd go shopping together and I'd help her with her housework and all because she [...] has arthritis in her hands, so I done all the heavy work. But at the same time it wasn't very fair for me rearing my own family and being expected to look after someone else's home as well. (Emer, b. 1970s, LHSC)

Like Grace, Niamh (b. 1960s, LHSC) saw parenthood – and more specifically the opportunity to be a good parent – as an alternative path to adult responsibility and individual self-fulfilment. However, this path undoubtedly had consequences for her own and for her children's life chances. Thus both Niamh and Grace dropped out of education – Niamh abandoned her plans to complete third-level education, while Grace, whose transition to parenthood occurred at a much earlier age, did not complete the Junior Certificate school exams. We will explore the discourse surrounding public concern about unmarried parenthood in more detail below.

In summary, this section has shown how the extension of early adulthood and the unbundling of family formation transitions must be understood in the context of the changing intergenerational relationships associated with the shift from a small property-owning society to one dominated by wage labour, especially in the service sector. These changing relationships comprised a shift in power away from the older generation in favour of young adults, leading to greater complexity in the sequencing of transitions associated with family formation. However, power relationships, centred on class and gender, continue to structure variations in the 'packages' of transitions, with different consequences for the life chances of young adults and their families. In light of concerns about the consequences of 'untimely' transitions to parenthood, some sociologists and policy makers have argued in favour of strategies to promote marriage. Before moving on to consider marriage as a public issue, we briefly discuss arguments that young adults are increasingly adopting an approach to family based on **relationships of choice**.

Young adults extending families and kinship

As we saw in Chapter 2, some social theorists have argued that, in the context of growing **individualization**, 'families of choice' are superseding 'families of fate'. The suggestion is that people are increasingly constructing **personal communities** comprising circles of relationships that are 'kin-like' in terms of the meanings and commitments associated with them, but are chosen on the basis of egalitarianism and the quality of the relationship they provide, rather than in terms of formal and hierarchical kinship ties. In this context there may be a 'suffusion' of friend-like and family-like relationships in contemporary personal communities (Pahl and Spencer, 2004). According to Weeks et al. (2001), this is the context in which gay and lesbian people claim the language of family – they have been innovators in a process that is nevertheless part of a wider societal change.

As we noted in Chapter 2, we must be cautious about assuming that family-like but non-kin relationships have become more important in individuals' personal communities over time (Pahl and Spencer, 2004; Jamieson et al., 2006); there is considerable evidence that the relationships anthropologists refer to as **fictive kin** have been significant in family and household relationships across a wide range of historical and societal contexts (Tadmor, 2010). However, it is also clear that in contemporary western societies non-kin relationships are more important amongst young adults before they form partnerships and families of their own (Pahl and Pevalin, 2005; Wall and Gouveia, 2014). Pahl and Pevalin (2005) suggested that in Britain this may be attributable to the increased geographical mobility of younger people who left home to pursue higher education or job opportunities in the changing socio-economic conditions associated with late modernity.

Research on Irish emigrants sheds light on continuities and changes in the significance of kinship supports and obligations amongst young adults, revealing the extent to which extended family ties stretched across geographical space. Louise Ryan's (2004) study of female Irish emigrants to Britain during the 1930s revealed a complex tension between active agency on the part of individuals and the constraints of family obligations. Most of the women repeatedly referred to the ways in which they played out family obligations. They sent money home, they paid for younger family members to join them, they found jobs for siblings, cousins and neighbours and provided accommodation for as many as they could fit into their flats or houses. Some women also remarked that they had been 'sent for' when elderly relatives were seriously ill. Such emergency visits to Ireland often involved caring for the sick person over several days or even weeks (Ryan, 2004: 362)

The LHSC interviews similarly reveal how, in the 1930s and 1940s, emigrant siblings (especially young women) remained embedded in 'transnational familial networks' centred on hierarchical intergenerational relationships. Patricia's (b. 1933, LHSC) older sister was working as a nurse in England, but returned home regularly, playing a pivotal role in the dynamic of family life: 'Oh, but she was such a person, you know? She'd come on holidays, she'd have something for seven of us, you know? ... she'd come and clean the house, left things, and helped my mother'. Her sister acted as an advocate for Patricia within the family sibling hierarchy: 'I remember her saying to me, "You are to go to [secondary] school and you're to go on to be a teacher."' When this emigrant sister died suddenly Patricia felt that her own life options were closed off.

Rates of emigration were exceptionally high in the 1950s. In a study of people who did not emigrate during that period, Breda Gray (2011) observed that their life narratives 'inhabit acutely uncertain periods of waiting in young adulthood when many of them imagined potential homes elsewhere only to spend the remainder of their lives in processes of "homing" or making homes for themselves in Ireland'. Retrospectively, female respondents evaluated their lives in Ireland positively through 'morally inflected' ideas about the kinds of families they were able to build at home, and male respondents through the idea that they were able to have a more 'relaxed' lifestyle than those who emigrated.

Emigrants who left Ireland during the 1980s did so in the context of the rapid transformations in patterns of family formation during early adulthood that we have described. Compared to earlier cohorts, the requirement to maintain extended family ties in order to meet obligations at home was considerably reduced. Nevertheless, O'Connor (2010) found an 'imperative to remain transnational' amongst 1980s emigrants to Australia. Arriving during early adulthood, they experienced considerable homesickness as a result of being separated from their families of origin, especially during family events and crises. However, once emigrants began to establish families of their own in Australia, they experienced a tension between having spouses, partners, children, and future grandchildren in one place (Australia) and extended family in another place (Ireland).

Just as Gray (2011) found that ideas about the quality of family life in Ireland structured experiences of emigration and non-migration in 1950s Ireland, Ní Laoire (2011) found that returning emigrants from within the cohort that left during the 1980s framed their decision to return in terms of an idea about Ireland as a good place to raise children. Corcoran (2003: 11) similarly found that highly educated Irish migrants who returned from Britain and North America during the economic upturn of the 1990s cited personal and familial reasons as the basis for their decision to return. The 'moral resources' of familial, friendship and communal affiliations were perceived to be 'more readily accessible in Ireland than in the host society'. Doreen (b. 1945, LHSC) described her decision to return from England in the 1970s in terms of the greater safety and happiness that she believed Ireland offered to children, and her own desire to be near her extended family of origin:

> my mother, thank God, was still alive at the time and I had great support. Like, in England, Frank and myself and the children, apart from our friends and neighbours ... Christmas was spent [as] Frank, myself and the kids, you know? There was no support, no family calling. Which I found brilliant when I came back, that we could sit into the car and go in and see my mother.

We explore further how parents mobilize support from family, friends and neighbours in Chapter 5.

This discussion of emigration has revealed continuities and changes in the tensions young adults experience as they strive to establish independence and families of their own, while also maintaining connections with their extended families of origin. While it is clear that friends play a greater role during young adulthood than in other life stages – and perhaps to a greater extent in contemporary social and economic contexts – family and kinship relations remain central to the personal communities of young Irish adults. For most, the obligation to provide material support to their families of origin may have given way to the desire to maintain extended family ties in order to receive support and to maintain a sense of security rooted in ideas about 'good' families. For single mother Emer (b. 1970s, LHSC), establishing an independent home was an important step in creating the 'comfortable' environment for her children that she craved while growing up in a home marred by alcoholism and violence. None the less, Emer felt a strong obligation to regularly call in to her mother who lived around the corner, and she was very critical of her other siblings for not doing the same; 'I know my blood runs the same way, but I can't believe how selfish they are, like they wouldn't ring my mother up and say "I am going to such and such a place, would you like to go?"'

Marriage as a public issue

Our discussion so far has shown how marriage has been displaced from its pivotal position at the heart of the transitions to new family formation in the context of extending young adulthoods. Irish people continue to exhibit a preference for raising children within marriage, but they no longer see marriage as a necessary precursor to sexual partnership, cohabitation or childbearing. However, evidence that children raised in families headed by married parents exhibit higher levels of well-being and have better life outcomes (see Chapter

3), has led some social scientists and policy advocates to argue that govern-ments should play a more active part in promoting marriage. In Ireland, the Iona Institute (www.ionainstitute.ie) draws on social science research to argue that state policy should maintain marriage as a special status (com-pared to civil partnerships) and resist demands to make it possible for same-sex couples to marry.

Internationally, some states have adopted policies to try to restore the status of marriage. In the UK, the Conservative-led government has recently moved to restore a transferable tax allowance for married couples (including gay married couples and those in civil partnerships). Writing in support of the proposal, Prime Minister David Cameron emphasized that 'there is something special about marriage: it's a declaration of commitment, responsibility and stability that helps to bind families. The values of marriage are give and take, support and sacrifice – values that we need more of in this country' (*Daily Mail*, 27 September 2013). In the United States since 1996 individual states have had the opportunity to use some of their welfare budgets to develop 'Healthy Marriage Initiatives' oriented towards assisting disadvantaged couples to form and sustain 'healthy relationships' (Hawkins, Amato and Kinghorn, 2013). However, evaluations of the projects show that they had no effect on outcomes such as the likelihood of marrying, or remaining married, or on the quality of couples' relationships (Wood et al., 2012).

In light of evidence that growing up in a one-parent family mediates the effects of poverty on life chances – rather than independently causing poverty – many social science researchers argue that policies oriented towards alleviating poverty amongst all families are likely to be more effective for reduc-ing the negative outcomes associated with 'untimely' transitions to parent-hood (see Chapter 3) and with unstable relationships. **This is discussed further in Chapter 5.** This position is supported by the fact that countries vary con-siderably in the extent to which single parenthood is associated with poverty (Chambaz, 2001; Brady and Burrawoy, 2012). Brady and Burawoy found that states with universalized social welfare models (which prioritize providing support to all families and households) do a better job of reducing the penalty attached to single motherhood than states which provide targeted benefits to particular kinds of families.

Ireland has a targeted approach to supporting lone parents through the One-Parent Family Payment (OFP). As described above, the first income support payments for lone mothers (other than those to widows, which had been in place since the 1930s) were introduced in 1973. At that time: 'There was an underlying assumption that unmarried mothers did not participate in the labour market due to their work in the home' (Murphy, Keilthy and Caffrey, 2008: 7). In the 1990s, however, there was a shift towards thinking of lone parents as potential workers, with the addition of an 'earnings disregard' to facilitate employment. A 2006 government discus-sion paper proposed a move towards universalism through the introduction

**Panel 4.4   Looking at the data: what it means to be a good parent –
Emer's story**

Emer (b. 1970s, LHSC) was determined to adopt a different style of parenting from that which she had experienced herself. Referring to her younger brothers and sisters she explained that:

> I was babysitting since I was ten and changing nappies and I think it was when I was around thirteen I thought I'd like my own child, 'When I grow up I'm going to have my own kids and I am not going to treat my kids the way [my parents] treated their kids'. You see they are very aggressive sometimes with their kids and they'd run at them with sweeping brushes and I'd be sitting there and my heart would go out, that is not a way to treat them, they are human beings as well, even though they could be little brats.

Emer's boyfriend was initially keen to set up home together, but backed out once the baby was born. Emer saw being an unmarried parent as something that 'worked out' for her, offering her a decent life different from that in her home of origin, marked by alcoholism and violence. But she also prioritized being there for her children:

> They say that things happen for a reason, you know, so I look at my oldest fellow and I am delighted because my life could have turned around the worst way, but then again I could have been a career woman, I could have had my own car and my own home but I wouldn't have time for a man or a family. And then I could have been a junky or an alcoholic ... or I could have been fighting at the weekend and could have been a very aggressive, emotional person exploding all the time, I don't know. At least it was better with him because I couldn't afford it as well, I hadn't got the time, I hadn't got the energy. So it worked out.

Emer saw herself as part of a positive family tradition stretching back to her grandmother who raised six children on her own as a widow: 'she was a very strong woman and she would do anything to help her kids and [...] I feel I am like that'.

of a means-tested parental allowance to support all low-income families. Subsequent reforms have centred on 'activation' – encouraging entry to the labour force in order to avoid poverty traps. This has entailed the removal of the One-Parent Family Payment once children have reached the age of seven, accompanied by a transition payment for one-parent families where the youngest child is between seven and fourteen years of age. The transition payment is intended to support lone parents taking up part-time or flexible employment in order to meet their childcare needs. However, the absence of affordable childcare continues to be a major obstacle to working, both for lone parents and for poor two-parent families (Murphy 2012). **We discuss the challenge of working outside the home and childcare for Irish families in more detail in Chapter 5.**

Aside from the issue of whether or not policies oriented towards addressing poverty do a better job of addressing the societal consequences of lone parenthood, there are questions about the intrinsic merits of policies oriented towards encouraging single parents to marry. As Cherlin (2003: 28) observed: 'it is hard to support healthy marriages without concurrently supporting unhealthy marriages ... If low income single mothers are encouraged to marry, the kinds of families that would be formed often would not match the healthy, two-biological parent, steady-breadwinner model that policy makers envisage'. We need to think about why young parents choose not to marry in the first place. In the LHSC interviews participants invoked **moral rationalities** (Duncan and Edwards, 1997) centred on what it means to be a good person – and more specifically a good parent – to explain the path they took. These moral rationalities were at least partly rooted in their own family histories, and those of their parents.

Each of the unmarried mothers described throughout this chapter (Emer, Grace, Niamh and Ruth) saw settling down and marrying their children's fathers as the possible endpoint of a process, not as something that would inevitably accompany parenthood. In this respect, their approach to marriage is similar to that of other young adults in contemporary Ireland. As Cherlin (2004: 855) observed, marriage has become 'a status one builds up to'. Paradoxically, then, the displacement of marriage within the sequence of early adult family life transitions has had the unexpected effect of enhancing its prestige. Fine-Davis (2011) found that the single most important factor influencing cohabiting couples' decision to marry was the cost of the wedding, mentioned by 80 per cent of the cohabitants in her sample. The next most important factors were the need to have a secure income and meeting the high cost of housing. Gillis has shown how weddings evolved in relatively recent times as expensive displays 'to sustain the marriages of our dreams and nostalgic yearnings' (Gillis, 2004: 990). More specifically, weddings are public displays affirming the status of the couple's relationship. Until comparatively recently weddings marked parental and community approval of the marriage (indeed parents often paid for the wedding) and legitimized couples' plans to have children. Now, it seems, weddings have become a statement that couples have 'made it': weddings demonstrate to family and friends that couples have earned the status of married adults. No longer a precondition for full adult status within society, marriage is now a declaration that a status has been achieved.

This long-term shift in the cultural significance of marriage provides part of the context for contemporary debates surrounding marriage equality for same-sex couples. Civil partnership was introduced in Ireland in 2011. In 2015 a referendum was held on extending the status of marriage to lesbian and gay couples. But why was there a demand for this change to the Constitution when civil partnership was already available? In their report *Missing Pieces* (Fagan, 2011), the Marriage Equality Campaign identified 160 differences in law between civil partnership and marriage. But notably, the authors stressed that even if the Civil Partnership Act had been amended to address those anomalies and omissions, 'this will not achieve equality for same-sex couples. Even if the two institutions are indistinguishable in terms of the legal rights they offer, they will still differ greatly in terms of the social meaning and status they confer on a couple'.

Those who argue against extending marriage to lesbian and gay couples refer to the social scientific literature that we have already discussed, indicating that two biological parents appear to be better for children in terms of their life outcomes. But trying to disentangle the effects of being raised by same-sex parents from all the other factors impinging on children's well-being is even more difficult than trying to establish the independent effects of growing up in a single-parent, non-marital or step-family. This is partly because the numbers of couples and children involved are comparatively small for the purposes of statistical analysis, and also because we do not yet have much longitudinal data on same-sex couples and their children. However, most social scientists agree that there is no evidence that growing up with same-sex parents is likely to be harmful to children (Manning et al., 2014).

But will married gay and lesbian couples have to 'construct a marital world with almost no institutional support' (Cherlin, 2004: 851)? We agree with Kefalas et al. (2011: 870) that 'Cherlin's prediction of the deinstitutionalization of marriage is probably premature', given the continuing cultural and social prestige that marriage enjoys as an achieved status. In the context of the extension of early adulthood, and the transformation of intergenerational relationships that we have described in this chapter, people find it increasingly important to 'get marriage right'. Furthermore, while most people aspire to marriage, not everyone finds themselves in a position to 'get it right' – and the chances of doing so vary across socio-economic groups (Kefalas et al., 2011: 869). It is worth remembering, however, that the capacity to achieve the conditions for marriage has always varied historically across social groups: over half of all people aged 30–34 remained unmarried in Ireland in 1930 (Fahey and Field, 2008: 15). It is the pathways to marriage that are different in the twenty-first century.

Summary and conclusion

This chapter has introduced the idea that early adulthood has emerged recently as a new phase in Irish family life, placing it in the context of longer term changes in social values, ways of making a living and the social construction of adolescence. We have seen how marriage has become displaced from its role as the linchpin of family-formation as the timing and sequencing of the transitions to adult family life have become 'unbundled'. We have also compared the experiences and consequences of 'untimely' transitions to parenthood in the present and in the past and considered debates about the changing meaning of marriage in the context of demands for marriage equality for same-sex couples.

While the focus of the chapter has been on transformations in the processes of family formation in early adulthood, we have also identified continuities in the life experiences of people during early adulthood. Intergenerational tensions and ambivalences surrounding adolescents' and young adults' desire for independence emerge as a consistent theme across each of the *Family Rhythms* cohorts. At the same time, maintaining extended family ties and the desire to be the best possible parents for their children continue to be at the heart of the moral rationalities that govern young adults' family life practices, even in the face of disruptive or untimely transitions such as emigration or unanticipated pregnancy. In the next chapter we move on from the process of family formation to explore in more depth the experience of caring in the 'middle years'.

Key concepts and ideas in Chapter 4

- Unbundling of transitions to family formation
- Timing and sequencing of transition to family formation
- Independent household
- Orderly and disorderly transitions to family formation
- Inheritance and the exchange of wealth across generations
- Matchmaking
- Marriage as a companionate relationship
- Emergence of youth culture
- Suffusion of 'friend-like' and 'family-like' relationships
- Transnational familial networks
- Moral rationalities

5.1 Mrs Flynn with her children, taken at Leperstown, near Dunmore East, Co. Waterford, circa 21 September 1933. The Poole Photographic Collection, courtesy of the National Library of Ireland

5

Working and parenting in the middle years

Well it's great, it's fantastic, we have [...] friends of ours who unfortunately can't have children and you can see the difference, the hole in their eyes, and they'll tell you, well they may or may not tell you but I think there's a difference, there's a huge gap, so I think it's great, it's absolutely fantastic, there's nothing nicer that having them [children] jump on top of you or wondering where you are. (Sam's father, GUI)

The quotation above summarizes a widely held belief about being a parent – that it is a wonderful experience and that those who are childless have something missing in their lives. Interestingly, however, survey research has consistently shown that, on average, people with children are less happy and report lower levels of life satisfaction than those without (Margolis and Myrskylä, 2011; Hansen, 2012). The discrepancy may be explained by the fact that parenthood confers rewards in terms of meaning – for example, providing a sense of purpose in life, or the feeling that one is part of something larger than oneself – rather than in terms of being happy or satisfied on a daily basis (Hansen, 2012). This is a good illustration of how qualitative research can sometimes better capture different aspects of social life than quantitative.

Nevertheless, it is worth thinking about the factors that give rise to relative unhappiness amongst those with children. Generally, parents report more unhappiness when their children are young and still living with them. Longitudinal research shows a big drop in happiness amongst individuals when the first child comes along. Unsurprisingly, perhaps, those who experience the greatest increases in financial pressures when they become parents (people in lower socio-economic groups and those parenting alone) also experience more unhappiness and lower life satisfaction. But given prevailing beliefs about motherhood, it may be surprising to find that children seem to reduce happiness for women more than for men. The research also shows that the relationship between children and unhappiness varies across countries. Margolis and Myrskylä (2011) found that, globally, the negative association

127

between children and happiness turns to a positive association amongst older parents, especially in countries where parents rely on their adult children for support in old age. In the rich world, the parenthood/happiness nexus varies across different types of welfare state regimes: in those countries that provide strong support to young families, and that promote gender equality, the negative effects of being a parent are weak or non-existent.

This chapter explores trends in the social meanings and textures of parenthood, showing how these are interrelated both with the changing intergenerational relationships described in Chapters 3 and 4, and with the transformation of gender roles in Irish society. We begin with an examination of the demographic patterns that frame these social changes, and then discuss how the meanings, values and attitudes surrounding partnership and parenthood have changed since early in the last century. Later we examine changing gender roles within the household economy. We then examine how parenthood alters adult partners' relationships with wider kinship and community circles, before proceeding to discuss some policy issues surrounding the transformation of partnership and parenthood. In this last section we focus on how institutional change has not kept pace with family household practices and on the enduring problem of intimate partner violence and the controversies that surround it.

Demography: the changing contexts of parenthood

The **fertility transition** has been the most significant demographic change impinging on the experience of parenthood. **The fertility transition is discussed in more detail in Chapter 1.** As in other European countries, Irish fertility – that is, the average number of births per woman – began to decline from the 1870s onwards (Guinnane, 1997). However, compared to many other countries, Irish family sizes were still rather large during the first half of the twentieth century. Women born in the 1930s in Ireland had, on average, between three and four live births compared to the average of between two and three that prevailed elsewhere in western Europe. However, more rapid changes in fertility behaviour began amongst women born in the mid-1940s. The proportions of all 'higher-order' births – that is, third, fourth or more children – have declined steadily since the 1960s (Fahey and Field, 2008: 32). Figure 5.1 shows the decline in **completed fertility** during the twentieth century. It shows how the middle cohort of people interviewed as part of the LHSC study – those born between 1945 and 1954 – were part of the national cohort of people that changed their fertility behaviour most rapidly during the twentieth century, so their stories are particularly interesting for understanding this change.

As we saw in Chapter 2, increasing fertility control at the beginning of the twentieth century – in the absence of new contraceptive technologies – can be understood partly in the context of changing gender relations. Below we will

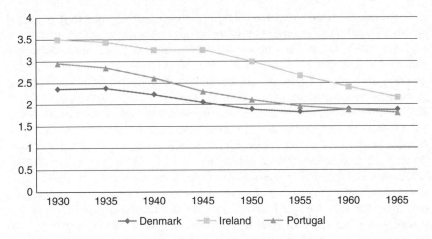

Figure 5.1 Completed fertility by generation: Denmark, Ireland and Portugal, 1930–65

Source: Eurostat 1999: pp. 104–105

explore in more detail the long-term trend towards an ideal of companionate relationships between adult partners. From the 1980s onwards, however, family gender roles underwent a sea change, alongside a dramatic increase in the employment rates of mothers of young children. As we will see later in the chapter, mothers' participation in the labour force is not a new phenomenon. However, during the 1980s the proportions of married women in employment began to increase rapidly, from less than a third in 1983, to almost one half in 1997 (Fahey et al. 2000: 254). While there is a continuing trend for women to withdraw from the labour force when their children are young, the proportion of married or cohabiting mothers of pre-school children working outside the home exceeded 60 per cent in 2007 (Russell et al., 2009: 19). In the context of falling employment rates during the recession, that proportion fell back to 57 per cent in 2011 (CSO, 2012a: 22).

As recently as 1994, amongst couple households with dependent children, the **male-breadwinner model** (where only the male partner was in employment) predominated. However, by 2000, this traditional family work strategy applied to just 38 per cent of such households (McGinnity et al., 2007: 202). In 2010, the percentage of all couples (not just those with children) in dual-earner households was 41 per cent. In 15 per cent of cases the female partner worked part-time (Watson et al., 2012: 27). As Watson et al.'s work has shown, especially in the context of the Great Recession, the transformation in gendered family–work strategies has been accompanied by the emergence of an increased gap between high-work intensity households (where both partners are in paid employment) and work-poor and workless households.

Alongside the transformations in family size and gender roles that impacted on Irish families during the twentieth century, rates of marital breakdown also increased. At the foundation of the Irish state in 1922, limited divorce was available under inherited British legislation; however in 1937 divorce was banned under a clause in the new constitution (Bunreacht na hÉireann) prohibiting the introduction of legislation to dissolve marriage (Fahey, 2012: 245). Political pressure to amend the constitution began to emerge in the 1980s, but the first referendum to introduce divorce was defeated in 1986. Divorce was eventually legalized in 1996, following a second referendum. Under Irish divorce law spouses must have lived apart for periods amounting to four years within the previous five in order to be eligible. While there was a sharp increase in the number of divorces immediately subsequent to legalization, the Irish divorce rate (that is, divorces per thousand married persons) subsequently stabilized as one of the lowest in Europe (Fahey, 2012: 249; Lunn et al., 2010: 42).

However, the divorce rate underestimates the extent of marital breakdown in Ireland. Following the rejection of the first referendum on divorce in 1986 the government reformed the law on judicial separation, making it more easily available on 'no fault' grounds from 1989.

An additional raft of legislation had been introduced in piecemeal form from the 1960s onwards to regulate de facto separations. As a result of the distinctive timing and pattern of Irish legislation on separation and divorce, there are at least as many separated people in Ireland as divorced. In 2006, more than one in ten ever married people in Ireland had been separated or divorced (Fahey, 2012: 251). Fahey suggested that focusing on divorce gives a misleading impression of the extent of family instability in Ireland: 'A comprehensive view of all kinds of relationship instability, including separation and divorce plus non-marital childbearing and lone parenthood, indicates that Ireland had already moved far along the path of family instability before divorce was introduced' (2012: 256). Nevertheless, the history of separation and divorce in Ireland does give a distinctive complexion to the pattern of family change for people in the middle years – the subject of this chapter.

As the population of Ireland continues to age, people in the middle stage of life are likely to experience greater pressures as a result of having to care for children and elderly parents at the same time. This phenomenon, often referred to as the **sandwich generation**, is due to a combination of greater longevity in old age (see Chapter 6) and the tendency for younger adults to postpone parenthood (see Chapter 4). A recent report from *The Irish LongituDinal Study on Ageing* (TILDA) study (McGarrigle and Kenny, 2013) found that 31 per cent of women aged fifty to sixty-nine have both living parents and children, and that many provide substantial practical support to both older and younger generations.

Of course the experience of caring for elderly parents (and other older relatives) in the middle years is not a new one: in the past, because childbearing continued over a longer period of life and because healthy old age was shorter, the period of caring for small children and elderly relatives often overlapped. The LHSC narratives provide many examples from the 1930s and 1950s of parents providing regular assistance to their own parents and also to aunts and uncles while raising their own young families at home. However, the TILDA study found that 50 per cent of 'sandwich generation' women today are in employment, revealing how many families that care for older people face different challenges today than in the past. **We will discuss some of these intergenerational continuities and changes in more detail in Chapter 6.** Here we begin by examining continuities and changes in the construction of partnership and parenthood.

Values: the transformation of partnership and parenthood

Rather than parenting being an unchanging biological fact of life, a destiny, it is also an experience shaped by dominant social, cultural and historical forces, changing from time to time, from place to place. Similarly, ideas and expectations about partnership have changed significantly over time. As we saw in Chapter 1, in his classic study Lawrence Stone (1977: 4) described the evolution of a long-term shift, originating in the seventeenth century, away from spousal relationships characterized by 'distance, deference and patriarchy' in favour of 'affective individualism'. Paradoxically, while ideal relationships between husbands and wives were increasingly based on love and companionship, this shift was also associated with the exclusion of women from public life. Middle-class family life became centred on the welfare of children, and women were expected to be sensitive mothers and intelligent companions to their husbands.

The material requirements for this middle-class family ideal were not available to most people throughout the period examined by Stone. However, as we discussed in Chapter 4, Burgess (1948) argued that by the twentieth century a companionate family ideal, focusing on the quality of interpersonal relationships rather than ideas about custom and duty, became increasingly prevalent as a result of urbanization and industrialization. During this period, experts who emphasized the special responsibility of mothers for the well-being of infants and children also became more influential in shaping public norms (Davis, 2012; Ryan, 2012). In the most industrialized societies of Europe and North America, by the middle of the twentieth century, the ideal of the companionate family, with its equal but different roles for mothers and fathers, seemed for the first time available to a majority of families.

While it may seem plausible that upper and middle-class family ideals percolated through to other social classes, it is important to remember that we know comparatively little about the values and inner feelings that structured intimate family relationships amongst working people in past centuries. Laslett (1977) suggested that because the age gap between spouses in western

Europe has been quite narrow for many hundreds of years, it is reasonable to assume that their marriages have always been companionate compared to those in world regions where brides tended to be significantly younger than grooms. French historical anthropologist, Martine Segalen (1983) argued that early twentieth-century folklorists and ethnologists viewed peasant family practices through the lens of middle-class ideals and so tended to see evidence of male dominance when other interpretations were possible. For example, they viewed women's practice of eating after the rest of the family as evidence of their lower status, when in fact this might simply have reflected their desire to eat quietly once their work was done. In the LHSC narratives, Denise (b. 1945, LHSC) recounted how, during family meal times growing up, her mother always dined separately, before serving the food to the rest of the family as 'that was her time ... she loved to have her meals in peace'.

Ethnographic research on rural Ireland presents a mixed picture of relationships between husbands and wives in the early to middle decades of the twentieth century. These studies emphasize the complementary character of men's and women's work roles but also portray differences of status and authority between husbands and wives (for a review see Shortall, 1991). Arensberg and Kimball (2001 [1940]: 47–49) emphasized how personal relationships and work roles were indistinguishable within marriage: 'Each learns to expect of the other not only the loving consideration of husband or wife but the proper skills of farm economy'. Transgression of 'proper' gender roles led to ridicule or graver charges of 'unmanliness' or 'unwomanliness'. John Messenger (cited in Shortall, 1991) described women as the 'strong' person in marital partnerships – a theme echoed in many of the LHSC narratives. Liz (b. 1946, LHSC) grew up on a small farm in the Mid-West and she remembered her father as a 'lovely, quiet man'. Her mother in comparison was a hard task master and the disciplinarian as 'someone had to do it'. She assigned the children their work around the home, and if there was any misbehaviour 'you'd hear her voice'. Sharon (b. 1951, LHSC), who grew up in the rural Border region, similarly remembered her father as a 'very gentle, quiet man', but her mother 'was strict' and 'would have been in control of the money'.

Older people often described their parents' relationship as characterized by undemonstrative affection. Seamus (b. 1916, LHSC) remembered that his farming parents 'got on well, they had hardships' and the essence of their companionship was in their weekly journey on a Saturday into town together to look at the shops. Simon (b. 1928, LHSC), whose father was a senior banking official, described his parents' relationship as 'Victorian' in that they 'would never show affection in public [but were] a very loyal, devoted, loving couple'. Most of the older LHSC participants recount that demonstrations of love between parents 'just wasn't done' at that time, but that affection within families was shown through doing 'practical things' such as a mother making sure her children were kept dry on their walk to school in the rain (Laura,

Panel 5.1   Landmark Irish study: *Traditional Families?* by Damian F. Hannan and Louise A. Katsiaouni (1977)

Hannan and Katsiaouni's *Traditional Families?* takes as its starting point the widely accepted portrait of the Irish farm family presented by Arensberg and Kimball – that is, a family with a rigidly defined division of labour, dominated by a patriarchal father figure, and structured around the **primogeniture** inheritance system. 'It has been continuously reproduced in sociological readings on family and kinship patterns', write the report's authors, 'despite the fact that there has been remarkably little systematic research to check the continuing accuracy and reliability of their model' (p. 1).

Setting out to check if the Arensberg-Kimball model was still valid for the early 1970s, Hannan and Katsiaouni found that the anthropological depiction of the typical Irish farming family was 'completely invalid now'. Many 'traditional' approaches to farming and running the family farm, they discovered, had been largely replaced by more 'modern' behaviours, attitudes and outlooks. For instance, rather than decision-making being the exclusive preserve of the male head of household, a trend had emerged where both spouses made decisions jointly. Mass-media consumption had become commonplace among most families, whereas in the past, newspapers, televisions and even radios were rare. An industrial approach to farm production – with the use of heavy machinery and chemical inputs like synthetic fertilizers – had largely replaced more indigenous, low-tech farming methods. Now most households engaged in paid work beyond the family farm, often travelling to distant towns, cities and countries to do so. Such work-related mobility in farming families was uncommon in former decades. What's more, the strictly differentiated sex roles prevalent on the traditional farm – men worked the farmyard and the fields, women the kitchen and the pantry – were fast collapsing, or at least being complicated, in contemporary farming communities.

While a quarter of the couples Hannan and Katsiaouni interviewed (and a greater proportion of younger couples) had relationships characterized by 'a joint consultative model of decision-making ... with a mutually supportive emotional structure' (p. 182), up to a third of rural families continued to display 'the rather rigid sex-role and decision-making patterns characteristic of the traditional farm family' (p. 182). Nevertheless, their study showed that Irish families in the 1970s, and farming families in particular, had entered a brave new world – a world increasingly influenced by modern communication technologies, media, and rising aspirations. A world we today would surely recognize.

b. 1928, LHSC) or a husband teaching his wife how to swim (Rob, b. 1953, LHSC).

As the twentieth century progressed, people placed more emphasis on the emotional quality of interpersonal relationships and increasingly viewed their partnerships as egalitarian, even though men's and women's roles remained clearly demarcated. In his study of 'New Dubliners', carried out around 1950, Alexander Humphreys (1966: 142–143) found that married couples saw themselves as 'partners' or 'pals', and that their relationships were characterized by greater comradeship and freedom of communication than that of their rural parents. New urban husbands were much more likely to 'walk out with their wives, attend movies with them and go out visiting or to parties with them'. Nevertheless, sex segregated socializing remained widespread and men's and women's economic roles continued to be clearly demarcated in families where husbands were the main, if not sole breadwinners: 'husbands prevalently scorn housework and fear being ridiculed as a "molly" if they be discovered at it. The wives themselves are inclined to think the man helpless at this sort of work' (Humphreys, 1966: 141). Nevertheless, Humphreys observed that these new urban women had much more equality within their marriages than their rural parents, with more control over the family finances and an increased say over family decisions.

By the later decades of the twentieth century, as growing proportions of married women entered the labour force (see the discussion below), the idea of marital partnership comprising equal but separate spheres had once again been transformed. By the early 1990s, more than three-quarters of Irish adults agreed that both husband and wife should contribute to the household income (O'Sullivan, 2012). Similarly, attitudes towards the importance of full-time mothering for child well-being changed significantly. As a working mother in the 1980s Audrey (b. 1945, LHSC) experienced negativity from other parents: 'Neighbourhood wise they were all waiting for my children to be delinquent, I could certainly see that, terrible children, mother works, latch key kids'. Similarly, during her childhood in the 1980s, Lorraine (b. 1969, LHSC) experienced negative comments about her mother's part-time work which upset her:

> I remember [my friend next door] saying to me that we must be really poor because my mam had to work ... obviously her mam had been talking about it ... there was some comment passed, 'You couldn't keep your house clean when you're working'. Oh no we're poor and our house is manky [laughs]. (Lorraine, b. 1969, LHSC)

In 1988 more than half of Irish adults agreed that family life suffers when the woman has a full-time job, but this proportion had shrunk to 37 per cent by 2002 (Hilliard, 2007: 37). The proportion of adults who agreed that a pre-school child suffers with a working mother decreased from 57 per cent in the 1990s to 35 per cent in the 2000s.

Growing support for working mothers has been accompanied by an increased emphasis on **active fathering**, whereby fathers have hands on involvement in the day-to-day care of their children (Ralph, 2015). But, despite widespread recognition amongst the GUI parents of the importance of sharing the load, mothers continued to invest the lion's share of time and energy in child care and domestic chores, even in dual-income homes. While the oldest LHSC participants subscribed to a **male-breadwinner model** of household labour, younger fathers confessed – usually with a sense of remorse – that they were largely absent during much of their children's childhoods due to long working days.

Anthony (b. 1946, LHSC) was promoted to a senior role in the 1990s that required long days at the office, which he felt 'imbalanced' him, even when he was at home, 'I was not present for a lot of them, in my head'. Bernard (b. 1951, LHSC) conceded that he possessed little in the way of fathering skills: 'I was never much now to tell you the straight truth even here at home or anything I was never much for minding children and even the grandchildren today I'll say, "my skills aren't great", I won't be long with them and we all have a row'. In other words, these participants, and many of their generation, were little equipped in the art of fathering.

The GUI qualitative interviews show that, despite changed expectations, like their counterparts in earlier cohorts, some contemporary fathers regret that they do not have sufficient time to be with their children and that after a working day: 'sometimes you are just too tired' (Ruby's father, GUI). The father of nine-year-old Tina (GUI) explained that his work regularly took him away from the family home from early morning until late at night, and he felt powerlessness to change things: 'You don't think about the difficulty of it. You just do it. It has to be done. I would change it if I could'. A number of the child respondents observed that they did not feel as close to their fathers as to their mothers because of the former's work schedules: 'My dad works a lot and I don't really get any time because as soon as he gets up, he showers and [is gone] again' (Robert, age 9, GUI).

Just as Irish people's beliefs about gender roles within marriage have been transformed, so also have their attitudes towards divorce and single parenthood. Tony Fahey et al. (2005: 128) showed that between 1981 and 1999, attitudes towards divorce became more 'liberal' amongst all age cohorts. By 2002, almost 60 per cent of people agreed that 'divorce is usually the best solution when a couple can't seem to work out their marriage problems' (Hilliard, 2007: 35). The proportion of adults who disapproved of 'pre-meditated' lone parenthood decreased from 57 per cent in 1981, to 35 per cent in 1999. Nevertheless, attitudes towards lone parenthood remain ambivalent in Ireland – 65 per cent of respondents continued to agree that children need both parents to grow up happily in the most recent wave of the European Values Survey (EVS, 2011).

In summary, quantitative survey data have shown that Irish values and attitudes towards partnership and parenting were transformed in a strikingly short period of time during the twentieth century, with particularly significant changes occurring in the 1980s (Fahey, 2014). Nevertheless, qualitative data add texture and nuance to this picture by revealing how changes in practices do not always map on to changing attitudes in a straightforward way. For example, similarly to how Humphreys (1966) found that urban couples in the 1960s joked about men's inability to do household tasks, contemporary couples in the GUI interviews joke about how men do not participate equally in decisions relating to children, despite general agreement that parenting should be a shared responsibility:

> *Interviewer*: How are decisions about things to do with the children made within the family?
> *Mother*: They'd be joint decisions, yeah? No?
> *Father*: No
> *Mother*: Who makes the decisions?
> *Father*: Get a grip on reality would you! Who do you think makes them? So, I can suggest but ... it'd basically be [Mother] that makes the decisions. (Sarah's parents, GUI)

As we will see in the sections below, both men's and women's capacity to achieve equality in partnership and parenthood continues to be constrained by obstacles in the economic and institutional environments, and by how people display family in their everyday life practices. In the following section, we begin by exploring how the transformation of gender relations has impacted on the social organization of households.

Gender in the household economy

As we saw in Chapter 1, in the semi-subsistence households that predominated in agricultural societies before industrialization, there was no clear boundary between 'productive' and 'reproductive' labour. The business of caring for house and children was just as important to the economic survival of the household as that of producing crops, livestock and other commodities for consumption and sale. At least in part because many of these activities took place in the same household space, peasants and artisans did not demarcate 'housework' as a distinct activity in the manner that we often do today.

Nevertheless, work was divided by gender, and much scholarship has shown that men's and women's work was valued differently (e.g. Honeyman and Goodman, 1991; Rose, 1993; J. Gray, 2005). The work done by women was held in lower esteem than that done by men. As we have seen, during the 'industrious' revolution the increased contribution of women's work in the production of commodities for sale had profound effects both on the overall development of world regions and on individual family-households, which in many areas became increasingly dependent on the sale of such commodities for their survival (see Chapter 1). Writing in the 1770s, Arthur Young (1892: 256) noted that in Co. Mayo: 'In their domestic economy, they reckon that the men feed the family with their labour in the field, and the women pay the rent by spinning'. Estimates of the labour costs of producing linen before the introduction of factories on a large scale show the importance of women's contributions – in preparing the ground for sowing flaxseed, weeding the crop, preparing the flax for spinning and, of course, in spinning the yarn (Crawford, 1991; J. Gray, 2005). Men were responsible for the heavier work associated with harvesting the flax and 'retting it' to break down the fibres, and also, until the introduction of mechanized systems, for weaving the linens. Outside the textile districts, women played an important role in other cash-generating activities: in dairying and the manufacture of butter, for example, and in the keeping of poultry and the sale of eggs. Furthermore, it was noted in the 1830s that: 'The women ... are not excused from the labours of husbandry, and during the more busy periods of the year may be seen with their husbands or brothers assisting in the business of farming' (Day and McWilliams, 1992: 12).

Despite the importance of women's work in the pre-industrial household economy, there is evidence that both contemporaries and later students of industrialization underestimated its value. For one thing, men appear to have had more opportunity to spend their earnings on leisure activities than women, whose lives consisted of almost continuous work (J. Gray, 2005). The tasks assigned to women had the character of being easily taken up and put down, which made it easier to combine them with taking care of children. Any lulls in agricultural or household activity could be filled by a task such as spinning and young women often combined socializing with spinning. These spinning gatherings (which landlords sometimes elevated into formal competitions), not only provided an opportunity for young people to socialize – they also represented an acknowledgement of the importance of women's work for the wellbeing of families and households (Medick, 1984). At such events a man on the lookout for a wife might have an opportunity to observe how well a woman could spin. While women's work continued to be poorly paid compared to men's, there is some evidence that as they brought more monetary income into the household, women acquired greater freedom to mix in the public domain and to consume luxuries such as tea and purchased clothing (J. Gray, 2005). This is significant because, while the lower social value placed on women's work has consistently affected the balance of power between men and women in families, it is important also to understand how this has varied and changed over time.

Gender and industrialization

As we saw in Chapter 1, nineteenth- and early twentieth-century industrialization saw the separation of home from workplace in urban manufacturing
centres. During the first phase of this process, the family economy shifted away
from a system based on the co-ordination of family labour, to one based on
pooling family wages. Under these circumstances it was difficult to combine
waged work with caring for young children. Female industrial employees
tended, if possible, to withdraw from the labour force when their children
were young, and to work intermittently across their lives in order to meet the
requirements of family survival (Hareven, 1993). Outside the industrial north-
east, in Ireland the shift away from tillage agriculture during the second half
of the nineteenth century, and the increasing use of agricultural machinery in
the twentieth century, meant that women became less likely to engage in field
work (Daly, 1981: 75). Nevertheless, especially on small farms in the western
part of the country, women's work remained important. Joan (b. 1916, LHSC)
remembered that:

> the custom was, here anyway, in [this part of the Mid-West], women took part
> in working, saving the hay and the turf and the potatoes, everything, women did
> their part ... [From the age of twelve] I was working with machinery, cutting hay,
> you name it, drive the horse to town and I just took it as a matter of course ... and
> I think I enjoyed it, it was a challenge.

Other changes in agricultural production, such as the introduction of creamer-
ies and the mechanization of dairying, resulted in some formerly female tasks
being increasingly carried out by men (Bourke, 1990). On the other hand,
the Congested Districts Board and Irish Agricultural Organization Society
introduced a number of schemes to improve poultry and egg production by
women from the 1890s onwards. They were comparatively unsuccessful in
persuading men to take up this branch of agriculture (Bourke, 1987), perhaps
because in Irish custom poultry were closely associated with women. When
Mandy's (b. 1965, LHSC) grandfather lost most of his land in an unsuccessful
business venture, her grandmother was determined to bring in an income for
the family:

> she got a poultry instructress to come out and show her how to, you know,
> manage the chickens properly ... Got hen houses built, you know, borrowed
> money from people to build her hen houses and she had turkeys going and she
> had geese going and she had eggs going. (Mandy, b. 1965, LHSC)

In urban areas, women engaged in a range of income-generating activities
that could be combined with care of home and children, such as keeping
lodgers and dressmaking (Daly, 1995: 76). Because her father was frequently

out of work, Betty's (b. 1947, LHSC) mother worked from home as a dress-maker especially 'when things were really bad' and as a young girl Betty often assisted her mother with the hand-sewing. Increasingly, from the early twentieth century onwards, families aspired to the ideal of a 'family-consumer economy', whereby men earned a 'family wage' sufficient to support their wives and children, while women focused on enhancing the family's stand-ard of living through good management of their husband's income. This has sometimes been attributed to a desire on the part of working-class women to emulate the higher-status homemaker role of middle- and upper-class women (Daly, 1995: 76), but there is also evidence that many women were happy to leave the drudgery of poorly paid, manual work if they could afford to do so (Bourke, 1994). **See Chapter 1 for more on industrialization and the transfor-mation of household economies.**

Gender and the growth of service sector occupations

From the 1960s onwards, the proportion of clerical occupations, which might be expected to attract women, began to increase in Ireland. However, in the 1930s a marriage bar, prohibiting the continued employment of women after they married, had been introduced to the civil service and was widely adopted throughout white-collar and professional occupations. In contrast to many other countries, where similar bars were removed in the 1950s, the Irish marriage bar lasted until 1973. Siobhan (b. 1950, LHSC) entered the civil service in the late 1960s and she described in detail how women's orientations towards working were beginning to change:

> most of the men I worked with are still civil servants ... [T]he women didn't [stay] because there was a marriage bar and obviously anybody who got married left ... But I think an awful lot of us didn't anticipate staying forever because we thought we would get married. And I did a degree at night and a lot of my moti-vation initially for doing the degree was that if I got married I'd need another qualification to get another job and I saw myself as doing something like teaching so I did a degree. As the thing wore on I think I was more career-orientated in doing that and the marriage bar, I mean I finished my degree in [the early 1970s] and the marriage bar was abolished in 1974 so ... And already at that stage a few people had been kept on, on a temporary basis after they got married. [But] the marriage bar was a huge influence on our career planning ... We all assumed we were going to get married. It was a much stronger assumption and much deeper ambition to be married and we married at a younger age.

While the marriage bar entrenched the male breadwinner–female home-maker ideal, in practice many women in the LHSC interviews recalled taking part-time and piece work whenever they could, to help support the household – practices that may not be very well captured in cross-sectional, quantitative data. In some instances, young children were placed with close relatives, or childcare was provided by older siblings so mothers could take up paid employment outside the home, often in seasonal or temporary positions. When they were first married in the late 1960s, Linda (b. 1950s, LHSC) and her husband struggled on his single salary and Linda returned to the clerical job that she had worked in before she married. As 'money was very, very tight' the couple sent their infant daughter to live with Linda's mother. After a few weeks, when Linda came to visit, her daughter, 'was walking and I hadn't been there to see her take her first steps. Her granny had bought her first shoes and she didn't know me ... I was roaring crying'. Unable to cope with this separation from her daughter, Linda took her back home after six months. While her two children were young, she dropped in and out of part-time, low paid work and 'had various people roped in, be they young girls or mothers, who minded them'.

As we saw earlier, married women's labour force participation began to grow steadily in the 1970s and then increased sharply in the 1980s, and continued to grow rapidly from the mid-1990s. Nevertheless, today a significant proportion of women continue to leave the labour force when children come along. In 2011, 86 per cent of women in a partnership without children were in employment, compared to 51.5 per cent of mothers of children aged four to five years (including lone mothers), and 73.8 per cent of fathers of children in the same age category (CSO, 2012a: 22)

Explanations of the gendered work-family division of labour

Why do women continue to be more likely than men to leave the labour force in order to meet the demands of caring for children (despite the emphasis on the importance of **active fathering** discussed above)? It might simply be that, in most households this is the most economically rational strategy: on average, women's lifetime earnings are lower than those of men (Becker, 1991 [1981]). However, the gender pay gap has narrowed considerably since the 1990s: the CSO estimated in 2011 that, controlling for differences in the number of hours spent at work, on average women's earnings were 94 per cent of men's (CSO, 2012a). Russell et al. (2009) found that in 1994 women whose husbands had higher earnings than they did were somewhat less likely to be in the labour force, but that by 2005 that difference had disappeared. (This change may have been due to the introduction of tax individualisation in 2000. See the discussion below.) Furthermore, there is a relationship between women's lower lifetime earnings and the pattern of withdrawing from the labour force when children are young: when women go back to work later in life they do so with lower accumulations of experience and credentials than their counterparts who worked continuously, making it more difficult for them to compete for higher paid positions.

According to an alternative argument, the gendered division of labour

---

Panel 5.2   Looking at the data: mothers' participation in the workforce in couple households – preference or constraint?

Daniel's mother (GUI) gave up work when her first child was born and explained, 'I wasn't going to put her out to someone else to be minded'. When she was interviewed in 2009, she was a full time homemaker. She described how her commitment to full time parenting was based on values handed down by her parents:

> maybe it's because I'm old fashioned, and my parents would have said, if you ever have children, if you ever decide to have children you've got to be a parent, you can't have everything in life, you're either one or the other, you either stay at home with your children, 'cause it's only for a short few years, or you don't have children, so it was probably the way we were brought up ourselves as well. (Daniel's mother, GUI)

By contrast, Karen (b. 1974, LHSC), was about to return to the workforce when she was interviewed in 2007 and framed her decision to return to work in terms of the benefit to herself, but also because she wanted to be a good example to her children:

> why would you go through all that heartache of studying until you're twenty-five and feck it all up? No. I think it would be silly not to [return to work] because [the youngest] girl is going to be at home for a few years and anyway, in the end I'm her role model ... what I do has an impact on her so if you want the best for her you have to look after yourself first you know. (Karen, b. 1974, LHSC)

Like Karen, Paula's mother (GUI) also wanted to set a good example by going out to work, but in reality her circumstances dictated how often she could participate in work outside the home. When she was interviewed in 2009, she worked part-time:

> I wouldn't give up work completely because I do think it's important for me and I think it's important for the children to see that the mother is meant to work and go out they are not just the mammy at home ... [that] they have to have responsibility and that there's not somebody there to find them all the time, somebody there to pick up after them all the time. If I could work school hours all the time that would be perfect but it's not a perfect world. (Paula's mother, GUI)

For most people 'external constraints' (McRae, 2003) governed their family–work strategies at least as much as their preferences. Both the financial costs of childcare and the logistics of co-ordinating work, childcare and school schedules impinge on parents' choices. Lorraine (b. 1969, LHSC) described how, after building a career in the public service, she eventually had to take a career break when her second child was born, despite having the opportunity to job share after the birth of her first child, an arrangement that she felt had given her 'the best of both worlds':

> I had a minder when I just had [my son] ... and she was lovely, really nice and he was really happy up there and it was all great. And then when I got pregnant with [my daughter] she said she wouldn't be able [to mind two] ... so I got a new minder and it just didn't work at all, just [my son] was really unhappy ... I was kind of hoping that maybe it was just teething problems ... but no, it was a disaster. So I went into the Personnel Officer in the morning and said, 'Look, this is not working. I think I'm going to need to take a career break'.

at home and at work can be attributed to women's preferences. Catherine Hakim (2002) argued that changes in gender roles have increased women's opportunities to choose whether to remain in the labour force or not, without really affecting men's choices. Women tend to cluster in three groups according to their preferences: career oriented women who prioritize work over their domestic role; homemakers for whom paid work is always a secondary consideration; adaptive women who move in and out of the labour force in response to variations in economic opportunities and state policies.

Gender stereotyping also acts as a constraint on parents' decision-making around sharing work-family responsibilities. In their analysis of what constitutes a 'good father' in modern Irish culture, McKeown et al. (1998: 28) documented the stress felt by fathers around combining the 'investment' role of parenthood – that is the provision of material security that was traditionally assigned to breadwinner fathers, with the highly prized 'involvement' role of modern parenthood – that is the hands-on caring for children. For contemporary Irish fathers 'Investment without involvement no longer carries the esteem that it once did'. Yet, as they learn new ways of being a father, contemporary Irish fathers are without role models from their own experience of being fathered, and their own identity as carers may be ambivalent (Hanlon, 2012). Consequently fathers in employment may be conflicted between the demands of work and their desire to be more involved with their children's lives.

This point is evident in the interviews with GUI parents from two-parent homes. Many of the fathers in employment expressed disappointment or guilt at being 'the gone person' (Rachel's father, GUI) that is pulled away from home by the demands of work. Amongst fathers that are out of work, particularly where their partner has continued to earn an income outside the home, the 'enforced loss of the traditional provider role ... challenges their self-image as both men and fathers (McKeown et al., 1998: 29). After the birth of twins Christine and Karen (age 9, GUI) their father decided to stay at home full-time to mind the family of five while their mother continued working, an arrange-ment that made the most sense financially. Although their father had been involved in the day-to-day care of the twins since their birth, his decision to leave the workforce to become a full-time carer marked him out for taunts by his male friends:

'Is it a plane, is it a bird, no it's nappy man'. I used to get an awful time ... Now they come up and shake my hand and some of them are doing it now them-selves. I would meet women down the town with the two girls and they would say, 'How do you do it? I can't wait to go back to work. (Christine and Karen's father, GUI)

In summary, contemporary parents – both mothers and fathers – develop strategies for managing the dual and sometimes conflicting demands of care and work in the context of financial and institutional constraints, guided by **gendered moral rationalities** (Duncan and Irwin, 2004) that centre on what they believe to be best for their children. These strategies tend to reproduce unequal gender relationships within both families and the workplace, even though this is not usually people's conscious intention.

In a classic article feminist economist Heidi Hartmann (1979) argued that the emergence of the **male-breadwinner model** early in the twentieth century created a vicious circle for women: on the one hand their weaker position in the labour market meant that they entered a partnership 'on bad terms' and compensated for their lower earning potential by taking on a greater share of responsibility for childcare and housework (see the discussion below). On the other hand those same domestic responsibilities limited women's oppor-tunities to improve their labour market position. Since the later decades of the twentieth century the terms of partnership and parenthood have shifted in a more egalitarian direction: the gap in pay between men and women has narrowed, as has the difference in time that each gives to domestic responsi-bilities. The gender stereotypes that inhibited men from prioritizing time with children over time at work have weakened. These changes have been driven, in part, by increases in education and the growth of female-typed white collar and professional occupations in Ireland. Nevertheless, social institutions have not quite kept pace with changing family rhythms, such that partnership and parenting in the middle years continues to be characterized by gender differ-ence and inequalities of power and status. We discuss this topic further below, where we focus on the gender division of caring labour and housework within families.

Panel 5.3   Landmark Irish study: *Gender Inequalities in Time Use* **by Frances McGinnity and Helen Russell (2008)**

McGinnity and Russell's research on behalf of the Equality Authority was the first examination, in an Irish context, of the distribution of paid and unpaid work between men and women using diary evidence. The study allows an assessment of the impact of increased female participation in the labour force in recent decades on gender roles within the family. The research was ground breaking in that it drew attention to the usually neglected area of unpaid domestic work when assessing differences in total workload between the sexes. Unpaid work (such as housework) is difficult to quantify, and McGinnity and Russell managed this by using data from the Irish National Time-Use Survey (2005). Analysing over 600 households' time-use diaries – where male and female participants recorded their activities in a diary at fifteen-minute intervals on one week day and one weekend day – they found that, on aggregate, Irish women worked forty-minutes more per day than Irish men, when both paid and unpaid workloads were taken into account.

In terms of labour force participation, a distinct gender gap was evident, where men spent considerably more time engaged in paid employment than women – who instead spent more time in unpaid caring and household work. Where men were engaged in unpaid domestic labour, it was largely in social / emotional care and outdoor gardening and household repairs. Women, meanwhile, did the bulk of the core domestic tasks of cooking, cleaning, shopping and the physical care / supervision of children. The massive rise in the number of women active in the labour market in recent decades, however, had not led to greater gender equality in the household – rather, women simply took on a 'second shift' of housework after their working day in paid employment. Although women reduced the time they spent on household work when they had a paid job, it wasn't an exact 'one-for-one reduction'; even when they undertook a similar amount of paid work as men, women continued to do more of the housework than their male partners.

Meanwhile, the arrival of children did little to enhance gender equality. When compared with couples without children, the study found that women – regardless of whether they were in paid work or not – disproportionately took on more unpaid work than men after the birth of a child. Parenthood, then, resulted in a reallocation of time commitment in couples, with a more traditional division of labour emerging. In an international perspective, the outlook from Ireland for those advocating a more progressive, egalitarian division of labour is somewhat disheartening. Scandinavian, British and French households all display far more equal gendered divisions of unpaid domestic labour.

Partnership, parenting and community life

According to Gerstel and Sarkisian (2006) marriage is a 'greedy' institution. Citing evidence that married people (both men and women) are less involved with family and friends, and disengaged from some kinds of neighbourhood and community relationships, they suggest that 'Ties to relatives and friends, like intense political and religious engagement, may depend on an unfettered life'. This evidence, according to the authors, contradicts the frequently articulated assumption that decreasing rates of marriage and traditional family relationships lie behind a perceived decline in social connectedness and community engagement – in social capital (see e.g. Putnam, 2000). But in other ways, Gerstel and Sarkisian's argument is consistent with the older view that we encountered in Chapter 1: that as societies modernize, families become more centred on the conjugal relationship, and extended kinship ties become less important.

Should we conclude, then, that conjugal family life and strong communities are inversely related? The debate is, to some extent, a false one and is rooted in assumptions about the 'decline' of extended family ties and of community that, as we saw in Chapter 1, are either false or unproven. As a result of demographic ageing, certain kinds of kinship relationships – such as siblings and cousins – have become less available to adults during their 'middle years'. At the same time, because of changing family practices and greater longevity, relationships with parents and grandparents, and relationships arising from re-partnering, have become more available (Murphy, 2010). However, as we know from Chapter 2, the timing and pace of this process has varied across European societies and, of course, while kin availability is necessary for people to have extended kinship ties, it does not determine the quality of those relationships or the frequency with which people are in contact with one another. Murphy found a clear north–south distinction in Europe, with people in the Mediterranean countries being much more likely to maintain regular contact with extended kin beyond the household. In this respect – as in some others – the evidence suggests that Ireland is more like southern Europe than its northern neighbours (although Murphy's study included data only on Northern Ireland).

Unfortunately, we do not have sophisticated quantitative evidence on changes in the availability of kin in Ireland over time. Early in the twentieth century, Arensberg and Kimball (2001 [1940]) described the rural townlands of Co. Clare as being characterized by a close inter-meshing of kinship and neighbour relations. Their research emphasized the importance of 'cooring' – exchanges of labour amongst kin and neighbours, especially at peak times of the agricultural year when household resources were insufficient. The intertwining of kin and neighbour networks in small-farm communities served to minimize class and status differences between households. However, Damian Hannan (1979) argued that that there were differences between circles of neighbours and kin that Arensberg and Kimball failed to identify: neighbour groups were of greater significance in the exchange of seasonal labour and everyday mutual assistance, but kinship groups were more important for coping with long-term crises and for providing emotional support. Other critics have argued that, far from suppressing class differences, cooring was an opportunity for larger farmers to exploit small-farm households in labour exchanges (Gibbon, 1973).

The LHSC interviews include some interesting contrasting accounts of labour exchanges amongst farm families in the first half of the twentieth century. Daniel (b. 1947, LHSC) grew up on a small farm in the west of Ireland where 'they were all small farmers and they were all in the same predicament'. During his childhood, Daniel remembered a system characterized by mutual exchanges where 'everyone borrowed from one another. The neighbours were very close and worked together and when the thrashing came along you went from house to house'. By contrast Seamus (b. 1916, LHSC) described how when he was a teenager in the south-east during the 1930s, labour exchanges benefitted the big farmer at the expense of the smaller farmer, those whom he called the 'cottage men':

> you see if the big farmer had the thresh and you might have two or three days he'd make you work and you'd be there in the morning early [...] He'd be looking over you the whole time [...] There could be thirty men in, at the threshing and he'd be spotting everything [...] [He'd] shift you to another job if you weren't pulling your weight [...] [And] then you'd have two or three days. The big man always had the majority for everything.

Many of the narratives of older LHSC participants show that extended kin, especially unmarried aunts and uncles, often provided regular support to struggling parents during periods of hardship. Irene (b. 1928, LHSC) grew up on a small farm in the south-east, and had an impoverished childhood during the economic depression of the 1930s and 1940s. Her two unmarried uncles who were living nearby in the paternal farmstead regularly assisted her parents in feeding and clothing their nine children: 'They always gave a couple of calves to my father to kind of rear and sell and get extra money because things were very hard in those years'. Nora (b. 1950, LHSC) described the weekly visits of her aunt, 'a single lady', who lived and worked in the nearby town: 'She'd have sweets and she would always bring rashers and sausages for the tea. You see, because you wouldn't have them in the country shops'. Such relatives were often involved in the significant occasions of a child's life. For example Nora's aunt 'was there for everything, for First Communion and Confirmations, and because she worked in a drapery shop she would have lovely clothes. We always got the best from her'.

According to the original assumptions of modernization theory, we might have expected extended kinship relationships to become less important to parents in the middle years as Ireland became more urbanized and fewer people worked in agriculture. In his study of kinship in a rural community in the 1970s Hannan (1979) found that, on the contrary, more modern and economically successful farm families had larger local kinship circles than did traditional farmers. Sean (b. 1952, LHSC) was born in a town in a border county, and when his father died suddenly during Sean's infancy his mother moved her family in with his granny and two unmarried aunts who were living nearby: 'There wasn't a social welfare system at the time to support her or us ... her mother was the only support she had'. As we saw in Chapter 2, sociological researchers 're-discovered' kinship in the 1950s and 1960s, especially amongst the urban working class, where local kinship ties provided everyday support and assistance. Nevertheless, both social scientists and other commentators continued to expect urban, and especially suburban, families to be less well integrated to extended kin and local community circles, especially as more adults live in dual-earner households.

In their classic study of East End families, Young and Wilmott (1957: 146) described how moving to a suburban council estate led to working-class families being 'more self-contained in bad times and in good'. However in a later study of the middle class suburb of Woodford, Wilmott and Young (1960) found that young couples had created a circle of contacts with similar functions to the extended kinship networks of the East End. In Ireland, Humphrey's (1966) study from the same period found that, compared to those living in older inner-city neighbourhoods, residents of recently developed housing estates in Dublin – such as Drimnagh, Kilmainham and Inchicore – interacted more formally and less frequently with their neighbours. But Gordon (1977) showed that middle-class suburban residents in Cork were more likely to include non-kin in their social networks than urban working-class people, regardless of the numbers of kin available to them.

Elizabeth grew up in the 1970s and 1980s in a suburban council estate in the south-east and recalled the informal childcare arrangement between neighbours whereby if both of her parents were away at work she could drop into a neighbour's home after school. The practice of dropping in and out of neighbours' houses continued for the next generation of children in the housing estate where her sister was living in 2007: 'I was there one Sunday, and she was out playing with some kids and there was kids coming in and out of her house ... this was just all day, in and out, and in and out' (Elizabeth, b. 1970, LHSC).

The *New Urban Living* study (Corcoran, Gray and Peillon, 2010) of four suburban areas in the Greater Dublin Area revealed that between one third and a half of all residents were embedded in nearby 'family circles' comprising at least one extended family member that they visited regularly and with whom they exchanged help and support. Parents tended to rely on kin for help when their children were very young, but once their children started primary school, parents began to establish closer ties with neighbours.

Residents with large numbers of neighbours and local friends in their personal networks had higher rates of local social participation and civic engagement than those with substantial kinship networks. Homemaker parents of pre-school children without local family circles were amongst those who felt most 'isolated' in the suburbs, a theme echoed by some of the GUI parents. Daniel's parents (GUI) moved to a commuter town in the greater Dublin area after the birth of their first child. New to her role as full-time homemaker, Daniel's mother felt particularly isolated as 'there was no one here during the day', and she joined a local 'mother and baby' group in an attempt to make some contacts. However her involvement with this group was short lived, as many of these mothers returned to work and continued to interact through a shared local childminder.

In a similar vein, the primary school gate acts as a focal point for the development of local social ties, especially for parents who must develop relationships with neighbours to help cope with the logistics of working and childcare (Hansen, 2004). As we saw in Chapter 3, children also facilitate the development of neighbourly relations amongst parents through their own friendship networks. Thus there is considerable evidence that contemporary dual-earner couples are not socially isolated or disengaged. They develop networks of support and participation beyond the nuclear family, especially when they live in communities where many households are at the same family life-stage (Swisher et al., 2004). **Child-centred community networks are discussed in more detail in Chapter 3.**

In summary, then, it is clear that there is continuity and change in the ways in which parents engage with extended kinship circles and the wider community. Parents in the middle years continue to mobilize networks of both extended kin and community connections for sociability and social support. Differences in the extent to which they rely on neighbours rather than kin are linked to family life stage and social class. While adults may withdraw from community engagement for a time during the early stages of family formation, once children reach school-going age adults in the middle years acquire access to new non-kin networks. It may be reassuring to learn that, in general, Irish conjugal families continue to be embedded in rich networks of kin and community, but it is important not to be overly sanguine about the extent to which these relationships can meet all the challenges faced by contemporary families. As we have seen, not everyone has access to such networks of social support. Olagnero et al. (2005), drawing on research in Ireland and Italy, showed that, in poor inner-city communities, reliance on kin may be a defensive response to living in a dangerous environment that inhibits participation in neighbour networks. Finally, as we will explore further below and in Chapter 6, reliance on kin and neighbours – and especially on grandparents – for support with childcare can bring challenges of its own.

Gender inequality in partnership and parenting as a public issue

As we have seen in the sections above, the social organization of partnership and parenting has been structured by gender in different ways across varying social and historical contexts. At first glance, adults' arrangements and practices with regard to their personal relationships, parenting and the division of labour within the home might seem to be intrinsically private issues. However, in this section, we show how these private concerns have consequences for public life and are, in turn, at least partly determined by public policies and institutional constraints. We focus on two key issues to illustrate this: balancing work and home life, and intimate partner violence.

Working and caring

As we have seen, as recently as the middle of the last century, both sexes considered housework and childcare to be the natural preserve of women. Women believed men to be incompetent at this kind of work, and in turn men feared loss of face and status amongst their peers if they were seen engaging in domestic activities. By the end of the twentieth century, however, more than 90 per cent of Irish adults agreed that men should take the same responsibility for home and children as women. Nevertheless, in their everyday lives, men's and women's practices do not necessarily follow this ideal. In her classic study, Arlene Hochschild (1989) suggested that the increased participation of married women and mothers in the labour force had not led to greater gender equality in the distribution of unpaid housework and caring work; instead, women found themselves putting in a 'second shift' at home, giving rise to a gender 'leisure gap'.

Consistent with international research, the Irish National Time-Use Survey, carried out in 2005, revealed that women spent more time on unpaid housework and childcare than men, both on weekdays and on weekends (McGinnity and Russell, 2007). See Panel 5.3, p. 144. On the other hand, fathers of young children tended to put in longer hours at paid work. All told, controlling for age, family and employment status, the study found that Irish women committed an extra thirty-nine minutes per day to work, paid and unpaid. As McGinnity and Russell (2007: 35) noted, their greater responsibility for caring and domestic work had 'significant consequences for women's access to (independent) income and status, since these activities are not financially rewarded, nor do they command a high level of social status, and this is particularly true for housework'.

As we saw in our discussion of changing gendered household economies, the perpetuation of a 'traditional' division of labour in the home has consequences for women's participation in the labour market. Guided by **gendered moral rationalities** couples may prioritize women's commitment to homemaking and childcare in their family strategies, but this in turn limits women's capacity to achieve full equality with men because it affects their lifetime earnings. From another perspective it has also been argued that the gender division of labour is harmful to men because it acts as a constraint on the quality of their relationships with other family members, especially with their children (McKeown et al., 1998). Even though gender roles have become less segregated in recent decades, regret at not having had enough time to spend with their children is a consistent theme in the interviews with men across all four cohorts examined for this book.

As the ideal of engaged fatherhood becomes more salient, the reproduction of traditional gender roles, especially once children come along, may give rise to greater family life dissatisfaction amongst men as well as women. There is evidence that unhappiness about the domestic division of labour can lead to significant strains in couple relationships, increasing the risk of divorce (Cooke, 2006). In their study of couples seeking help from the Irish marriage counselling service Accord, McKeown et al. (2002: 59) found that 'dissatisfaction with the way one's partner shares housework and childcare is an important contributory factor in the marital distress of both men and women', although this was not necessarily related to how household and childcare tasks were actually distributed. Conversely, greater male participation in family and home life increases family satisfaction, especially amongst men (Forste and Fox, 2012).

In this context, it is interesting to note that some researchers have found evidence of a pattern of female **gatekeeping** in relation to domestic chores – especially to childcare (for a review see Bianchi et al., 2012). Interviews with married and co-habiting GUI parents often revealed a joint perception that childcare was the mother's domain, as betrayed by the response of both mothers and fathers to the interview question 'who makes the decisions?' In the majority of cases, both parents stated that the mother made all of the day-to-day decisions on childcare and related household issues, even when both partners worked, and that mothers then decided when to involve the father in a decision as 'there is no point in hassling him for every little thing' (Tina's mother, GUI). Even for the weightier decisions, the mother usually took the lead and later presented her decision to the father for him to consider. For example, Paula's mother (GUI) stated that, '80 per cent of [decisions] come from me and go through [my husband]'. As a result, some of the fathers joked that rather than having any active role in the process, they 'get told what is decided by the family' (Tina's father, GUI). Some of the mothers saw themselves as better equipped to make decisions on the children, and their partners seemed to buy in to this assessment: 'He'd be a bit kind of scattered in terms of organisation, so in general I'd come up with the thing and I'd say, you know, "What do you think?"' (Eoin's mother, GUI).

In many cases fathers appeared happy to surrender decision-making to the mother, and their rationale was often that mothers 'would have the day to day running of the kids really' (Taylor's father, GUI). In one case, a mother described having a more domineering partner, but she was able to 'manipulate things, to put words into his mouth' (Luke's mother, GUI). In terms of the division of labour in couple households, it was apparent that most of the mothers undertook the majority of the physical, managerial and recreational aspects of parenting, such as helping with homework, dropping off and collecting children from school and activities, and cooking and cleaning, while fathers tended to engage in more recreational activities with children. In addition, both in couple households and separated households, mothers often described themselves as the main 'disciplinarian'. For example Alan's mother (GUI) complained to her husband during the interview: 'you're the fun one! I'm the party pooper'.

Panel 5.4   Looking at the data: gatekeeping or gendered roles?

During their interview, Damien's parents (GUI) discussed the roles they take in parenting Damien and his younger brother. At the time of their interview, Damien's mother was working part-time outside the home and his father was working full-time.

Mother: I guess that I kind of feel sometimes that I'm missing the relationship with them. Not missing out, but I feel like I have so much of a mother role to play that I feel that I'm constantly setting the rules and telling them what's next. Like, 'You can't do this' or 'You have to do this first'. And you find you don't have the fun. [Speaking to Father] Now you do the fun things, like you bring them in the summer, you go to the beach with them, you go to the park with them, you do all of those things.
Father: I think the hard part for her is that [Speaking to mother] you spend so much time with him that the fun time
Mother: Yeah, we do have fun times
Father: Well not even so much the fun time
Mother: Yeah, but you get more one-on-one fun time. Like what I do is more, like, I bring them to the activities
Father: But even when you're here, they're in and out and they want different things. I think they put more demands on you
Mother: Yeah, so I feel I'm more kind of
Father: Laying down the law?
Mother: Yeah, I feel like I'm giving out more, you know (Damien's parents, GUI)

As we have seen, there are a number of reasons why the 'private trouble' of allocating housework and childcare tasks between couples is also a 'public issue'.

But if governments, employers and other organizations want to promote more egalitarian sharing of unpaid household tasks, they need first to know why this gendered division of labour persists. A range of possible explanations has been examined in the sociological literature. They can be summarized under three main headings: (a) household decision-making; (b) gendered ideologies and practices; (c) policies of the welfare state.

Household decision-making

These explanations centre on the idea that partners must allocate limited resources of time and income in making choices about the household division of labour. They can be divided further into three variants: rational choice, family adaptive strategies and household bargaining perspectives. According to rational choice models, partners make the most efficient possible use of their resources. One model centres on time as a resource: women do more housework and childcare because they have more time available to them; as we have seen, women tend to work shorter hours than men do. An alternative model centres on earnings: women do more housework and childcare because their earnings are generally lower than men's; it makes more sense for men to invest more effort into their paid work, and for women to support them in doing so by taking on a greater share of domestic work. Quantitative empirical research lends most support to the second argument: differences in earnings are the best predictor of differences in the share of domestic work within partnerships (Coltrane, 2000; Lachance-Grzela and Bouchard, 2010).

But critics have identified a number of problems with rational choice perspectives. First, as we saw earlier, there is a reciprocal relationship between differences in earnings and differences in the time allocated to domestic household work. This means that power inequalities between men and women are reproduced through 'choices' about the allocation of labour to paid and unpaid work. Choices that seem rational at the level of households are not necessarily rational for all of the individuals who live within them. In an intriguing study Bittman et al. (2003) found that gender 'trumps' economics amongst high-earning women. Generally, as women's earnings relative to their partners' grows, their relative contribution to housework and childcare declines, and that of their partners increases. However, amongst highly paid women whose salaries are greater than their partners the trend seems to reverse: such women do proportionally more household work. Studies like this one suggest that something in addition to rational economic choice is at play in household decision-making: deeply held ideas about 'proper' gender roles, including status differences between men and women, are part of the mix.

As we learned in Chapter 1, in the 1970s, Marxist-Feminist theorists developed the idea of family-adaptive strategies to understand the interrelationship between socio-economic transformation and family change. In traditional peasant societies, they argued, household divisions of labour were based on enduring customs and expectations, reproduced in everyday practices and experience. As societies industrialized, families coped by adapting their customary household practices to new circumstances. From this perspective, in contemporary societies, gender differences in the household division of labour could be due to institutional 'lag' – that is, failure on the part of societal institutions to 'catch up' with changing circumstances. Thus, for example, normative career paths continue to emphasize intensive efforts during those periods of life when childbirth and childcare also demand considerable attention, making it difficult for both partners to devote equal attention to their careers. Similarly, schools, social services and other public offices continue to function on the basis of an assumption that carers will be present in the home during the day.

McKeown et al. (1998) documented how the everyday practices of Irish public services do not just reinforce traditional roles for women, they also actively exclude men from parenting. The persistence of these institutional constraints could be due to a kind of cultural 'inertia', or, as Heidi Hartmann argued, the constraints could have been institutionalized historically in support of groups who benefit from the hierarchies of capital and patriarchy. But how are such hierarchies perpetuated within individual households?

The household bargaining approach attempts to incorporate differences of power and status in models of household decision-making (Sen, 1990; Breen and Cooke, 2005). The idea behind this approach is that partners negotiate entitlements to consumption and leisure not just on the basis of their perceived contribution to the household economy, but also on the basis of unequal power due to differences in the perceived consequences for each of them if the family-household failed. Women are unable to negotiate the same entitlement to leisure as men so long as they perceive their 'breakdown position' to be worse – for example, because of their weaker earnings potential in the context of caring for children on their own. Household bargaining models differ from rational choice models in two key ways: (1) they incorporate the principle that household choices arise from negotiations (or struggles) between unequal partners; (2) they include an acknowledgement of cultural or ideological factors by recognizing that people do not have perfect knowledge about their circumstances – what matters is how they perceive their relative bargaining positions. In the longer run, there is a limit to how wide the gap between perception and reality can be. Thus, for example, from this perspective we might explain rising rates of separation and divorce as a consequence of improvements in women's breakdown position (through greater opportunities to earn an independent living, and state support for lone parenthood), such that they are no longer willing to remain in unsatisfactory relationships (Cooke, 2006).

Gendered ideologies and practices

If models of household decision-making are to incorporate cultural or ideological factors in their explanations, they have to take account of gender as sets of ideas and practices that guide perceptions. According to the liberal feminist or sex-role-socialization thesis gender roles are largely the product of learned beliefs about the attributes of men and women. As ideas about the gender division of labour change, people begin to modify their behaviour, but inevitably changes in practice lag behind changes in values. International survey research does show that gender role attitudes – especially those of male partners – do affect household division of labour, but to a much lesser extent than relative earnings (Coltrane, 2000). In a broader sense, the gender role socialization perspective is weakened by the evidence that both men and women tend to agree that household tasks should be shared.

An alternative approach, rooted in the qualitative sociological tradition, emphasizes how, in their everyday practices, individuals enact different roles by **doing gender**, regardless of their formal beliefs about the proper roles of men and women. In a classic article, West and Zimmerman (1987:140) described gender as something that is 'accomplished' in interaction with others: '[Sex] category and gender are managed properties of conduct that are contrived with respect to the fact that others will judge and respond to us in particular ways'. This way of thinking about gender is very effective for understanding how men and women drift into traditional roles, especially following the birth of a child, even though they may have started out with more egalitarian ideals. As they find their way through the unfamiliar challenges associated with coping with a new baby, for example, people develop patterns of behaviour in interaction with one another, co-constructing their own and others' expectations and perceived expectations about how each should behave. The advantage of this way of thinking about gender is that it allows us to better understand the 'bricolage' of social change and also how some couples achieve different outcomes from the 'norm'. For example, Henry's father (GUI) explained how he and his partner fell into a pattern of role reversal, leading to strains in their relationship that are unusual compared to those usually described in the sociological literature:

> *Interviewer*: And have you encountered any difficulties as parents?
> *Father*: Well we have. The impact on our lifestyle, well the impact on Tania's lifestyle rather than my lifestyle because my lifestyle is very sedentary, before I met Tania I never went out much. I don't go out drinking or anything like that. Tania and myself were together for ten or fifteen years before we had Henry and my lifestyle changed dramatically because she is very outgoing and I just fell in with that. But then when Henry was born you see we did have an enormous tension, huge and it still isn't resolved because she wants her lifestyle to more or less continue and I felt that was impossible. I immediately cut down my work to

half time and she wanted to continue whole time. She became very upset, quite upset about the fact like she feels that I became totally absorbed with Henry and sort of let go of our relationship in that sense but that is gradually getting better so yeah it was a huge ... Then I was happy to be staying at home. (Henry's father, GUI)

Policies of the welfare state

Much of the scholarship on gender divisions of labour within the home has centred on the economic, social and cultural factors that impact on couples' (and single parents') decisions and strategies relating to managing the responsibilities of working and caring. However, it is important also to recognize how state policy shapes these processes (Fuwa, 2004; Neilson and Stanfors, 2014). The Irish Constitution (Bunreacht na hÉireann, 1937) includes an Article (41.2) that emphasizes a traditional understanding of the gender division of labour:

> In particular, the State recognises that by her life within the home, woman gives to the State a support without which the common good cannot be achieved.
>
> The State shall, therefore, endeavour to ensure that mothers shall not be obliged by economic necessity to engage in labour to the neglect of their duties in the home. (Bunreacht na hÉireann, Article 41.2)

Consistent with the changes in values and practices that we have described in this chapter, there have been moves since the mid-1990s towards altering the language of this article in favour of a more gender-neutral format. Most recently, members of the Constitutional Convention voted in favour of amending the article to make it more gender neutral and to include carers beyond the home.

While the Constitution includes a lofty aspiration towards supporting care-work within the home, in recent times, Irish state policy has, in practice, focused on encouraging women to work. Changes in the taxation of couples and parents provide a good illustration of how national values and state policy towards gender, work and care have been transformed. From 1967 until 1980, the Irish tax system treated married couples as a single unit for taxation purposes. While there was a 'married man's allowance', the joint tax-free allowance awarded to married couples meant that, if both partners were in employment, their tax bill was greater than that of an unmarried couple, each of whom was taxed individually. On the other hand, if one partner was not earning an income, a married couple received a tax subsidy compared to an unmarried couple. When this system was ruled to be unconstitutional in the Supreme Court, the government responded by introducing, in 1980, a system of doubling tax bands to married couples. This meant, in effect, that a couple's tax was calculated by assigning half their joint income to each partner, and taxing each of them as though they were single. Couples were able to transfer both allowances and tax bands in order to minimize their income tax liability (Callan et al., 2007: 24).

Both the pre- and post-1980 systems tended, in different ways, to discourage married women's participation in the labour force. The principal difference was that the pre-1980 system imposed a tax penalty on marriage for dual-earner couples, whereas the post-1980 system conferred an advantage on marriage. In 2000, at the height of the 'Celtic Tiger' boom, the Irish government began to 'individualize' the tax system by progressively reducing the transferability of tax bands. The intention was to move to a situation where each individual, whether married or not, had the same tax band which could not be transferred to a spouse. Interestingly, the government was confronted by some vigorous public opposition to tax individualization, which was perceived by some groups as a strategy to 'force' women into the labour force by disadvantaging traditional family-caring arrangements. In response to these criticisms a 'carer's allowance' was introduced to provide some additional tax relief to families where one partner was working as a full-time carer in the home.

The public outcry in response to the introduction of tax individualization surprised many, since it seemed to go against the trend towards greater emphasis on gender equality and individual autonomy within marriage and (later) civil partnership that had become well established in the 1980s and 1990s. However, if we consider the **gendered moral rationalities** revealed in our analysis of the LHSC and GUI interviews above, it is possible to understand how many Irish people might be unhappy with the emphasis on tax individualization while simultaneously subscribing to the principle of gender equality. Irish government moves towards promoting greater female participation in the workplace did not take account of the ethic of care (Murphy, 2011) at the heart of most parents' family strategies.

Comparative welfare-state research has shown that countries that provide high levels of public support for childcare also have high levels of female participation in the labour force (Hegewisch and Gornick, 2011). In Ireland, childcare costs are amongst the highest in Europe (Murphy, 2012). During the Celtic Tiger boom the Irish government sought, initially, to address the problem of high childcare costs for parents through an 'Early childcare supplement' to the universal children's allowance. Subsequently, in 2010, this was removed in favour of an Early Childhood Care and Education, (ECCE) scheme that provided free part-time pre-school places for all children for one year. This will be extended in 2016.

These approaches have avoided contentious public debates surrounding gender roles through their focus on the needs of children, irrespective of parents' family–work strategies. However, for many parents who wish to work in the paid labour force – including single parents – while the ECCE initiative provides welcome support that also benefits their children, it does not address the financial and logistical challenges associated with combining work and care, and so is unlikely to contribute significantly to altering the trend for a considerable proportion of mothers to withdraw from paid work when their children are young. In particular, the absence of affordable childcare, together with family unfriendly work practices, tends to exacerbate the gap between high work-intensity and work-poor households that has opened up during the recession (NESC, 2013: 27).

In summary, this discussion has shown how what might seem to be the most personal of issues – who cleans up the house, picks of the children from school, remembers dental appointments and co-ordinates after-school activities – is deeply implicated in public issues relating to labour force participation, productivity, the structure of careers and the organization and delivery of public services. Just as in other countries, Irish individuals, families, employers and the state have struggled to find a balance between meeting the needs of the economy and the requirements of caring for children and others. Historically, meeting the requirements of care has depended on a gendered household division of labour in which one partner had lower levels of participation in formal economic activity than the other. However, even at the middle of the last century, when the breadwinner-homemaker ideal was at its height, many families struggled to achieve a satisfactory balance between the demands of caring and an adequate standard of living. Furthermore, this model placed those who were not participating in the formal economy at a disadvantage, especially if family households broke down, leading to the perpetuation of power inequalities between men and women. Since that time, both states and households have moved towards an ideal of increasing labour market participation amongst all adults, and dual-earner households have become the norm.

While some other countries have adopted a strategy of 'de-familializing' care in this context, Ireland has joined the 'liberal' group of welfare states in promoting private solutions through a market-oriented configuration of policies (Korpi et al., 2013). **See the discussion of comparative welfare regimes in Chapter 2.** The consequence of this strategy has been a continuation of a pattern of comparatively high female withdrawal from the labour force when their children are young, and the emergence, during the Great Recession, of a growing gap between households that are work-poor and those that are work-rich but time-poor (Watson et al., 2012). Many families rely on informal care by extended family members, especially grandparents, to enable parents to participate in the labour force. **Grandparent's care of grandchildren is discussed in more detail in Chapter 6.** However, as we will see in Chapter 6, this solution brings challenges of its own.

Intimate partner violence

Ruth (b. 1970s, LHSC) described how, when she was growing up in the 1970s her family's 'private' pain took place in public view. Referring to her mother:

the neighbours used to say 'how the woman isn't dead', everyone knew but back then people never said anything either. I suppose it can be like that now, but people kind of kept their doors closed, people knew what was happening. But I remember thinking, 'Are we the only family that this happens to?' But obviously we weren't, a lot of that goes on, especially with men drinking a lot. I'd say everyone knew, they'd have to know, she'd be covered in bruises, black and blue from head to toe and she'd run off and leave him and we'd be left at home and it was horrible. I remember thinking, 'Jesus, will one of them die or someone die or me die, to get out of this house'. (Ruth, b. 1970s, LHSC)

What used to be called 'wife-battering' was, at one time, treated within the social science literature as an issue that affected a small number of dysfunctional families, or as a feature of distinctive subcultures – of the poor, or of particular ethnic communities (Elliot, 1996). However, beginning in the 1970s, feminist writers and campaigners began to highlight the pervasiveness of violence against women, and to argue that it was one aspect of the domination of women by men within patriarchal societies. From the perspective of family studies, growing evidence that the family home – which has often been depicted as a private haven from a harsh public world – is also the place where people are most likely to experience violence and abuse, formed part of the emergence of critical perspectives on the family as an institution characterized by inequalities of power and by conflict (see Chapter 1).

However, almost as soon as family violence was 'discovered' as a feminist issue, social scientists faced continuing challenges relating to attempts to identify just how pervasive a problem domestic violence is, and the extent to which it is a problem relating specifically to gender inequality, or to other aspects of the social organization of the family. These challenges centre on methods of data collection, changing definitions of what constitutes violence, and the extent to which the contexts and consequences of acts of violence are included in their measurement.

According to feminist scholars, explanations of domestic violence must take account of the 'overwhelmingly obvious fact' that 'men of every clan and culture victimize women more than the reverse' (Hunnicutt, 2009: 557). In this view, violence against women must be understood as an aspect of **patriarchy** – a set of social relations whereby men as a group dominate women as a group (Hunnicutt, 2009: 557; see Chapter 1). Some feminist theorists have drawn attention to the institutionalization of domestic violence in the past to support their argument that violence against women is a common feature of patriarchal societies, rather than of particular social and cultural contexts (Dobash and Dobash, 1998). However, historians have argued that how people judged and responded to intimate partner violence in the past depended on their interpretation of the context, and varied across time and place. In a study of local court records in Württemberg, Germany, David Sabean (1990) was able to show how the content of complaints about violent behaviour and abusive language altered between the eighteenth and nineteenth centuries in the context of changing gender roles in household production.

At the end of the nineteenth century, 'wife-battering' was treated as just one aspect of the problems associated with poor, immigrant communities in industrializing urban centres. The drunken Irishman who beat his wife was a focal image in child-protection, temperance and social purity campaigns in both the United Kingdom and the USA (Gordon, 1988). At this time, sympathy for violently abused women was underpinned by a late Victorian image of the 'long-suffering, devoted wife'. In Ireland, by comparison, Steiner-Scott (1997) has shown how nationalist discourse contributed to relative public silence around domestic violence, partly because of a reluctance to play into negative stereotypes of Irish emigrants, and partly because of the promotion of ideas about the 'purity' of married life in Ireland compared to the industrial cities of Britain and the USA which were thought to have dehumanized Irish men. Nevertheless, court cases arising from violent domestic incidents featured prominently in Irish newspaper reports in the latter decades of the nineteenth century. According to Joanna Bourke, as women's contributions to household production declined, allegations of domestic violence centred increasingly on accusations of poor housework. On the other hand, Arensberg and Kimball referred almost casually to the belief in the small rural community they studied that a man married to a woman perceived to be infertile had the right to 'bounce a boot off her now and then' (quoted in Steiner-Scott 1997).

Paradoxically, in the United States, public sympathy towards female victims declined during the twentieth century. According to Ramsey (2013), 'misperceptions of women's growing independence' created an 'exit myth', a belief that women could 'just leave' violent relationships if they were unhappy in them (Ramsey, 2013). In Ireland, according to Steiner-Scott (1997: 142), 'The new State showed in many ways that it was reluctant to inquire too closely into what was considered to be the private domain of the family'. As in other western countries, public discourse about wife-beating declined during this period.

As a result of feminist mobilization, violence against women in the home re-emerged as an issue in the 1970s. In Ireland, the organization Women's Aid was established in 1974. But how prevalent is intimate partner violence in Ireland in the present? Researchers have attempted to establish this in a number of ways: by looking at the numbers of people seeking help; from crime statistics; by examining reports from medical professionals; and from survey evidence.

• In its annual one-day 'census' Safe Ireland reported that 467 women and 229 children were receiving support from a domestic violence agency on 5 November 2013. Of these, 115 women and 155 children were accommodated in refuge. However, Safe Ireland believes that the figure is 'dwarfed by undisclosed prevalence' since most Irish women 'did not contact any organisation following the most serious incident of violence'.

- Incidents of domestic violence that come to the attention of An Garda Síochána (Irish police service) are not recorded separately from other forms of assault in the official statistics. 1,320 breaches of a domestic violence order (such as where a person has been barred from the home of someone they have previously victimized) were reported to An Garda Síochána in 2012 (CSO, 2014a: 79, table 15.1).

- In 1996, Bradley et al. (2002) distributed questionnaires to women attending twenty-two general practices in Ireland. They found that 39 per cent of the women who responded had experienced violent behaviour by a partner. Almost half of the women who experienced violence had been injured as a result. However, relatively few had been asked about violence by their doctor. Of all the women who answered the questionnaire, 77 per cent favoured routine inquiry about domestic violence by their GP. The authors noted that comparison with community-based random surveys suggested that 'women who experience domestic violence are over-represented in general practice'.

- The first survey evidence on violence against women was collected through a postal questionnaire issued to 1,483 women on behalf of Women's Aid in 1995. Of the 679 women who responded, 18 per cent (101) of those who had ever been in a partnership (575) stated that they had been subjected to some form of violence (including mental cruelty) at some time in their lives by a current or previous partner. In 2003 the Economic and Social Research Institute carried out a survey on domestic abuse and violence with a representative sample of more than 3000 adults, on behalf of the National Crime Council. That study found that 15 per cent of women, and 6 per cent of men, had experienced 'severely abusive behaviour [that is, behaviour likely to cause physical injury, or high levels of fear or distress] of a physical, sexual or emotional nature from a partner at some time in their lives' (Watson and Parsons, 2005: 24). A recent Europe-wide survey carried out on behalf of the European Union Agency for Fundamental Rights (FRA 2014: 28) found that 15 per cent of Irish women (aged fifteen years or older) had experienced violence of a physical or sexual nature from a current or previous partner. Prevalence rates in European countries ranged from 13 per cent to 32 per cent in this study.

As the above summaries show, the prevalence of domestic violence is likely to be either over- or under-estimated in research based on self-reported data or carried out in clinical settings. Survey-based evidence has, since the 1980s, been thought to yield more reliable estimates of the prevalence of domestic violence. However, this has generated new controversies, particularly relating to the finding that men also report having experienced violence from a partner. Especially when individual incidents of violence and abuse are enumerated, rates of violence against men can be as high as those against women. For example, in the National Crime Council study described above, when all incidents of abuse were counted (without distinguishing between 'severe' and 'minor' incidents), 29 per cent of women and 26 per cent of men reported having experienced some form of violence by a partner.

This apparent **gender symmetry** was first observed by scholars at the University of New Hampshire who pioneered the use of survey research to study domestic violence (Straus and Gelles, 1986). In contrast to the feminist perspective on domestic violence as a consequence of male dominance, or patriarchy, these authors argued that aspects of the culture and structure of modern societies were to blame. First, they suggested that individuals in contemporary societies are exposed to widespread cultural messages – for example on television or in computer games – that violence is an effective solution to problems. Second, they argued that, compared to more traditional family settings, modern conjugal families are isolated from wider networks of kin and community. Furthermore, they are the only places where people spend extended periods of time with members of the opposite sex and with people in different age categories. More public spaces – such as workplaces and educational institutions – tend to be segregated by gender and age. In this context the family can become a 'pressure cooker' in which violence can break out when people are under stress.

The suggestion that domestic violence was not differentiated by gender led to bitter controversy, both within the academic community and in wider public debate. The organization Amen was founded in Ireland in 1997 to provide support and to campaign for greater recognition for male victims of domestic abuse. On their website, the organization argues that there are myths surrounding men's and women's violence (Amen, 2015). Society, they claim, accepts 'excuses' from women, including 'post-natal depression, stress, PMT, eating disorders, personality disorders, menopause, addictions, childhood traumas, provocation, self-defence etc.', but men are expected to take responsibility for their violence without excuse, and in contrast to women, will automatically be considered to be unfit parents if they are violent towards their partner. By contrast, the organization Women's Aid counters what they claim is the myth that domestic violence is not gender-based: 'The vast majority of the victims of domestic violence are women and children, and women are also considerably more likely to experience repeated and severe forms of violence and sexual abuse' (Women's Aid, 2015).

Amongst scholars, there have been efforts to show that the 'Contact Tactics Scales' used by the New Hampshire researchers fail to distinguish incidents of violence according to their context and consequences. The National Crime Council study used the statistical method of 'latent class analysis' to distinguish the group of people who had experienced 'severe abuse' – that is, abuse

---

Panel 5.5   Timeline of law and policy developments on domestic violence in Ireland

1. 1976 Family law (maintenance of spouses and children) Act introduced barring orders which enabled perpetrators to be removed from family home for a maximum of three months
2. 1981 Family law (maintenance of spouses and children) Act extended duration of barring orders to a maximum of twelve months and introduced protection orders from the initiation of court proceedings
3. 1989 Judicial Separation and Family Law Act permitted judicial separation on the grounds of unreasonable behaviour of one spouse towards another, among other things.
4. 1996 Domestic Violence Act provided for enhanced protection for spouses, children and other dependents whose welfare or safety was in jeopardy because of the conduct of another person in the domestic relationship, expanded powers available to the Gardaí and extended the range of instruments available to the courts.
5. 1997 Publication of report by the Taskforce on Violence against Women (established in 1996). The report highlighted the need for co-ordinated service provision across a range of government departments.
6. 1998 Establishment of a National Steering Committee on Violence against Women to oversee regional planning committees, promote public awareness and advise on the distribution of funding and the development of policies.
7. 2003 National Domestic Violence Intervention Agency established under the aegis of the Department of Justice, Equality and Law Reform. Ceased operations in January 2007 due to lack of funding.
8. 2007 Establishment of Cosc (The National Office for the Prevention of Domestic, Sexual and Gender Based Violence) as an executive office of the Department of Justice and Equality. Cosc is responsible for delivering a 'whole of Government' response to domestic, sexual and gender-based violence.
9. 2010 Publication of the National Strategy on Domestic, Sexual and Gender-Based Violence 2010–2014.
10. 2011 Cosc established the National Steering Committee on Men with the aim of improving protection and services for men who are or may become victims of domestic violence.

Sources: Kearns et al., 2008; Cosc www.cosc.ie/en/Cosc/

---

that was sustained over a period of time, led to physical injury, or had a serious impact on the victim's life – from the group that had experienced comparatively minor incidents. Women clearly predominated in the group that were severely abused, being more likely to have had injuries requiring medical attention, and to have been very frightened or distressed by their experience (Watson et al., 2005: 58–59).

In an influential mixed-method study, Nazroo (1995) used qualitative data to show that the motives and consequences of women's violence were different from those of men. Recently, Johnson and Ferraro (2000; see also Kelly and Johnson, 2008) have moved the debate forward by arguing that we need to 'unpack' different kinds of domestic violence that may require different explanations. In particular, Johnson and Ferraro argue that it is useful to distinguish **common couple violence**, where both partners 'lash out' in the context of an argument, from **intimate terrorism**, where one partner uses violence as a tactic within an overall pattern of control of the other. Johnson and Ferraro argue that most of the violent incidents captured in survey research fall within the category of 'common couple violence', whereas the violence encountered by those providing services to victims is more likely to come under the heading of 'intimate terrorism', and to be perpetrated by men.

This section has provided a brief overview of the substantial sociological literature on intimate partner violence and on research and policy developments in this area in Ireland. In her memory of being the daughter of an abused woman in the 1970s, Ruth (b. 1970s, LHSC) expressed the view that 'everyone knew' but people kept their doors closed and said nothing. Clearly, there have been significant changes in attitudes, practices and policy relating to intimate partner violence in Ireland since that time, but there are continuities as well. A study on attitudes to domestic violence in Ireland, published by Cosc in 2008, found that Irish people exhibited an extremely high level of awareness of domestic abuse and considered it to be unacceptable. Most people believed that they would intervene if they witnessed domestic abuse. However, people felt more reluctant to become involved if the victim was someone outside the family milieu, such as a neighbour they didn't know well. 'Not wanting to interfere in other people's business and the concern or fear of making things even worse are the main reasons given for not interfering' (Horgan et al., 2008).

Summary and conclusion

This chapter began with evidence that, despite the fact that most people want to be parents, there is evidence that becoming a parent reduces peoples' happiness and satisfaction with life – at least for a time. Being a parent is challenging and demanding for people in the 'middle years' who may also find themselves caring for their own elderly parents. The transformation of values and practices relating to gender roles has, in some respects, added to these challenges. Women have benefited from changing values and opportunities for participation in the labour force, but this has not led to an equal sharing of domestic responsibilities leading to a 'leisure gap'. Together with the absence of state and institutional supports for childcare, this has left many families with difficult choices about how to manage the 'instrumental' and 'expressive' requirements of family life (see Chapter 1). For men, the emergence of a norm of 'involved fatherhood' may be frustrated in practice by economic, institutional and practical obstacles, leaving many men feeling sad about being 'the gone person' in the family.

Finally, gender is also a controversial issue at the heart of public discourse surrounding the 'dark side' of the family – domestic abuse. We saw how, on the one hand, children act as a catalyst to increase adult participation in community relationships. On the other hand, the experience and research on intimate partner violence shows how – in the past and in the present – there continues to be a tension between respecting the privacy of the family and preserving the well-being of all of its members. In our next chapter, we explore the intergenerational relationships between grandparents, children and grandchildren.

Key concepts and ideas in Chapter 5

- Active fathering
- Common couple violence
- Completed fertility
- Division of labour
- Family–work conflict
- Gatekeeping
- Gendered moral rationalities
- Gender roles
- Gender inequality
- Gender stereotyping
- Gender symmetry
- Intimate partner violence
- Intimate terrorism
- Parenthood
- Preference theory

6.1 Children fishing with nets at lake/pond, Herbert Park, Ballsbridge, Dublin, 1969. The Wiltshire Collection, courtesy of the National Library of Ireland

6

New grandparents: older people in the family

I get on brilliantly well with my grandparents and I see [them] very much (Lizzy, age 9, GUI).

Grandparents have become increasingly significant for children. Fewer than one in five of the oldest people in the *Family Rhythms* study said that a grandparent was an important person in their childhood, but more than half of all contemporary children identified a grandparent as someone who is close to them (Figure 6.1). This is partly because more grandparents are available to young children today. Across all age groups, most people could remember at least one grandparent, but just about a third of those born before 1935 could remember two or more, compared to 60 per cent of those born around the middle of the century. Three-quarters of the nine-year-olds in the GUI qualitative study mentioned two or more living grandparents in their interviews. (It is not true, as is sometimes suggested, that few children in the past had the opportunity to know any grandparent (see Gourdon, 1999 and Herlofson and Hagestad, 2011)).

But longer and healthier life is just part of the story behind the changing significance of grandparents in contemporary families. In this chapter we will also explore changes (and variations) in the social construction of grandparenthood. How have our understandings and expectations about older people's roles in families changed? We will see how power relations across the generations changed as Irish society moved away from an economy based on small-property holding to one centred on wage labour, and again in the context of changing gender roles and the restructuring of the adult life course. During most of the second half of the twentieth century grandparents hardly figured in sociological depictions of family life. As societies modernized, it was assumed that intergenerational ties beyond those of parents and children would become relatively unimportant. Today, as social research reveals the growing importance of multi-generational relationships (Bengtson, 2001;

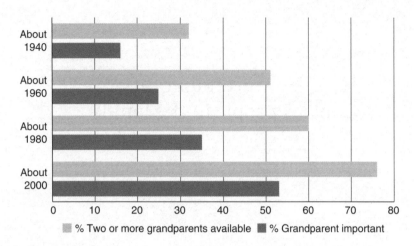

Figure 6.1 The changing importance of grandparents for children in the
            Family Rhythms study by participant's year of birth

Source: Authors' calculation (see text for details)

Harper, 2003; Arber and Timonen, 2012) grandparenthood has become
central once again to understanding families.

Demography: the coming of the Third Age

As we described in Chapter 2, a reduction in the risk of dying at all ages (but
especially in infancy) was a central component of the set of changes referred
to as the 'demographic transition'. Together with reduced fertility, this led to
what Peter Laslett (1987) called the **secular shift in ageing** that took place in
most European societies between 1950 and 1960. The transition occurred,
according to Laslett, when two conditions were met: (1) a quarter of all adults
had passed the age of sixty; (2) at least half of all males surviving to age twenty-
five can expect to live to age seventy. Ireland had already met the first of these
criteria in 1926 (51 per cent of men who had survived to age twenty-five could
expect to live to age seventy (Survival, 2015)), but has not yet met the second
(those aged sixty or more years comprised 16 per cent of the population in 2011
compared to 13 per cent in 1926 (CSO, 2015)). A number of factors explain
this phenomenon. First, the emigration surge that occurred in the middle of the
twentieth century combined with a baby boom in the 1970s to keep the ratio
of older to younger people comparatively low. Second, compared to other countries, Ireland made comparatively poor progress in improving the life expectancy of older people during the twentieth century (Fahey and Field, 2008).
    Until the 1920s, increased life expectancy in European societies was

primarily due to reductions in infant and child mortality. However, since the 1950s, most of the change can be attributed to the extension of life in old age. This is sometimes referred to as the **longevity revolution**. In 1926, at age sixty-five, the average life expectancy for men in Ireland was 12.8 years, and for women it was 13.4 years. By comparison, in 2010, the average life expectancy for sixty-five-year-old men was 17.7 years, and for women 20.8 years. This places Ireland at around the European average for old-age life expectancy (see Figure 6.2). Length of life is not the only criterion for understanding the demographic impact on intergenerational relations. Old age inevitably brings increasing health difficulties that change the nature of our relationships with other family members. According to the European healthy life year index, Irish men and women can expect to live an average of eleven healthy years after the age of sixty-five (Eurostat, 2014a).

One consequence of the extension of healthy old age is that contemporary grandchildren are more likely to know their grandparents into adolescence and even adulthood (Gourdon, 1999; Bengtson, 2001). We also need to consider how demographic change affects the supply of kin available to older people. On one hand, as we will explore in more detail below, fewer grandchildren

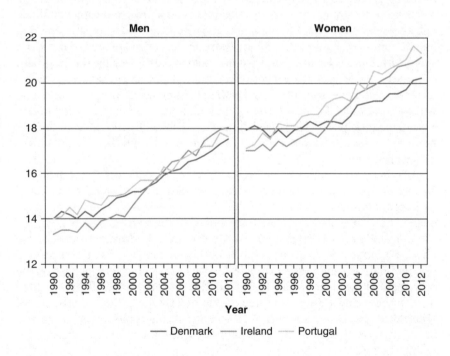

Figure 6.2 Life expectancy at age sixty-five: Denmark, Ireland and Portugal, 1990–2012

Source: Eurostat (2014b) Eurostat Database Life Expectancy by Age and Sex demo_mlexpec

(as a result of declining fertility) may create the potential for closer relationships with cherished members of the youngest generation (A. Gray, 2005).
On the other hand, high rates of non-marriage in Ireland in the past, together
with high rates of emigration, have left some older people with comparatively
thin networks of family and kin on whom they can rely for help and support
(Kamiya and Timonen, 2011: 40). Nevertheless, as we will see, changing patterns of marriage and migration mean that most older people are embedded in
extended family networks and, in many cases, are themselves sources of vital
help and support to others. Finally, the changing family life paths that we have
discussed throughout this book – the transformation of childhood, the unbundling of early family life transitions, changing gender roles in the middle years
and higher rates of separation and divorce – all have consequences for the role
of grandparents in family life.

The changing social construction of grandparenthood

Describing the emergence of the *Third Age*, Laslett (1987) explained that,
before the 'secular shift in ageing', individual life courses could be divided into
three main phases: (1) a period of dependency and growth during childhood
and adolescence; (2) a middle period of independence, work, procreation and
familial and social responsibility for those in dependent phases of life; (3) a
short period of decrepitude and old-age before death. During the twentieth
century a new phase emerged between adult independence and decrepitude –
a comparatively healthy Third Age with fewer immediate responsibilities and
with opportunities for new forms of individual achievement and fulfilment.
This new phase was made possible in part, of course, by the extension of life,
but also by the institutionalization of retirement through the introduction of
old-age pensions.

Together with the advent of compulsory schooling, the introduction of
the old-age pension was central to the restructuring and standardization of
life courses in modern societies (Kohli, 2007). Previously, amongst property
owners, the concept of retirement was linked to the transmission of land. For
those dependent on their labour for survival, work ceased only when they were
physically unable to continue (Thane, 2003). On small farms, the success of
the stem-family system as described by Le Play (see Chapter 1) depended on the
retirement of the older couple. In Ireland, this process was vividly represented
in Arensberg and Kimball's ethnographic description (2001 [1940]: 118):
'The old couple relinquish the farm, they enter the age grade of the dying, and
direction of the enterprise of the group passes from their hands to those of the
young people'.

As we will discuss in more detail below, the transition was sometimes
associated with tension between the old and young adult generations.
Interestingly, while Arensberg and Kimball (2001 [1940]: 121) acknowledged

the significance of the old-age pension for land transmission, they believed that it had been 'incorporated into Irish farm life without upsetting, but rather reinforcing, the matchmaking pattern'. However, there is other evidence that before the introduction of the pension the custom in Ireland may have been to delay transmission of land until the death of the father (Guinnane, 1997). Indeed one of Arensberg's and Kimball's (2001 [1940]: 121) respondents told them that 'there is no chance that the old people would give up the land but for the pension, and there is no hurrying them'. In any case, the pension introduced the idea of retirement as a stage of life defined by nominal age – rather than a transition negotiated within families – and, in Thane's (2006: 63) words, 'the spread of retirement created a new cultural barrier between the lives of older and younger people'.

In the next section we will discuss in more detail the changes in intergenerational power relations that accompanied this shift. First, how did the institutionalization of retirement affect the social construction of grandparenthood? Of course becoming a grandparent does not wait for retirement, although there is some evidence that it speeds up the decision to retire, especially amongst women (Van Bavel and de Winter, 2013). In Ireland the TILDA study revealed that about half of those aged fifty to sixty-four – that is, people who are too young to receive the state pension – provide regular care to grandchildren and great-grandchildren, and of course this is likely to underestimate the proportion that had actually grandchildren (McGarrigle and Kenny, 2013). Nevertheless, as Attias-Donfut and Segalen (2002: 283) explained, the introduction of the pension at the turn of the twentieth century altered the structure of intergenerational family ties and created the potential for a new kind of grandparenthood: 'By freeing the family of its traditional role of caring for its ageing members, public solidarity ... contributed towards the emergence of new ties which were founded on the basis of the autonomy of generations'.

Around the middle of the twentieth century, sociologists within the structural-functionalist tradition asserted that families in modern societies were increasingly neglecting their older members: 'the older person ... must seek elsewhere for the satisfaction of his needs – financial, health and social. In western cultures he turns to the Government or other organizations' (Burgess, quoted in Aboderin, 2004: 31). This belief in a growing unwillingness to provide for older kin was linked to the argument that industrialization and urbanization led to the breakdown of the extended family and the emergence of an 'isolated' conjugal family form centred on the relationship between parents and children. **See Chapter 1 for a detailed discussion.** As a consequence of these changes, it was argued, older people found themselves 'trapped in a role-less role'. In fact there is little evidence to support this argument, which was elaborated in the context of the visible destitution of many older people in the United States during and after the Second World War (Aboderin, 2004). However, the belief that older people have become less valued than in the past has a long

Panel 6.1   Looking at the data: grandchildren's feelings towards their grandparents

Compare Martin's account of the granny who lived with his family on their farm in the south-east of Ireland during his childhood in the 1950s and 1960s, with that of Shirley who was nine years old when she was interviewed in 2008.

[Granny] was very nice to us [...] she'd look after us and tell us stories. She'd help us to say prayers when we were young and she'd teach us prayers. I suppose she did everything every granny did and oh she was very nice to us. And she'd be there in the kitchen you know when we'd come home from school and she'd always have a smile and she'd talk to us and ah ... but as I said she was getting old at the time. (Martin, b. 1947, LHSC)

Interviewer: And how do you get on with your granny?
Shirley: Great, she is one of the best members of the family.
Interviewer: And why do you say that?
Shirley: She is really kind and she is barely ever angry. (Shirley, age 9, GUI)

Of course grandparents, and grandchildren, differ so not all relationships are good:

[He] was a vicious old mill of a man, you know what I mean, we were afraid of him ... We were very much afraid of him because he ... might hit you with a stick, he had a walking stick and he'd hit you with it. (Desmond, b. 1945, LHSC)

She's a bit mean to me most of the time, and I don't really get on with her that much ... [She's] mostly judging, and if I say something she'll say that I'm wrong or that that's not true or something like that. (Audrey, age 9, GUI)

However, Desmond and Audrey's experiences of their grandparents are very much in the minority in our data.

history and remains a common theme in everyday public discourse. Thane (2003: 105) suggested that it 'expresses persistent cultural fears of ageing and neglect, and real divergences in experience in most times and places, rather than representing transparent, dominant reality'.

In direct contrast to the argument about the 'abandonment' of older people in modern societies, other scholars suggested that, because nuclear family

households have long predominated in north-west Europe, older people have always been vulnerable to loss of support from their adult children (Laslett, 1988). However, more recent research has challenged this argument about the distinctiveness of the north-west European family pattern, arguing that the likelihood that elderly people lived with their children depended on the proportions of younger and older people in the population – on the supply of kin available to live with the old (Ruggles, 2011). Even when older people were not living with relatives, they may have been living nearby (Kok and Mandemakers, 2012). As Thane (2003) rightly observed, we cannot infer anything about how well older people were treated and valued within their families from evidence about their living arrangements.

In fact, neither argument – that families valued and cared for older people more in the past, or that they have always been comparatively neglected in western societies – stands up to the evidence. As Thane (2003: 102) argued, 'The relationships between older people and their close relatives show striking long-run continuity and closeness in 'western' culture, even when they do not share a household'. Arensberg and Kimball (2001 [1940]: 163) observed that in rural Ireland in the 1930s older people were 'objects of respect and a mild sort of veneration on the part of all younger members of their families'. Our qualitative life histories similarly reveal a striking continuity in the affection that young children had for their grandparents across all four cohorts.

Grandparents, similarly, greatly value their relationships with their grandchildren, often speaking of the joy and happiness grandchildren had brought into their lives. Older people consistently told us that becoming a grandparent allowed them to have a closer relationship with young children than was possible when they were busy parents, and they felt that this enabled them to occupy a distinctive niche in their grandchildren's lives – to be 'all the things you would have liked to be for your [own] children' (Brigit, b. 1946, LHSC).

> Time and love ... Listen to them. Because it's very important. And I think, to learn by your own mistakes with your children, that you could be ... a great parent to your grandchildren [laughter]. That you can listen. You don't criticise. You just listen. And advise, obviously, if they ask for it. But, like, I mean, you just listen, is the most important. (Doreen, b. 1945, LHSC)

> I think it could be a calming influence on children really, when you slow down and when parents are young they have an awful lot of chores to do and an awful lot of demands on their time and probably a lot of debt as well and trying to cope and you have more time and more experience to lend to them and show them interesting bird life or the environment that maybe can be skipped over when you are a young parent and you don't have the time for those [things]. (Daniel, 1947, LHSC)

A number of grandparents mentioned introducing children to the joys of nature as an aspect of their role. There is some evidence that grandfatherhood provides men with an opportunity to interact more fully with young children, in ways that gendered parenting norms had prevented them from doing in the past. Bernard (b. 1951, LHSC) loved being with his little granddaughter but felt that his 'skills aren't great', because as a father he 'never had time, worked too hard ... 'twas all I was ever used to'. On the other hand, stories of grandfathers who had 'a way' with grandchildren stretch back to the oldest cohort in the study. Joan (b. 1916, LHSC) remembered her father babysitting her own children when she and her husband were busy milking cows: 'I'd come in and the whole place would be upside down and whoever the culprit [was] would hide behind him and he'd say, "They'll get sense yet"'. Across all ages many grandparents saw their role as 'spoiling' their grandchildren with sweets and money, something that those who were grandchildren in the 1970s and 1980s – and contemporary nine-year-old grandchildren – were all too aware of.

Jennifer Mason (Mason et al., 2007) and her colleagues have shown how discourse on contemporary grandparenting in Britain is governed by a high degree of consensus around two norms that sometimes come into conflict with one another – being there, and not interfering (see also Breheny et al., 2013). This theme is also very prevalent amongst grandparents in Ireland. Audrey (b. 1945, LHSC) expressed it concisely: 'When you can be of use, be of use but mind your own business. Share the joys and share the sorrows and mind your own business'. The life history narratives revealed a certain amount of tension around the boundaries of 'being there' without interfering. Parents sometimes resented what they saw as implicit criticism by grandparents, or felt guilty about wanting a bit more independence from grandparental influence. Some grandparents, on the other hand, felt a bit excluded from their grandchildren's lives and were indeed critical of their grandchildren's parents. This negotiation of boundaries reflects the extent to which the grandparental role is an ambivalent one – that is, it imposes contradictory expectations about attitudes and behaviours in **intergenerational relationships** (Luescher and Pillemer, 1998; Bengtson et al., 2002; Connidis and McMullin, 2002). Later we will discuss in more detail changes in the context within which ambivalent intergenerational relationships are played out in Ireland.

To conclude this section, however, as Attias-Donfut and Segalen (2002) highlighted, grandparents are essential to the affirmation of a sense of collective identity that transcends more than one generation. Thus even in urban contexts, grandparenthood echoes the institution of lineage that governed traditional rural societies **See the discussion in Chapter 1.** In the *Family Rhythms* interviews, a number of respondents spoke about the role of grandparents in maintaining their connection to the land. As we saw in Chapter 3, the experience of spending summers on grandparents' farms was quite common, especially amongst those who grew up in the second half of the twentieth century. As well as offering a welcome opportunity for greater freedom, this

---

Panel 6.2   Landmark Irish study: *Grandparenthood in Modern Ireland* by Francesca Lundström (2001)

Francesca Lundström's pioneering study on the role played by grandparents in Irish family life used a qualitative methodology to capture grandparent's own views on their family role. Prior to the report *Grandparenthood in Modern Ireland* no systematic research into Irish grandparenthood had been undertaken and there was an obvious dearth of information on the demographic profile of Irish grandparents, their level of involvement in family life and the degree and nature of support given by grandparents to their families. Lundström's study described Irish grandparenthood at the outset of the economic boom, and identified many experiences and issues that have since became even more salient in the context of changing family patterns. The research was first proposed by the charity Age Action Ireland in 1992 in recognition of the 'overwhelmingly negative attitudes towards aging and older people', as a means of uncovering the very positive life stage of grandparenthood. When the research commenced in 1999, with funding from the Department of Social, Community and Family Affairs, a second objective was added of identifying issues and concerns pertinent to Irish grandparents that might be addressed by policy and service planning.

Lundström interviewed fifty-eight grandparents (forty-four grandmothers and fourteen grandfathers with an average age of seventy years) from a diversity of backgrounds. The research included a demographic questionnaire with interview participants on items such as their geographic proximity to their grandchildren and the degree of contact with their children's families. The questionnaire revealed interviewees had an average of ten grandchildren, which was considerably more than the US or UK, and a quarter were also great-grandparents. In the qualitative interviews grandparents discussed their views on becoming and being a grandparent, which were mostly positive; where negative feelings were reported this was usually in response to a pregnancy outside of marriage and/or a teenage pregnancy. The study also highlighted the sometimes negative impact of marital breakdown on maintaining a relationship with a grandchild.

The supportive role played by grandparents in family life was also studied in detail and the report identified six types of caring for grandchildren undertaken by Irish grandparents. Caring for grandchildren for blocks of time was the most common type of care given, for example when the mother of a grandchild returned to work after maternity leave. While many grandparents described caring for their grandchild as 'a joy', some found care work tiring and a strain, and some were ambivalent about the risk of being 'taken advantage of'. Some interviewees supplied financial support to their families including buying clothing and equipment for grandchildren. In terms of spending time together, the age group 60–69 was the most likely to engage in recreational activities with a grandchild and involvement in such activities tapered off with encroaching old age. The study also uncovered a gender division between grandmothers and grandfathers in terms of the types of activities undertaken with grandchildren.

A major finding from the study was the persistence of strong extended family bonds between Irish grandparents and their families. While very few lived in three-generation homes in 1999, most interviewees lived within ten miles of their grandchildren and saw them at least once a week. Lundström suggested that the frequent contact between grandparents and their families might be due to the typically close proximity of kin in Ireland. The study also captures some interesting reflections by grandparents on the modern family: interviewees commented on the shift in the balance of power between the generations that had occurred during their lifetimes; most interviewees avoided interfering in parenting decisions around rearing and disciplining a grandchild; some interviewees were concerned that in the dual-earner home parents might tend to acquiesce too much to the demands of their child.

contact with rural life formed an important part of their sense of who they were as adults: 'there would be no aspect of a farm that I probably wouldn't be familiar with, I'm not saying I would turn out to be a farmer but I wouldn't be as removed from agriculture as say my nieces are' (Mandy b. 1965, LHSC, referring to time spent with her grandfather). Martin (b. 1947, LHSC) spoke eloquently about his desire to pass on a familiarity with country life to his granddaughter:

> Everybody in the country has somebody belonging to them [in Dublin] ... So I think it's important for children growing up in Dublin that they would be down the country in their early years growing up into teenagers so that they will always have it in their background ... [I]t gives them freedom and ... it gives them background. It probably makes them who they are at the end of the day.

Of course not everybody has an ancestral connection to the land in Ireland. Other respondents talked about how their grandparents connected them to the past through their work, such as Graham (b. 1931, LHSC), whose sense of identity and place was linked to his inheritance of the trade of stonemasonry from his grandparent. Others spoke of how their grandparents provided a template for their own way of being in the world, including their potential as human beings. Remember single mother Emer (b. 1970s, LHSC) who saw herself as part of the same tradition as her grandmother, who raised six children on her own? **See the discussion in Chapter 4**. In Attias-Donfut and Segalen's (2002) words, 'Grandparents provide the basis for an identity that everyone needs'.

Older people in the economic life of families

This section focuses on grandparents' (and other older relatives') roles in the production, sharing and distribution of 'economic' resources within families. As we have seen throughout this book, in family life the practices that give rise to material subsistence transcend those that we normally think of as 'economic' to include activities relating to caring and nurturance. In order to understand changing intergenerational practices relating to the economic life of families in this sense, we must also consider intergenerational relationships within and between **households**, the institutions at the heart of family economic life.

As we have seen, questions about the extent and form of intergenerational co-residence have been central to the extensive literature on historical family systems and household economies in Europe. **This topic is discussed in detail in Chapter 1**. Despite questions about how widespread multi-generational households were in early twentieth-century Ireland – or how many we should expect to find given prevailing demographic conditions, experiences of living with grandparents are sufficiently common amongst the oldest two cohorts in our study – and sufficiently unusual in the youngest two cohorts – to demonstrate that a profound shift in the nature of intergenerational exchanges occurred during the twentieth century. As Ruggles (2007) showed for the United States, long-term decline in intergenerational co-residence can be explained principally by growing economic opportunities for the younger (adult) generation. He found that before 1930, intergenerational co-residence was more likely to occur amongst high-status, property-owning families. By contrast, after 1950, that relationship was reversed – intergenerational co-residence became more common amongst lower-income families, when adult children were unable to afford to live independently. In Ireland, a similar process appears to have taken place during a more compressed period of time. The implications of these changes for intergenerational relationships can be illustrated through a life sketch of one of our respondents (see Panel 6.3, p. 178).

As early as the 1930s, Arensberg and Kimball (2001 [1940]: 122–123) observed that 'The theme of strife between mother and daughter-in-law ... appears very frequently in conversation and in jokes'. At that time, the burden of adapting to this potentially conflict-ridden situation fell on the daughter-in-law, who 'must learn a nice balance between her new freedom and new full status and the continued control and the vested interest of her mother-in-law'. As the social and economic context changed during the twentieth century, both the older and younger generation of women appear to have become less

Panel 6.3   Looking at the data: Sally's story

Sally (b. 1949, LHSC) was born into a farming family in the south-east of Ireland. She has warm memories of her paternal grandmother who lived in the family home until she died: 'I'll always remember coming home from school and if my mother wasn't there, it was kinda acceptable, Granny was always there to give the dinner to us'. After a short time working in Dublin Sally married a farmer and moved in with his mother and brothers in the 1980s. She was, however, at pains to emphasize that, in contrast to her own mother's experience, in her case the mother-in-law lived in an extension built on to the house.

> we had the same situation here but Granny here had ah, her own apart-ment but my mother was all in the one kitchen [overlapping] She found it hard ... I remember her saying she found it hard when she got married first and the granny being such a hard worker expected I think mammy to be working as hard and when she was expecting me I think she was awful sick which I was as well with my first and she said she remembered going out and sitting in the hay barn [laughs] just to get a break. Yeah she did find it hard she said. (Sally, b. 1949, LHSC)

Despite her separate living arrangements, Sally found her own mother-in-law to be helpful when she was raising her children: 'Coming home yeah with the baby, well Nana was here again, possibly the same with my mother, great support as I say I would run to Nana if there was, if I was worried'. At the time of her interview around 2005, Sally had become a grandmother herself, and was enthusiastic about helping her daughter:

> Oh its gorgeous [being a grandparent] yeah absolutely love it, we love it sure we see her at the weekend. She's a year [old] and seeing her, things now I hadn't time when ... mine were growing up, I realise that now to enjoy them. You're so busy like I was I suppose cooking dinner for all these men and I hadn't time to enjoy them. Now I'm enjoying her ... [There will be] ... another little one ... in five weeks' time, so I help [my daughter] out. I have been going up and down [...] a good bit ... Helping out but aw she's gorgeous yeah, we love her to bits. (Sally, b. 1949, LHSC)

Sally's story vividly illustrates Ruggles' (2009) argument, showing how the interplay between the transformation of intergenerational relationships and changing social and economic structures led to the reconstruction of grandparenthood that we described above. Sally was born into a world where the power of the older generation was rooted in their control over property and the means of making a living. Even after the heir married and took over the management of the farm, the old couple often remained economically active and, in the case of Sally's grandmother, rather dominant in the female sphere. However, when Sally married into her husband's farm, norms about gender and family life were changing and they arranged for her mother-in-law to have her own distinct living space. This arrangement represented a new accommodation to the requirements of both generations.

willing to tolerate this situation. An older respondent, from much poorer rural origins than Sally (b. 1949, LHSC) reflected on how it would be nice to have children living nearby now that she was getting frail, but would only have considered this option if she had been in a position to provide for separate accommodation:

> It doesn't always work to have anyone living in the house with you either, you know, like your son or your son-in-law unless that is the way you are used to ... except if you had another part built on to the house so they'd have their own door and as long as two women wasn't standing in one kitchen. (Monica, b. 1932, LHSC)

Sally (Panel 6.3, p. 178) and her husband were in better circumstances than Monica (b. 1932, LHSC) at the time of her interview, being younger and quite active. Their son had, after an extended period of time, decided to return to take up farming alongside his father, but was yet unmarried.

Even amongst working-class families who did not own property, the difficulties faced by young couples starting out made them more dependent on older family members during the first half of the twentieth century. Many multigenerational households came about as a result of grandparents (or in some cases aunts or other relatives) taking in young children (Gray, Geraghty and Ralph, 2013; Gray, 2014). **This practice is discussed in detail from the child's perspective in Chapter 3**. Stories of sending children to live with grandparents on a semi-permanent basis began to disappear from the life history narratives of respondents born in the 1960s and 1970s and amongst those with rural origins were replaced by references to the custom of sending children on extended summer holidays to their grandparents' farm. Where experiences of children sharing a household with grandparents appear in accounts dating from the 1970s onwards, they are associated with crisis situations (such as parental separation) and they are depicted as problematic, temporary situations, best discontinued as soon as possible. Whereas formerly patterns of intergenerational co-residence were considered routine and unexceptional – if not always ideal – they were now treated as generally undesirable.

This shift can be understood in terms of a changing balance of power that emerged between the generations (Gray, Geraghty and Ralph, 2013). International scholarship has shown that, in other countries, a number of factors came together to alter intergenerational relationships between parents and their adult children around the middle of the twentieth century (Ruggles, 2007; Merchant et al., 2012). These included: demographic factors (the concentration of childbearing earlier in a woman's life); greater levels of educational attainment amongst the older generation; and increasing labour force participation amongst older women returning to work once they had raised their children. Most important, however, were the economic changes that permitted earlier marriage and household formation in the younger generation. As opportunities for making a living and establishing an independent household increased, young adults no longer depended on their parents to the same extent. Both adult children and their parents were increasingly able to act on a growing preference for living independently. From the perspective of grandparents, adult children and their spouses were now in a position to act as gatekeepers to their grandchildren and in this context the ambivalence associated with the grandparental role increased (see the discussion of ambivalence earlier in this chapter).

As we have seen, grandparents have historically 'taken in' grandchildren to ease the pressure on parents associated with poverty and large family sizes. International research, especially in the United States, has focused on the continuing role of grandparents in supporting families affected by poverty and high rates of non-marital childbearing (Fuller-Thomson et al., 1997; Minkler, 1999). New family practices, including single parenting due to non-marital births and separation or divorce, can present challenges for grandparents – especially paternal grandparents – in maintaining relationships with their grandchildren (Doyle et al., 2010). However, it should be remembered that other factors can separate grandparents from grandchildren – in Ireland, most notably, emigration. Kathleen (b. 1924, LHSC) described her feelings and those of her husband when her son emigrated with his family:

> good God yes it nearly broke my heart, the kids and especially [granddaughter]. And what broke my heart entirely was they were here and Daddy started crying here one day and it was very hard to take a tear out of Daddy, he wasn't one for whinging. And he said what I wouldn't say or expect either, but he did and he meant it, why didn't they leave us one of them. How could they, for God's sake?

Kathleen's husband's outburst reflected memories of the practice of 'sharing' children with grandparents, other relatives, and sometimes even friends. This practice became increasingly untenable in a world where parents economically and normatively had wrested independence from the older generation.

Grandparents are now considerably less likely to share a household with their adult children and grandchildren, but social and economic exchanges continue to flow upwards and downwards across the generations. As we saw earlier, there is scant evidence to support the view that flows of help and support between grandparents, parents and grandchildren have declined in contemporary societies; on the contrary, a wealth of recent research has demonstrated that most European families engage in such **intergenerational transfers** both 'upwards' to grandparents (and great-grandparents) and downwards to parents and grandchildren (Attias-Donfut et al., 2005; Dykstra and Fokkema 2011).

The TILDA study (Kamiya and Timonen, 2011) found that financial transfers flow mainly from parents to their adult children: about a quarter of older households in Ireland had given a gift worth 5000 euro or more to one of their children within the last ten years, whereas just 9 per cent of the older generation had received financial gifts from their children. Over one-third of older parents (that is, aged fifty or more years) provided practical, everyday help (such as shopping or everyday household chores) to their non-resident adult children. Forty-one per cent of older people received similar forms of everyday help from their children.

As you might expect, the flow of such transfers in kind changes with age: children are increasingly providers rather than receivers of everyday forms of assistance as their parents grow older. In a more recent report the TILDA research team (McGarrigle and Kenny, 2013) highlighted the experience of what is sometimes termed the **sandwich generation** – people who provide help and support both to adult children and to their elderly parents. Focusing on women living in the community (i.e. not in care homes or other institutions), they found that 31 per cent of those aged fifty to sixty-nine were in the 'sandwich'. Eighty-three per cent of women in this situation help their children in one way or another, while 58 per cent provide help to their parents.

Childcare is one of the most notable forms of help that Irish older people provide to their adult children. As we saw in Chapter 4, formal childcare costs in Ireland are amongst the most expensive in Europe, and it is likely that the provision of care by grandparents was a key factor enabling many mothers to participate in the labour force during the Celtic Tiger boom. As one single mother in the GUI qualitative study put it, 'there would be no-one working only for nanny' (Emmanuelle's mother, GUI). The TILDA study found that almost half those aged fifty or more years provided regular care for grandchildren (at least one hour per week); this was true of more than one-third of 'sandwich generation' women. From the perspective of the grandchildren, about 12 per cent of infants are regularly cared for by their grandparents; the GUI study found that 42 per cent of all infants in non-parental care were being minded by their grandparents (McGinnity et al., 2013).

In the qualitative data analysed for this book, many children described how grandparents eased the transition from school to home, picking them up and minding them until their parents came home from work. Of course,

Panel 6.4   Landmark Irish study: *The Irish LongituDinal Study on Ageing* **(TILDA)**

TILDA is the first nationally representative, **longitudinal panel study** of ageing in Ireland, and aims to 'make Ireland the best place in the world to grow old' by providing an evidence base for policy development. This longitudinal study follows a cohort of over 8,500 Irish people aged fifty and older, and collects an extensive range of economic (pensions, employment, living standards) and social data (contact with friends and kin, formal and informal care, social participation) every two years using a survey methodology. Participants can also take part in a detailed medical check-up of their physical, mental and cognitive health, and the combination of both datasets makes TILDA a very comprehensive, internationally comparative study of ageing.

The results from the first wave of TILDA, entitled *Fifty Plus in Ireland 2011*, offer a fascinating snapshot of contemporary older Irish people's lives. Most over-fifties, it transpires, live in close proximity to their children. Many make significant financial and non-financial transfers to their adult children, with the generational flow of resources rarely flowing in the opposite direction towards older family members. Community interaction is also strong among many of the over-fifties, with visits to kin and friends, community volunteering, and participation in leisure activities common among the majority of the sample. Social isolation is a problem for 7 per cent of the sample, who, interestingly, reported considerably poorer health states than those not experiencing social isolation. Sixty per cent attend weekly organized religious services; 80 per cent vote in general elections (well above the average electoral turnout).

The health profile of the over-fifties raises some concerns for practitioners and policy makers. One in five smoke; one in five take five or more daily medications; three in four are overweight or obese. There is also a noticeable discrepancy between participants' self-reported health status and objectively measured status; consistently people think they are healthier than they really are. Health-related behaviours differ markedly according to one's socio-economic position, so that the wealthier an individual is, the more likely they are to get screened for various diseases, especially cancers, and the less likely they are to be obese, a smoker, or to drink excessively. A majority of participants in the first wave of data collection reported a high quality of life and held a positive outlook on ageing – though there is a clear correlation between one's reported quality of life and one's objective asset worth. Publications and project information from TILDA are made available at www.tilda.ie.

as we have seen, grandparents were also there for children returning home from school, or on their way to and from school in the past: '[On] our way home from school ... we used to go in [to our grandmother] and she'd have the bacon and cabbage in the pot on the hearth and she'd give us the mug of cabbage water and say, drink that into you ... and that will bring you home until your mother gets you your dinner' (Kathleen, b. 1924, LHSC). For contemporary grandparents, however, the changing social construction of childhood discussed in Chapter 3 means that today there is a requirement to collect children from school and to co-ordinate schedules with their parents. As one grandmother in the Life History study explained, this can be complex and tiring, especially for older grandparents. Lillian (b. 1932, LHSC) was minding a pre-schooler and two school-going children for her daughter and son-in-law:

> He is a full time job now at three, you really have to keep an eye on him so [husband] would take him off for a walk and that works out great because he would get tired and he comes back then around twelve o'clock and he would either fall asleep here or fall asleep in the front room and he will sleep then from maybe twelve to half one or he will doze off and watch the television. And then the other two come in then about twenty to four and I have their dinner ready because they are hungry. I make them do their homework, although I find it hard to get them to do their homework when the little fellow is here because he is in on top of them and he wants the pens and pencils ... They are collected at a quarter past five. [My daughter] finishes work at five and by the time she gets up here through the traffic it could be a quarter past five or twenty past five. Now that is Monday to Friday.

Lillian explained that she had made the decision to mind her three-year-old grandchild two days a week (in addition to the school-going children on five days) 'because I just want a reason to get up on Monday morning'. Nevertheless, it is clear from the interview that this participant is ambivalent about her (and her husband's) ability to cope and she reassured the interviewer that if it got too much they could 'say it in the morning' to their son and daughter-in-law, 'we have that understanding with them'. At the same time, she feared that, in the absence of the childcare arrangement, she 'wouldn't see', her grandchildren, especially those that were at school.

Childcare is thus a focus for the intergenerational **ambivalence** that we discussed earlier. Some respondents commented negatively on the expectation that grandparents would take care of their grandchildren. Evelyn (b. 1923, LHSC) objected to the way a cousin was treated by her adult children: '[I]t is not like they are sitting at home on their bottoms but they are all out working and she is minding the kids and I don't think that is fair'. Parents, also, expressed some guilt about the extent to which they were imposing on their own parents for childcare, such as Elizabeth (b. 1970, LHSC):

she'd mind all the grandchildren when we work and she'd never moan or anything. Like if you ask her there is never any bother, you know and I kind of feel
guilty asking her because you know she is not going to say no, even if she doesn't
want to, you know.

Van Gaalen and Dykstra (2006) found that (in the Netherlands) when
adult children and their parents frequently exchanged financial and practical
support, they were also more likely to experience conflict in their relationships.
On the other hand, the subjective quality of such relationships was comparatively high. The authors suggested that such ambivalence occurs when there
are fewer options for escape – for example, by transferring responsibility for care
to professional providers or other siblings. Class, gender and life stage are key
factors here. In Ireland, reliance on informal childcare by grandparents is clearly
related to social class. The TILDA study found that women with a primary education were almost three times more likely to care for their grandchildren than
those with a third-level education (McGarrigle and Kenny, 2013).

Because responsibility for care is still strongly gendered, intergenerational
care remains at heart a set of negotiations amongst women. Across Europe,
mothers and daughters are more likely to be engaged in **descending familialism**
– that is, intergenerational relationships characterized by: 'living nearby, frequent contact, endorsement of family obligation norms, and primarily help
in kind from parents to children' (Dykstra and Fokkema, 2011). In Australia,
Horsfall and Dempsey (2013) found that, while grandmothers and grandfathers both actively engaged in caring for their grandchildren, grandmothers
tended to be positioned as nurturing co-ordinators of care, whereas grandfathers were freer to opt in or out of the physical or routine tasks and more
likely to focus on the educational and recreational aspects of caring for their
grandchildren.

There is some evidence in our study of similarly gendered patterns of care
when both grandparents are involved: grandfathers are often depicted collecting grandchildren from school, or bringing them to the park while grandmothers cook meals and supervise homework. As grandparents grow older, their
relationship with their adult children tends to shift towards **ascending familialism**, in which help in kind flows to them from their adult children. There
are differences across European countries in the form of intergenerational
relationships; familialism is most characteristic of southern and eastern countries, whereas more distant, autonomous intergenerational relationships are
found in greater proportions in northern and western countries. As we have
seen throughout this book, Irish families share many of the characteristics of
families in southern Europe, and the qualitative evidence presented here tends
to support the view that familialistic intergenerational relationships prevail.
However, as Dykstra and Fokkema (2011) caution, a mixture of family types
occurs within all countries, and the differences are linked to demographic and
social factors – such as life stage and social class – so we should be wary about

drawing the conclusion that there is a culturally specific form of intergenerational relationships in Ireland.

In summary, this section has argued that in the course of the twentieth century, demographic, social and economic changes in Irish society led to a shift in the balance of power between generations that had consequences for how resources were exchanged between grandparents, their adult children and grandchildren. During the first half of the century, the older generation had the upper hand, either because they provided access to property and the means of making a living to their children and grandchildren, or because, in the context of poverty and large families, they provided essential practical support during family formation. From the late 1950s onwards, new opportunities for making a living in Ireland, together with higher levels of education, allowed young adults greater independence from their parents. This included the opportunity to maintain separate households, an aspiration that seems to have been shared across generations, but which gave parents the power to regulate grandparents' access to their grandchildren.

Beginning in the 1990s, women's growing participation in the labour force created new opportunities and challenges for intergenerational solidarity. Grandparents have once again been called on to help with caring for grandchildren, but in a new institutional and socio-cultural context that makes childcare more demanding in many ways. Furthermore, an increasing proportion of women find themselves in the position of a 'sandwich generation', with responsibilities both for frail older parents and their non-resident adult children, including in some cases help with childcare.

Drawing on data from the *Changing Generations* qualitative longitudinal study, Conlon et al. (2014) showed that Irish women expressed intergenerational solidarity in different ways, depending on their social class position. Young women in lower socio-economic groups lived **enmeshed intergenerational lives**, and remained committed to caring for older family members in the future, even as they recognized that this would affect their own life chances. By contrast, young women in higher socio-economic categories lived freed lives oriented towards independence. The older women in these groups responded to their observation of the demands that intensive parenting placed on younger women by withholding expectations about their own care and assistance, but also, in some cases, by withholding or lessening their own provision of care to grandchildren.

In other words, these older women were initiating a sea change in intergenerational relationships, one oriented towards displacing the central role of care in women's lives. Just as the earlier transformations that we have discussed in this chapter depended on social, economic and institutional changes that altered the structures of dependence in intergenerational relationships – the introduction of the old-age pension at the beginning of the twentieth century and the emergence of new opportunities for making a living at the middle – so too, this innovation is currently only possible for those who can envisage, and

**Panel 6.5   Landmark Irish study: *Changing Generations* –
the intergenerational solidarity in Ireland project**

Changing Generations is a major qualitative study of **intergenerational solidarity** in Ireland – 'how people of different generations live together, help each other and depend on one another in their daily lives'. Against a backdrop of recession and demographic change, the study sheds light on the ways in which 'ordinary' Irish people support one another, and the degree of 'give and take' between the generations. *Changing Generations* also provides an evidence base for a national dialogue on intergenerational solidarity and justice in Ireland, by capturing how Irish people 'perceive the social policies that support individuals at different stages of the life course'. Participants are asked to consider their contribution to wider Irish society and what they receive in turn from the state.

The study sought to construct new understandings of intergenerational relations in Ireland, and adopted a constructivist grounded theory (Charmaz, 2014) approach whereby 'conceptualization and theorising are constructed "from the ground up", rather than with the view to testing or fleshing out any particular notions of or assumptions regarding solidarity'. Between September 2011 and July 2012 in-depth, semi-structured interviews were conducted with a national sample of one-hundred men and women covering an age span of eighteen to 102 years. Initially participants were recruited through local organizations, and from here recruitment snowballed out to gather further respondents that were less inclined to join such organizations and were potentially more isolated. Participants were drawn from five study sites with distinct levels of affluence and deprivation, and were purposively sampled for a balanced representation of high, middle and low socio-economic status 'to allow for theoretical exploration of the role of socio-economic status in shaping practices and perspectives'. To complement this data, interviews were also conducted with twenty leaders from the public, private and civil society sectors.

Changing Generations found considerable evidence of intergenerational solidarity within Irish families which was helping people to survive the current recession. Most often the older generation provided extensive support to the younger generations in the form of financial, housing and childcare support. The study found little evidence of conflict between the generations – younger participants felt older people's welfare entitlements were deserved, while older participants called for improved supports for some younger age groups. The researchers concluded that 'economic inequality, not intergenerational difference, is a more significant cleavage between groups living in Ireland today'.

Changing Generations is a collaborative research project between the Social policy and Ageing Research Centre (SpARC) at Trinity College Dublin, and the Irish Centre for Social Gerontology (ICSG) at the National University of Ireland, Galway. The research has given rise to many scholarly articles and reports, and a resource of materials for others that wish to carry out research projects or raise awareness about intergenerational relations in their own communities. All of these materials are available on the project website: www.sparc.tcd.ie/generations/

plan for, alternative sources of care late in life. As we will discuss further below, the extent to which public services will be able to meet the demands for elder care in ways that permit the development of 'freed' lives for women across all social classes, remains uncertain.

The kinship and community life of older people

Under the modernization perspective that dominated thinking about families around the middle of the twentieth century, the prevailing view was that older people had become increasingly isolated from wider kinship and community networks in modern societies. However, beginning with the community studies of the 1950s and 1960s, it became increasingly clear that older people were embedded in networks of kin, neighbours and friends, even in 'new' suburban areas (Wilmott and Young, 1960).

Phillipson et al. (1998) revisited three urban areas in the United Kingdom that had been the subject of landmark community studies in the 1940s and 1950, and found evidence of continuity and change. While older people were significantly more likely to live alone or as couples in the 1990s, they remained embedded in social networks comprising kin and friends. However, the kinship networks of older people in the 1990s tended to be somewhat more dispersed (and dependent on the telephone and car for contact). Furthermore, their respondents' personal networks (relationships with those who were important to them), were more focused in terms of generation than those of the past – that is, centred on people in their own age group and on their children. There were also variations by class and ethnicity – with dense local networks being more characteristic of working-class areas and some ethnic-minority communities.

International research has found that older people's networks also vary by age. Evidence from the United States (Cornwell et al., 2008: 200) suggests that, as they age, older people increase the frequency with which they socialize with neighbours, attend religious services and engage in volunteering. The volume of contact people have with people in their social networks increases following retirement, but then begins to decrease. 'The oldest have smaller social networks, they are less close to network members, and they have fewer non-primary-group ties than do younger adults'. Comparative European research has revealed variations in older people's social networks by region. In southern European countries older people are much more likely to co-reside with their adult children, and if they do not, have more frequent contact with them than do older people in northern countries (Hank, 2007). By contrast, older people in northern European countries are more likely to exchange practical forms of help and support with non-kin, and to be involved in clubs, voluntary associations and other organizations (Kohli et al., 2009).

Ireland appears close to the European average in terms of older peoples' social connections (see Table 1 in Ellwardt et al., 2014: 7). Data from a special module of the *Quarterly National Household Survey* (CSO, 2009) showed that amongst Irish adults aged between fifty-five to seventy-four more than 65 per cent saw relatives at least once a week, more than 70 per cent saw friends, and more than 85 per cent saw neighbours at least once weekly. Amongst the oldest adults aged seventy-five years or more, the proportion seeing friends at least once a week was smaller (64 per cent), while the proportions seeing relatives weekly was greater (72 per cent). The first wave of the TILDA study found that almost a quarter (23 per cent) of older Irish adults provided some form of help to neighbours and friends, while 17 per cent received help. Older people were less likely to provide help as they aged, but not much more likely to receive it (Kamiya and Timonen, 2011: 48). In a mixed-method study of an urban and a rural location in Ireland, Gallagher (2012: 98) found 'a rich landscape of relatedness consisting of multidimensional relationships based on kinship and friendship'. Not all older people are equally well-embedded in networks of kin and community; social isolation occurs more frequently in rural areas (Fahey et al., 2007; Walsh et al., 2012).

Much of the quantitative research on older people's social networks has focused on the numbers of kin, neighbours and friends available to them. However, qualitative studies reveal the extent to which older people themselves actively mobilize community and kinship relations, and provide a focal point for extended family relatedness. Gallagher (2012: 98) observed that the participants in her study 'co-created' the satisfying relationships they experienced. The *Family Rhythms* study revealed a consistent pattern of 'kin-keeping' on the part of grandparents – especially grandmothers – going back to the memories of the oldest participants.

In summary, then, contrary to earlier (and still widespread) beliefs that older people are more isolated and disconnected from family, friends and neighbours in modern societies, the evidence suggests that most older people play an active role in maintaining and promoting extended kinship and cross-generational ties, and in their local communities. However, it is important also to remember that there are variations in the nature and kinds of networks mobilized by older people in different socio-demographic groups. The oldest,

---

Panel 6.6   Looking at the data: in my grandparent's house

Many stories in the *Family Rhythms* study tell how a grandparent's house was the centre for extended family gatherings:

> every day whenever there was time, we used we used to go [...] up to the shop with my mother and I remember calling on those days [...] to a little house ... I remember my grandmother and she was a hardy woman up until the time of her death ... they all wore a shawl in them days, and long clothes of course. And they were great musical people, they were singing and playing accordions and all and that ... they were mad for that kind of thing, they were light-hearted. (James, b. 1924, LHSC)

> Sunday dinner was never at home, it was in my grandmother's house ... it tended to be the whole Sunday right up to say seven or eight o'clock at night, so you were there for the day and you know, maybe television was coming in and everything [was] changed a little bit. I remember in the earlier days my cousins would come as well on the same Sunday and we would have to put a play on and my aunt was the director. (Rob, b. 1953, LHSC)

> *Interviewer*: So tell me a little bit about your grandparents and your cousins and all, do they live around here?
> *Sarah*: Some of my cousins live a little bit far away
> [....]
> *Interviewer*: And would you get to see your cousins much?
> *Sarah*: At the weekend we go down to my Nanny's and they're probably there
> (Sarah, age 9, GUI)

---

those suffering from disabilities and some older people living in rural areas are more likely to suffer from isolation.

Intergenerational solidarity as a public issue

Throughout this book, we have emphasized how changing demographic patterns impact on the rhythms and textures of family life. Of all the consequences of societal ageing, the longevity revolution has had the highest profile as a public issue. However, public discourse in Ireland has rarely explicitly recognized the extent to which increasing proportions of older people in the population are challenges – and opportunities – for family life. As we have seen, the state played a central role in the transformation of intergenerational relationships through the institutionalization of retirement, linked to the introduction of the old age pension at the beginning of the last century.

Just as modernization theorists expected to find that older people would be neglected as the conjugal family took centre stage, some analysts feared that the welfare state, as it increasingly took on greater responsibility for the care of older people, would 'crowd out' the family. As older people began to live longer, there were concerns that the growing public burden of supporting them would lead to problems of intergenerational justice and even to conflict between the generations (Kohli, 2006). However, as we have seen throughout this chapter, in Ireland – as in other European countries – there is no evidence of a decline in intergenerational solidarity. Instead, as Kohli (2006) argued (and as we have seen throughout this chapter), private intergenerational exchanges within families have instead been 'crowded in' by the public generational contract. By freeing (or at least partly freeing) the younger adult generation from the responsibility of providing financially for their parents, the state created the possibility of grandparental support for childcare (facilitating female participation in the labour force) and also flows of financial support from grandparents to parents.

However, even though family processes and dynamics are at the heart of the changing generational contract, the Irish state has rarely developed policy towards the elderly from a whole family perspective. We can illustrate this point through a consideration of arrangements for the care of older people in their homes. Timonen and Doyle (2008) showed how Irish policy has historically focused on institutional care for the poorest, and the principle of state support for care in the community emerged only in the second half of the twentieth century. From the 1970s onwards, provision of home care packages through the regional Health Boards increased, but they remained at the discretion of individual Boards, leading to an uneven and fragmented pattern of service across the country that continues to the present day, despite the emergence of a 'mixed economy' of service provision incorporating public, non-profit and private organizations since the 1990s. Across the country, care packages are frequently inadequate to meet the needs of those who require them, often incorporate an element of 'cash for care', and generally rely on very poorly paid carers. In summary, just as childcare for working parents tacitly depends on a 'grey economy' of informal and unpaid care (frequently by grandparents), community care for older people in Ireland tacitly depends on extended family (and neighbour) support.

Is this what Irish people want? In 2007, Eurobarometer (2007) carried out a survey on people's attitudes and expectations about care across Europe. Figure 6.3 shows how people in Ireland, Denmark and Portugal responded to a question about what they thought an elderly father or mother should do if they were no longer able to live alone without regular help. Compared to Portugal,

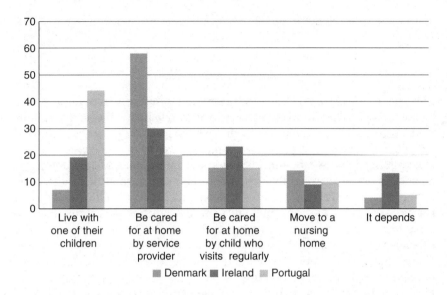

Figure 6.3 What should an older person do if no longer able to care for self?
(Per cent responses in Denmark, Ireland and Portugal)

Source: Eurobarometer (2007), Table QA7a

Irish people are less 'familial' insofar as they are much less likely to agree that an older person should move to live with an adult child. As we saw earlier, a clear preference for independent household living has evolved across all generations in Ireland since the beginning of the last century.

On the other hand, the Irish responses are more ambivalent than those from Denmark, with more people agreeing that a family member – rather than a public or private service provider – should visit and care for an older person in their own home. This solution, as Timonen et al.'s (2013) work shows, has consequences for the reproduction of class and gender inequalities over time. People from lower socio-economic groups are more likely to expect – and anticipate – family based care, but this has consequences for the life chances of family care providers. By contrast, people in higher socio-economic groups can plan (to some extent) to mobilize financial solutions that promote independence across the generations. Importantly, these patterns are linked to the Irish liberal welfare state regime: Irish, Danish and Portuguese people's expectations about what should happen are informed by their knowledge of the kinds of solutions that are available in the society in which they live. 'Intergenerational solidarities are simultaneously being constructed at the family level and at the societal level, and are at both levels powerfully shaped by socioeconomic resources that influence the attitudes and practices we adopt towards other generations' (Timonen et al., 2013: 178).

Summary and conclusion

This chapter has examined the transformation in intergenerational relationships in Irish families from the perspective of grandparents. We have seen how demographic changes, including the increase of healthy life expectancy in old age, have provided the context for changing patterns of residence and intergenerational flows of care and support in ageing societies. Most notably, the balance of power between the generations changed during the last century, as the parent generation acquired greater independence and the ability to act as gatekeepers to grandchildren. In recent decades, as parents increasingly require two incomes to support their households, many have become dependent on grandparents for help with childcare. However, because of the transformation of meanings and practices that has occurred in all dimensions of family life grandparenthood has become a more **ambivalent relationship**. Even though parents rely on them for help, grandparents adopt a stance of being supportive, but not interfering with parents' priorities and approaches to raising children.

We have documented evidence of considerable continuity in the warmth and affection between grandparents and grandchildren despite the changing family contexts for their relationships. Furthermore, most older people continue to be embedded in networks of kinship and community; many continue to be the focal point for the preservation of extended family ties. As we have shown, there is little evidence that there has ever been a widespread pattern of neglect of older people by their families, or that this has increased as societies have modernized. Nevertheless, there will be increasing challenges for Irish society as the number of older people requiring regular care grows in the years ahead. Ireland has relied on a mixed and grey economy to meet the demands of family caring: grandparents have provided much of the 'solution' to the problem of the absence of affordable childcare for many families. The extent to which families will be able to meet the requirements of caring for those grandparents as they themselves require more care remains uncertain.

Key concepts and ideas in Chapter 6

- Ambivalent relationships
- Ascending familialism
- Descending familialism
- Enmeshed intergenerational relationships
- Freed intergenerational relationships
- Institutionalization of retirement

- Intergenerational transfers
- Longevity revolution
- Sandwich generation
- Secular shift in ageing
- Standardization of the life course
- Third Age

Part III

Re-visioning family change in Ireland

7

Conclusion: resilient families

Scholarship on Irish families has benefited immensely in recent decades from important new quantitative data sources, including census micro-data and longitudinal panel data from the GUI and TILDA projects. Perhaps less well known are the major new qualitative resources that have become available to researchers in recent years. This book set out to 'revision' family change in Ireland, drawing on two significant qualitative datasets that have been deposited in the Irish Qualitative Data Archive: in-depth life-story interviews from the LHSC study and interviews with children and their parents who participated in the GUI study. Drawing on these qualitative longitudinal resources, our book has presented a rich account of continuity and change in the textures, meanings and rhythms of family life in the Republic of Ireland since the early years of the state. We have also consciously highlighted the value of revisiting past, sometimes almost forgotten, social science studies for helping us to understand the complex pathways of family change.

Our qualitative longitudinal focus is consistent with the recent turn to more inductive approaches in family studies towards understanding what people *do* in their everyday family practices, and away from questions oriented towards identifying the essential features of the family as a social institution. However, understanding changes in family practices over such a long period of time does require a macro-sociological framework. We therefore placed our qualitative analyses in the context of broad societal shifts in demography, value systems, household economies, and patterns of kinship, community and public life. In doing so, we benefited immensely from new insights from the quantitative research tradition and have, we hope, demonstrated the fruitfulness of bringing quantitative and qualitative research together.

The life course perspective in sociology is particularly useful for understanding the relationship between historical times and changing practices across peoples' lives. We examined changing life course patterns from the perspectives of different family life stages: childhood, early adulthood, the middle years and grandparenthood. This approach allowed us to obtain

197

comparative insights on diverse experiences of family life from different historical and generational points of view and on the associated challenges for social policy. For each family life stage we also placed the Irish experience in a comparative European context, focusing particularly on how the Irish experience compares to the contrasting cases of Portugal and Denmark. In this concluding chapter, we first summarize what we have learned about changing experiences from the perspective of different life stages before proceeding to draw out some of the general patterns and trends that our analysis has uncovered.

Childhood

In many respects, the transformation of childhood is at the heart of family change. As we saw, many scholars explain the **demographic transition** with reference to changes in the social and economic value of children that accompanied declines in infant and child mortality. Within the **structural-functionalist** tradition that dominated thinking about the family for most of the twentieth century, caring for children was understood to be the core function of the family as an **institution**. For contemporary researchers and policy makers, how children are affected by family change remains a primary concern. On the other hand, recent scholarship has also emphasized the importance of children's **agency** in shaping family life. Contemporary research and policy aims, as much as possible, to take children's own views and perspectives into account.

Our qualitative longitudinal approach allowed us to explore these issues from a 'child's eye' perspective, through the lenses of childhood memories from the LHSC project and contemporary children's voices from the GUI project. We saw, in Chapter 3, how demographic change has affected children by reducing the number of siblings with whom they share their everyday lives, and increased the salience of relationships with people in older generations, including grandparents. These changes have been accompanied by declines in the significance of children's contribution to the economic well-being of their families while they are still young, but by an increase in their responsibility for securing their own futures through the acquisition of cultural capital, especially in the education system.

The demographic and socio-economic changes affecting children's lives were intertwined with a transformation in the social construction and meanings of childhood. Compared to the first half of the twentieth century in Ireland, today childhood is expected to be a special, carefree stage of life. Nevertheless, children are subjected to new forms of surveillance and control by adults, partly in response to increases in perceived risks, but also in response to the impulse towards **concerted cultivation**, especially on the part of middle-class parents.

However, our qualitative data reveal how children have consistently 'pushed back' against adult constraints in different socio-historical contexts, finding opportunities for the construction of their own social and family worlds and, in the process, shaping the family and community lives of adults. We saw, for example, how children in the 1930s and 1940s reinforced and sometimes disrupted relationships between families and households in local communities on the journey from home to school. Today, parents and grandparents waiting at the school gate also find that their family and community lives are at least in part shaped by the requirements and practices of their children and grandchildren.

While the numbers of lateral kin available to them have undoubtedly declined, the GUI data show that many Irish children remain embedded in comparatively large extended family networks that they and their families continue to maintain through regular patterns of visiting and other exchanges. However, consistent with international research, there are clear class differences in children's life experiences in the context of wider family changes. Irish scholarship has shown how socio-economic disadvantage appears to intersect with diverse family living arrangements in ways that affect children's life chances.

We saw how the experience of moving in and out of different family living arrangements is not a new feature of children's family lives in Ireland. Indeed the ubiquity of the practice of sending children to live with extended family members – and even with family friends – on a semi-permanent or permanent basis during the early decades of the last century took us by surprise. Nevertheless, middle-class families' capacity to invest in their children's cultural capital in the context of dual-earner household living arrangements is likely, in Ireland as elsewhere, to continue to give rise to significant class differences in children's experiences and opportunities.

Early adulthood

In Chapter 4 we showed how many of the changes giving rise to diverse patterns of family life in contemporary societies can be understood as changes in the **timing and sequencing of early family life transitions** in the context of the emergence of a phase of life that scholars have dubbed 'early adulthood'. Amongst the oldest participants in the LHSC project, the period of life when they were no longer in education but were still not in a position to establish their independence as heads of their own households, was rather long compared to those born around the middle of the last century. However, in contrast to contemporary young adults, who are also experiencing a lengthening of the time before they can establish themselves as fully independent adults, young people in the first half of the century were subjected to severe restrictions on their freedom, especially with respect to courtship and sexuality. This ensured that the sequence of transitions leading to independent family formation followed the prescribed order of marriage, living together and childbearing.

We saw how, around the middle of the twentieth century, these transitions began to follow more speedily in a cluster or 'bundle' after leaving education – partly because young people remained in education longer, but also because ages at marriage declined. Especially from the 1980s onwards, however, the transitions became 'unbundled' and their sequence less ordered. Contemporary young adults are likely to have sexual intercourse for the first time long before they establish a cohabiting relationship with a partner, which itself is increasingly likely to precede marriage. Whereas in the past, having a child outside marriage led to social ostracization, today it may occur in the context of a continuing cohabiting relationship, accompany a transition to marriage or civil partnership, or mark a transition to lone parenthood, at least for a time.

Of course sex and pregnancy outside marriage are not really new experiences in Ireland. The LHSC participants' narratives uncovered widespread memories of how such experiences were disguised in the past. They also revealed how, just as today, middle- and upper-class people were often better able to cope with the consequences of disorderly transitions, that is, with transitions that received less support (or none at all) from social institutions beyond the family. The LHSC interviews also demonstrate the extent to which young adults in the 1930s, 1940s and 1950s were already beginning to rebel against the constraints on their lives, so that in many respects the rapidity of later changes can be understood as a response to pent-up demand. Indeed it is striking how, despite some ambivalence on the part of members of the oldest cohort, there is widespread acceptance amongst Irish people that the decline of authoritarian restrictions on young adult lives is for the better. We argued that these changes can be understood in the context of changing intergenerational power relations as Ireland moved, somewhat belatedly, from a social structure centred on small property holding to one with increasing opportunities for economic survival through waged employment.

Emigration was a widespread experience for young adults in the past that facilitated the persistence of authoritarian **intergenerational relationships**, but which also precipitated demand for change, especially amongst those who spent time as emigrants in the United Kingdom during the 1950s and the 1960s. Today, emigration has re-emerged as an integral part of early adulthood in Ireland, as the Great Recession has made it even more difficult for young adults to acquire economic independence. Research on the contemporary experience of emigration shows that, just as in the past, emigrants strive to maintain **transnational family networks**, and that relationships with their extended families of origin remain highly important to young Irish adults. This is the case even though friendships are more salient at this stage of life than at any other.

The **unbundling of early family life transitions** has caused some scholars and commentators to worry about the **deinstitutionalization of marriage**, especially in the context of research evidence suggesting that – on average – children may fare better when their parents live together as married couples. However, policy responses need to take account of the reasons why people postpone marriage and qualitative research can help to understand this. We saw how lone parents in the LHSC study invoked moral rationalities about what it means to be a good parent to explain the path that they took and how, just like other young adults, they saw marriage as the endpoint of a process of family formation, rather than the beginning. These findings reinforce the view that policies oriented towards improving young adults' opportunities for stable partnership and marriage, are likely to be more effective than policies oriented toward promoting marriage as an end in itself.

The middle years

Sociology books on 'the family' used to focus almost exclusively on that stage of life when people were raising children in independent households. As we have seen, demographic ageing – together with the ageing of family life transitions – means that this stage no longer dominates people's family lives to the extent that it did at the middle of the last century. Nevertheless, this life stage is of vital importance both for families and for society as a whole, since it is during these 'middle years' that people expend most energy caring for those who are younger or older, or sick or disabled, while also working and contributing taxes that enable the state to subsidize, to a greater or lesser extent, the work of caring.

In Chapter 5 we saw how changing gender roles have structured participants' experiences of the challenges of meeting the responsibilities of working and caring. We traced how the character of adult partner relationships changed from undemonstrative affection to an emphasis on companionship followed by a shared commitment to active parenting as women increasingly remain in paid employment following the birth of children. We also saw, however, that for many couples the ideal of egalitarian, shared responsibility is difficult to attain and we explored some of the factors leading to these outcomes. As with the decision to marry, in the LHSC and GUI parent narratives, participants invoked complex **moral rationalities** – rather than preferences or rational strategies – to explain how they had accommodated these competing demands in ways that they were not always entirely happy with and that often reproduced gender differences in unanticipated ways. In this chapter we also examined debates about the significance of gender in the international and national literature on intimate partner violence and revealed how the continuing tension between the private spaces of families and the public spaces of community and social life creates gaps in which some of the darker aspects of family life remain concealed.

Grandparenthood

As societies age, grandparents have become topical in family scholarship. There has been an upsurge of interest in questions about flows of help and support between older and younger generations and in the increasing significance of grandparents in the lives of children and young adults. In Ireland both the quantitative and qualitative data reveal the prominence of grandparents in contemporary family life, especially when it comes to helping with childcare. Ireland's 'new' grandparents are distinctive, in part because many started their own families at comparatively younger ages and, because of the increasing duration of healthy ageing, making them available to contribute to the family lives of their children and grandchildren. We also saw, in Chapter 6, how many are members of an innovative cohort that initiated some of the most significant changes in Irish family life.

However, we also saw that we often make inaccurate or misleading assumptions about the experiences of older people in families in the past. There is little evidence to support arguments about persistent or changing patterns of neglect of older people; indeed the LHSC life history narratives and GUI child interviews provide compelling evidence that grandparents have consistently been held in high regard in Irish families and that they continue to play a central part in facilitating family connectedness and providing a sense of family continuity over time.

Sociologists have described grandparenthood as an **ambivalent relationship** in which roles and boundaries have to be constantly negotiated. Certainly, we found evidence that power in **intergenerational relationships** has shifted in favour of parents despite their growing need for help, especially with childcare. Most of the stories in our data told of 'downward' flows of assistance from older to younger generations. However, narratives of isolation and anxiety about the future were also evident. While Ireland has yet to face the consequences of the **longevity revolution** to the same extent as other countries, it is clear that the potential for families to cope with the challenges of caring for the elderly will be stretched, and that the Irish welfare state is currently inadequate to the task.

There is a clear pattern of continuity in the importance of family bonds for Irish people, including those of extended family relationships. The image of the isolated conjugal family separating itself from wider family networks and abandoning elderly and other extended family relatives does not stand up to scrutiny in the Irish context. This does not mean that experiences of separation, loneliness and isolation never occur, but rather that they are not intrinsic features of Irish family systems. On the contrary, the evidence shows that Irish people make considerable efforts to maintain extended family ties, even in the face of separation through emigration.

Change in continuity: continuity in change

Having reviewed changing family experiences from the perspective of different family life stages, it is time to draw out some of the shared patterns and themes that have emerged in our study. Throughout the book, we have seen how four interconnected macro-sociological changes altered the contexts for how people enacted and accomplished family from the early part of the last century to the present. First, the demographic transition altered the supply of kin with consequences for the potential form and quality of different kinds of family relationships. Second, the intergenerational balance of power has been overturned because of the declining significance of property and the increasing importance of education and other forms of social and cultural capital for the economic well-being of families. Third, the social construction of different family life stages and the values and attitudes that frame people's sentiments towards family life have been transformed. Fourth, Irish state policy has shifted away from bolstering families as patriarchal, corporate entities towards promoting the well-being of individuals within families. In all these respects, Ireland has followed a trajectory that shares many features with those of other rich western societies, but there have also been differences in timing and scale that shaped the experiences of Irish families that we have highlighted throughout the book. By taking a life course perspective we have explored family change at the intersection of different temporal scales: those of individual lifespans, generations and historical periods.

Our qualitative longitudinal analysis shows how, in the face of these significant macro-social, economic and life-course changes, Irish families have been characterized by extraordinary **resilience**. By this we mean that Irish people have adapted their behaviour and life plans relationally, in the context of an enduring commitment to family ties. Recent sociological literature has drawn attention to the importance of moral reasoning in everyday life: people are guided in their choices and actions by judgements and beliefs about what they believe to be good (Sayer 2011; Skeggs and Loveday 2012; Inglis 2014).

Quantitative data derived from standardized questions on values and attitudes, while vital for understanding long term trends, does not capture this process and can therefore give rise to misleading inferences about the motivations behind changing family practices. Throughout this book we have met people struggling to do what was best for their families in the face of the challenges life threw at them, often with unintended consequences. We have seen how during the first half of the last century, young parents struggling with large families coped by calling on grandparents or unmarried relatives to take on the task of raising some of their children. We have heard the voices of young, unmarried mothers today striving to be the best possible parents for their children. We have encountered working mothers who are committed to being role models for their daughters, and fathers coping with the competing demands of earning a living and active parenting. We have learned of the feelings of ambivalence and guilt associated with Irish families' reliance on grandparental childcare today. There are many other examples we could mention, but the point is that there was never a time when Irish families could draw unthinkingly on a set of rules for family life; rather, family life has always been accomplished through a process of adaptation and **bricolage** (Duncan, 2011), whereby people make pragmatic choices guided by family memories, traditions and practices as they encounter new situations and challenges. In this way, family is always simultaneously a process of reproduction and innovation.

At the same time, it is important not to create the impression that family life is always harmonious, or that all families are equally successful at ensuring their own survival and well-being. Within families and extended kinship groups there are competing sets of interests that may vary according to different historical and social contexts and that inevitably give rise to conflict. For example, we have seen how, in memories that span the decades from the earliest part of the last century, children and young adults pushed back against the constraints and limitations imposed on them by members of the older generation. We have witnessed how women struggled against gender role expectations, often by working to ensure that their daughters had greater life chances than they had experienced themselves.

Furthermore, our study has consistently revealed the extent to which social class inequalities structure family experiences and practices. Perhaps nowhere is this more evident than in people's ability to cope with 'untimely' family life transitions. We saw, for example, how at the middle of the last century middle-class women were able to escape the harsh consequences of becoming pregnant outside marriage. In contemporary Ireland, similarly, new scholarship has begun to focus on how social class constrains family formation processes (Hannan, 2014), family strategies for caring for the elderly (Timonen et al., 2013), and different patterns of family coping with the recent economic crisis (Watson et al., 2012).

Through its inductive, qualitative longitudinal approach, our study also uncovered some less familiar aspects of Irish family life that are often hidden in census and survey data, or in analytical approaches centred on ideal-typical family forms. For example, while scholars have known from analysis of census data that early twentieth-century Irish households were often both extended and 'incomplete', consisting of non-marital kin, the life history narratives revealed a widespread pattern of active exchanges between marital and non-marital households within extended kinship groups, including practices of 'sharing' children and adolescents (see Gray, 2014). Furthermore, the frequency with which participants recounted tales of disguised pregnancies and unofficial adoptions of children born outside marriage raises questions, not just about the validity of official statistics about the prevalence of births outside marriage before the 1980s, but also about how we interpret changing attitudes to lone parenthood.

While the focus of our study has been principally on how Irish families have changed over time, we have also made comparisons with trends in other countries. This has been particularly appropriate for considering the consequences of state policy for Irish family life. We have seen how, in general, Ireland seems to fit best within the liberal group of countries that have focused on expanding individual rights within families, without greatly increasing families' claims on the state, especially with regard to caring. These policy choices have consequences for family patterns and the shape of family life. To illustrate these features, we have, where possible, presented Irish data in comparison with Denmark, which exemplifies the social democratic welfare regime and Portugal, which exemplifies the Mediterranean welfare regime (of course we are aware that neither country is a perfect exemplar of these **ideal type** representations). We have seen how Irish families seem to share some characteristics with southern European countries, but not others. While Irish family policy has, in many respects, shifted dramatically towards the liberalization of family roles and statuses, it has to date relied on a combination of market and informal solutions to the challenges associated with meeting the demands of caring faced by families. As the cohort of grandparents who have filled the 'caring gap' for many young families over the past two decades grows older, this approach is likely to further exacerbate the inequalities that are already opening up between families that can afford private, market based solutions and those that cannot.

Finally, we would like to return to a theme we discussed in the Introduction, namely, the question of what kinds of answers social science can provide to questions about families. We have emphasized in this conclusion how family practices must be understood in the context of people's moral reasoning about what is good. This means that social science cannot tell us what to do, either at the level of our individual families or at the level of social policy. However, it can provide us with better information about how the particular constraints and opportunities that we face as a society have come about and with some guidance about the consequences of the choices we make for families. The qualitative longitudinal approach that we have championed in this book has an essential role to play in this interaction between social science, social policy and family practices, first because it yields a more complex understanding of the process of inter and intra-generational change over time, and second because it provides distinctive insights on the changing meanings and interpretations that govern people's understandings and practices; it has the potential to ensure that both sociological understanding and social policy develop as part of a 'shared and iterative process' (Corden and Millar, 2007: 531).

At the conclusion of Chapter 1, we suggested that the debates and cleavages that had already emerged in the early decades of the twentieth century continue to concern social scientists, policy makers and members of the public today. As we debate how to legislate for assisted human reproduction or whether or not to permit same-sex marriage, questions are raised about how to protect the best interests of children while also extending the joys, benefits and protections of family life to a wider range of enduring intimate relationships. But our understanding of what makes families good has changed – it has become democratized, focused to a far greater extent on recognizing and meeting the individual needs of different family members than on the corporate well-being of families as institutions. While there are some voices who continue to express regret about the **democratization of family life**, research on changing values and attitudes demonstrates that the great majority of Irish people are in favour of it. As Fahey (2014: 67) noted, 'there is a new consensus on norms of family behaviour'.

And yet, as we have seen throughout this book, the opportunity to 'live up to' societal norms of family behaviour continues to vary by social class. For those with greater resources, new family practices – the reconstruction of gender roles, the separation of sex, childbirth and marriage, and the transformation of intergenerational obligations – provide opportunities for enhanced individual freedom while sustaining and sometimes even improving their social and economic life chances. For those with more limited means, new practices and freedoms are sometimes accompanied by challenges and compromises that may even perpetuate disadvantage across the generations. So when we query whether or not family change is progressive, or whether families promote cohesion or conflict, we have to ask for whom, and in what contexts?

The new family sociology, through its focus on practices, networks and displays, has re-visioned family change and diversity by opening a new window on family life; it has begun to meet the challenge of exploring how 'families create and maintain webs of meaning, how members use and adapt to the changing orthodoxies of what families do, and how they relate to each other' (Inglis, 2014: 74). Qualitative longitudinal sociology creates the possibility of exploring these processes through time in order to develop new explanations of how family practices give rise to innovation and change, as well as new understandings of family life in the past. However, there is a risk that these approaches tend to over-estimate the power of family adaptation and resilience, leading to complacency about the need for researchers and policy makers to look for the silences and ruptures that signal future problems for families. It is necessary, we believe, to avoid both over-estimating the challenges families face and over-stating the extent to which families are able to cope with whatever social and economic change throws at them. Most importantly, we must be attentive to how different groups of people have varying capacities to mobilize and achieve family relationships in ways that promote resilience in different socio-historical contexts. This book has aimed to provide a foundation for such a 're-visioning' of Irish family life.

Glossary of key concepts

A

Active agents: see **human agency**.

Active fathering: the 'hands on' involvement by fathers in the day-to-day care of their children.

Adaptation view: see **classic demographic transition theory**.

Agency: see **human agency**.

Agnatic systems: see **patrilineal system**.

Agrarian societies: societies that are characterized by sedentary agriculture that is productive enough to support classes of people who are not directly involved in subsistence production, such as political rulers, priests, soldiers and craftsmen.

Alliance: see **rules of alliance**.

Ambivalence/ambivalent relationship: intergenerational relationship in which roles and boundaries have to be constantly negotiated, resulting in mixed feelings and contradictory expectations.

Ascending familialism: intergenerational relationships characterized by the flow of resources from younger to older generations, for example from young adults towards their elderly parents.

B

Beanpole family structure: term to describe the increased relevance in contemporary families of vertical family relationships between, for example, great-grandparents, grandparents, parents and children. The emergence of the beanpole family is due to a combination of the following factors: the extension of life expectancy amongst contemporary grandparent generation, earlier marriage and childbirth amongst this grandparent generation than preceding and subsequent generations, and fewer births in the contemporary generation of children.

Birth cohort: a group of people born during a particular period or year. In this book four birth cohorts are presented: people born before 1935; between

1945 and 1954; between 1965 and 1974; and those who were 9 years old when interviewed between 2007 and 2009.

Bourgeois family: the middle-class, nuclear family form which emerged in the course of **modernization**. In this family form private family property is passed on from a father to his descendent heir, usually a son and is also associated with an emphasis on domesticity.

Breadwinner family: family form whereby fathers attended to children's **instrumental needs** through their work outside the home and mothers attended to children's **expressive needs** through their work inside the home. See also **expressive needs** and **instrumental needs.**

Bricolage: in family studies **bricolage** is used to describe how, as people encounter new situations and challenges, their choices are guided by family memories, traditions and practices (see Duncan, 2011). In this way, family is always simultaneously a process of reproduction and innovation.

C

Civil partnership: legally recognized union of two people with rights similar, but not the same, as those of a married couple.

Clan: descent groups where the common ancestor has become mythical, and no direct genealogical link can be traced to living individuals. Lineages may be subsets of clans. See also **lineage**.

Classic demographic transition theory: theory that the trend towards smaller family sizes in wealthy, industrial societies was mainly due to economic modernization. See also **demographic transition** and **innovation / diffusion view**.

Cognatic descent system: see **undifferentiated filiation / descent system**.

Cohort: see **birth cohort**.

Common couple violence: in research on domestic violence the term denotes when both partners 'lash out' in the context of an argument.

Companionate / companionship family: where bonds between family members depended on the quality of inter-personal relationships – on feelings of affection and love. This family form became increasingly prevalent as a result of urbanization and industrialization. See also **institutional family**.

Completed fertility: the number of children actually born per woman in a cohort of women up to the end of their childbearing years.

Complex marriage systems: societal rules that specify whom the individual must not marry. See also **elementary marriage systems**.

Concerted cultivation: the ways in which middle-class parents invest time in extra-curricular, structured activities for their children in the company of adults, which contrast with working-class parents' approach in which children spend unstructured after-school time in the company of peers. By doing so, middle-class parents are said to provide their children with a better preparation for middle-class jobs.

Conjugal family: also known as the '**nuclear family**', the **conjugal family** unit consists of parents and their children.

Conservative welfare regime: in Gøsta Esping-Andersen's (1990) distinction amongst the 'three worlds' of welfare capitalism, the Conservative welfare regime intervenes in the market to preserve existing status inequalities such as those based on institutions like the family. See also **social democratic welfare regime** and **liberal welfare regime**.

Convergence thesis: key proposition of twentieth-century **modernization theory**, which stated that around the world social institutions, including the family, would tend to converge as societies underwent the modernizing processes of industrialization and urbanization. Goode (1963) argued that the diverse family patterns that existed around the world were being altered by modernization to converge on a **conjugal family** form. See also **convergence to diversity**.

Convergence to diversity: term coined by Boh (1989) to describe the common patterns of growing diversity in family forms in advanced industrial countries. See also **convergence thesis**.

Cultural ideals: standards that a society use to define the ways in which members should be treated and / or behave.

D

Defamilialization: the degree to which individuals can uphold a socially acceptable standard of living, independently of family relationships, either through paid work or through the social security system (see Lister, 1994).

De-institutionalization of marriage: process whereby adult partnerships are no longer guided by a shared set of norms and expectations (see Cherlin, 2004).

Democratization (of family life): refers to increasing focus on the interests and well-being of individuals rather than the family as a corporate group. See also **informalization of relationships**.

Demographic transition: a shift from a demographic pattern of high fertility and high mortality, to one of low fertility and low mortality. See also **classic demographic transition theory**.

Demography: the scientific study of population. Demographers seek to explain shifts in the size and structure of human populations by examining trends in the number of births and deaths, and in patterns of ageing and migration.

Descending familialism: intergenerational relationships in which resources flow from older to younger generations. See also **ascending familialism**.

Displaying family: the concept of display refers to the ways in which family practices are embedded in wider systems of meaning: it refers to how people 'convey to each other and to relevant audiences that certain of their actions do constitute doing family things and thereby confirm that these relationships are family relationships' (Finch, 2007: 67). See also **doing family**.

Divorce rate: divorces per thousand married persons in a population.

Doing family: how families are enacted in everyday practices oriented towards others who are identified as family members. 'In this way ... family practices are reflective practices; in being enacted they simultaneously construct, reproduce family boundaries, family relationships and possibly more discursive notions of the family in general' (Morgan, 2011: 163). See also **displaying family**.

Doing gender: the idea that gender is constructed in everyday, human interactions. Feminine and masculine traits are therefore the product of social interaction. See also **doing family**.

Domestication of childhood: the development of dedicated spaces and activities for children within controlled environments, for example playtime that is supervised by and / or structured by adults.

Domestic group: see **household**.

Dual-earner economy: contemporary family form that arose in the mid- to late twentieth century when women who had once worked inside the family home moved into the cash economy and took paid jobs alongside their male partners. See also **family economy** and **family-consumer economy**.

Dual-systems theory: also known as socialist feminism, Hartmann's (1979) dual-systems theory argues that women are marginalized by their dual role in modern society as both paid employee and mother. Women are exploited both in the workforce and in the home as they are more likely to secure lower paid employment than men, and more likely to deliver 'unpaid services' in the form of housework within the home. See also **Marxist-Feminism, liberal feminism, radical feminism, structural-functionalism**.

E

Early adulthood: see **formal adulthood**.

Ecological fallacy: the logical error of making inferences about individuals based on observations about groups. See also **individualistic fallacy**.

Egalitarian individualism: social policy paradigm where the welfare and rights of the individual are not dependent on family status or role (see Fahey, 1998). See also **patriarchal familism.**

Elementary marriage systems: societal rules that specify the groups from which an individual must choose their spouse, thus ensuring different descent groups are socially linked through marriage. **See also complex marriage systems**.

Endogamy: marriage rules that prescribe the group from which a spouse must be taken. See also **exogamy**.

Enmeshed intergenerational lives: situation where young adults remain committed to caring for older family members, even as they recognize that this will affect their own life chances.

Ethnography: systematic study of a social group usually involving both observing and living amongst the group. Participant observation is a key technique of ethnography.

European marriage pattern: historic pattern of family formation in which couples married and commenced childbearing relatively late. During the period between reaching adulthood and marriage many young adults spent a period of time in service to allow them to accumulate savings that would help them establish their own home.

Exogamy: marriage rules that ensure individuals marry outside their own kinship group. See also **endogamy**.

Expressive needs: children's need for daily nurturance, love and care in order to grow up well, as provided by parents. See also **instrumental needs**.

F

Family adaptive practices: theory that families adapt their household strategies in response to external constraints such as changing institutions, economic circumstances and political contexts.

Family configuration: a way of studying family relationships that focuses on networks of personal ties or personal communities.

Family-consumer economy: from the end of the nineteenth century through the middle of the twentieth century men's wages began to rise, and growing numbers of women began to take on the specialized role of homemaker. In such families women contributed to the household economy not by earning an income, but by managing the household income to ensure the well-being of all its members. See also **family economy** and **dual-earner economy**.

Family economy: in agrarian societies all members of the household, both family members and servants, worked together to ensure the survival of the household as a unit of production and consumption. In such households there was no meaningful distinction between productive and reproductive labour. Work was differentiated by gender and age, and women's tasks tended to be consistent with caring for young children. Nevertheless, the importance of women's work for the survival of the family and household was recognized. See also **family wage economy** and **family-consumer economy**.

Family failure: a term sometimes used to refer to a failure to continue the family line through succession in agrarian society.

Family life cycle: the idea that family households move through a predictable sequence of stages from marriage to succession and family dispersal.

Family systems: family systems can be defined as preferred patterns of recruitment into households. They specify 'who should live with whom at which stages of the life course; the social, sexual, and economic rights and obligations of individuals occupying different kin positions in relation to each other; and the division of labour among kin related individuals' (Mason, 2001: 161). See also **stem-family system**.

Family wage economy: during the first phase of industrialization (from around the end of the eighteenth century through most of the nineteenth century), all household members pooled their labour to ensure their survival in the family wage economy. As much as they possibly could, men, women and children contributed wages to the household pot, for the benefit of the family as a whole. See also **family economy** and **family-consumer economy**.

Fertility rate: number of births per woman. See also **total fertility rate** and **mortality rate**.

Fertility transition: see **demographic transition**.

Fictive kin: people that treat one another as though they are related, despite having no biological or marital links.

Filiation: system whereby those considered an ancestor or a descendent of an individual are defined.

Formal adulthood: the transition of an individual to the status of adult. Hannan and Ó Riain (1993) described adulthood as 'comprised of a set of statuses which provide a basis for individual independence and for full civic status'. Until comparatively recently **formal adulthood** was associated with marriage and independent family formation. See also **timing and sequencing of life transitions** and **unbundling of family life transitions**.

G

Gatekeeping / maternal gatekeeping: term used in the study of the gender division of household labour to describe practices of mothers who are reluctant to relinquish responsibility over family matters.

Gender contract: power relationships between female and male members of a society that determine roles, responsibilities, privileges, status, sexuality and behaviour of men and women within households, communities, the market and the state.

Gendered moral rationalities: **moral rationalities** based on perceptions about gender roles, for example, ideas about what makes a 'good mother' and what makes a 'good father'. See also **moral rationalities**.

Gender stereotyping: generalizations about the characteristics of men and women. For example, the idea that women are the 'natural' parent and therefore fathers are not as good at caring for their children as mothers.

Gender symmetry: in research on domestic violence, the argument that women and men experience and perpetrate violence at similar rates.

Grand theory: 'A term coined by C. Wright Mills in *The Sociological Imagination* (1959) to refer to the form of highly abstracted theorizing in which the formal organization and arrangement of concepts takes priority over understanding the social world' (Scott and Marshall, 2009: 295).

H

Historical period: an amount of time defined chronologically.

Homogamy: the tendency to choose marital partners from within our own social class or ethnic group.

Horticultural societies: a society that generally combines gathering food from the wild with agriculture, using simple tools and long fallowing periods.

Household: the set of people who share a living space and pool their resources.

Household economy / household economics: practices of production and consumption that are organised within households. The theoretical approach is particularly associated with the work of Gary Becker. Family behaviour is explained with reference to the idea that members act rationally to maximise the well-being of their household.

Human agency: the extent to which people are planful, make choices and take action with reference to their understandings of their own potentialities and futures.

I

Ideal type: in Weberian theory **ideal type** aims to describe the essential characteristics of an institution. In family studies **ideal type** is an abstract statement of what were thought to be the essential features of the family as an institution. See also **cultural ideals**.

Incest: sexual relationship between two closely related 'blood' relatives. In every society **incest** is prohibited, but the definition of incestuous relationships varies to some extent across societies.

Independent household: the establishment of a family and residence of one's own that is separate to the home of the family of origin. See also **formal adulthood**.

Individualism: an ideology or stance which emphasises the needs of the individual. Individualism is sometimes contrasted with collectivism, where the needs of the group as a collective take precedence over the needs of each individual member. See also **individualization**.

Individualistic fallacy: the logical error of making inferences about the group based on observations about individual cases. See also **ecological fallacy**.

Individualization: societal process whereby values and institutions increasingly centre on requirements of individuals rather than as collectives. See also **individualism**.

Individualized marriage: marriage in which relationships are evaluated according to how well they meet each partner's sense of self and the expression of their feelings.

Inductive approach: in social research, an inductive approach commences with observation of a social phenomenon and from these observations generalizations are drawn out which are then used to build social theory.

Informalization of relationships: in family studies, this term describes the transformation of relationships between family members whereby more traditional, authoritarian models of parenting have started to give way to more democratic ones. See also **democratization (of family life)**.

Innovation / diffusion view: theory that modernization affected family sizes primarily through the diffusion of new values emphasizing **individualism** and self-fulfilment. See also **classic demographic transition theory**.

Institution: in sociology the term institution refers to a system of behavioural and relationship patterns that function across an entire society, which order and structure the behaviour of individuals by rules, norms or patterns of behaviour. Social institutions like the family have been thought of as comprising a set of interdependent roles governed by socially agreed rules of behaviour (see Cherlin, 2004). See also **role**.

Institutional family: proposed by Ernest Burgess (1948), where the bonds between family members are enforced by law, custom, public opinion and duty. See also **companionate relationship family**.

Instrumental needs: children's need for material conditions for survival, as provided by parents. For example food, clothing, housing and so on. See also **expressive needs**.

Intergenerational flow: refers to the movement of help and assistance between generations. See also **intergenerational transfers** and **intergenerational relationships**.

Intergenerational relationships: relationships between older and younger generation in families and societies. See also **intergenerational flow** and **intergenerational transfers**.

Intergenerational solidarity: the ways in which people of different generations in a society live together, help each other and depend on one another in their daily lives.

Intimate terrorism: in research on domestic violence, the term denotes where one partner uses violence as a tactic within an overall pattern of control of the other.

Intergenerational transfers: financial assistance or benefits in kind given from one generation to another. See also **intergenerational flow** and **intergenerational relationships**.

J

Judicial separation: according to Courts Service Ireland (www.courts.ie), 'When a couple cannot agree the terms by which they will live separately, either party can apply to the court for a decree of judicial separation [...] The main difference in law between divorce and judicial separation is that a divorce allows both parties to remarry whereas a judicial separation does not'.

K

Kin: the group of living persons who are related to us.

Kindred: the group of relatives we recognize through the genealogical links in our memory.

Kinship: a social **institution** that governs a society to a greater or lesser extent. In some societies, the institution of **kinship** governs all aspects of social life, including politics, the economy and religion. The kinship group to which an individual belongs may determine who they marry, and where they work and live.

L

Late modernity: a term used to signify a body of work that rejects the idea that society has transitioned to a new era of **post-modernism**. Proponents of late modernity tend to argue instead that in contemporary society there has been an intensification of some aspects of modernity. See also **post-modernism**.

Liberal feminism: liberal feminist theorists challenged **structural-functionalist** theories by arguing that gender roles within families were not given in nature; rather they were perpetuated through a process of socialization and can therefore be altered through tools such as education and anti-discriminatory legislation. They also emphasized the extent to which gender roles were not just different, they were unequal: the unpaid work of meeting the **expressive needs** of families within the home was of lower status within society – that is, less highly valued – than working for pay to meet the family's **instrumental needs**. See also **dual-systems theory**, **Marxist-Feminism**, **radical feminism** and **structural-functionalism**.

Liberal individualism: a political philosophy 'that stresses the importance of the individual and the value attached to individual freedom and individual choice. The philosophy is frequently contrasted with collectivism, where the collective rather than individual good is paramount' (Scott and Marshall, 2009: 342).

Liberal welfare regime: in Gøsta Esping-Andersen's (1990) distinction amongst the 'three worlds' of welfare capitalism, the Liberal welfare regime is oriented primarily towards supporting the market. Social welfare transfers in this regime are targeted towards marginalized and stigmatized groups. See also **social democratic welfare regime** and **conservative welfare regime**.

Life-chances: the opportunities each individual has to improve his or her quality of life.

Life-course: term denoting how an individual's life evolves over time, in a linear sequence of significant events through a series of socially defined transformations.

Life-course perspective: an examination of how a person's life evolves over time, within structural, social and cultural contexts. This method allows us to consider how key events in the life of an individual influence the decisions that they make, which thus direct the course which their life takes.

Life stage: term used to describe a period of time in a person's life, for example grandparenthood, middle age, adolescence, parenthood, childhood and old age.

Life transition: a period of significant change in an individual's life, such as setting up a first home with a spouse, or starting a family.

Lineage: a group of individuals who share a common ancestor. Lineages are at the heart of how **unilineal descent** systems are organized. See also **unilineal filiation**.

Linked lives: the principle of **linked lives** emphasizes how individual lives are embedded in sets of social relationships – especially those of family and kin – that travel with us through the life course.

Longevity revolution: since the 1950s, most of the change in life expectancy in European societies can be attributed to the extension of life in old age. See also **secular shift in ageing**.

Longitudinal data / longitudinal study: research that is conducted over a long period of time, usually many years. Data about key characteristics are repeatedly collected at specified intervals over this time period. See also **panel study** and **prospective data / prospective study**.

M

Macro-societal changes: large-scale social processes, patterns and trends of whole societies. See also **micro-practices**.

Male-breadwinner model: see **breadwinner family**.

Marital breakdown: deterioration of marital relationships leading to separation or divorce.

Marxist-Feminism: both Marxist and dual-systems theorists sought to understand families as sites where the processes giving rise to class and gender inequality intersected. They argued that the unpaid work carried out by women within the home acted as a kind of subsidy to capitalist employers and the state, making it possible to maximize profits by keeping down wages while also perpetuating inequalities between women and men. See also **dual-systems theory**, **liberal feminism**, **radical feminism** and **structural-functionalism**.

Matchmaking: practice of arranged marriage that was common in the stem-family system in Ireland, in which an inheriting son was 'matched' with a suitable bride.

Matriarchy / matriarchal family: society in which the mother or oldest female heads the family. Descent and relationship are determined through the female line. See also **patriarchy / patriarchal family** and **matrilineal system**.

Matrilatral ancestors: ancestry that is traced through the female line. See also **lineage** and **patrilateral ancestors**.

Matrilineal system: system whereby names, privileges, rights and obligations are passed from mother to daughter. See also **matriarchy / matriarchal family**, **patrilineal system** and **unilineal descent system**.

Matrilocal residence: where a married couple lives with, or near, the wife's family. This typically occurs in matrilineal societies. See also **matrilineal system** and **patrilocal residence**.

Micro-practices: small-scale interactions between people. See also **macro-societal changes**.

Modernization / modernization theory: in the decades after the Second World War, sociologists developed modernization theory to explain the rise of wealthy, industrial societies and to contrast them with poorer societies – both in the present and the past – that were thought to be more 'traditional'. Modernization was described as a set of fundamental, interdependent changes in the economy, the political system, social institutions and social values. See also **post-modernism**.

Modes of production: the Marxist concept of **modes of production** refers to the major ways in which societies are organized in order to meet the material needs of their members, for food, warmth and shelter, and to ensure their continuity over time.

Monogamy / monogamous relationship: a form of relationship in which an individual has only one partner during their lifetime, or at any one time.

Moral rationalities: term to describe how the actions of people are primarily guided by social and relational understandings rather than economic and rational choices. While economic considerations are important they are secondary to moral considerations. For example if a parent follows a **gendered moral rationality**, the decisions they make about their role in the family may be centred on what it means to be a good mother or father.

Mortality rate: number of deaths per population. See also **fertility rate**.

N

Nostalgic construction of childhood: Christopher Jenks (1996) described the **nostalgic construction of childhood** in late modernity as a prevailing belief that past childhoods were better than those of today.

Nuclear family: see **conjugal family**.

O

Orderly transition to family formation: term to describe a transition to **independent household formation** that is consistent with social norms and institutional constraints around the timing and sequencing of life transitions during a particular period. See also **timing and sequencing of life transitions**.

P

Panel study: used in longitudinal research, a group of research participants are followed over time and interviewed at specified intervals often over many years. A key feature of this research design is that repeated measures are collected from the same group of people at different points in time. See also **prospective data / prospective study.**

Patriarchal familism: social policy paradigm where the welfare of the individual is dependent on their inclusion in a cohesive family unit, and their legal status is defined by reference to family status. See also **egalitarian individualism**.

Glossary of key concepts

Patriarchy / patriarchal family: in this family structure the father is the head of household, and all titles and inheritance are traced through the father's line. See also **patrilocal residence**, **matriarchy / matriarchal family**.

Patrilateral ancestors: also known as 'agnatic', ancestry that is traced through the male line. See also **lineage** and **matrilatral ancestors**.

Patrilineal system: also known as 'agnatic', system where names, privileges, rights and obligations are passed from father to son. See also **matrilineal system**, **patriarchy / patriarchal family** and **unilineal descent system**.

Patrilocal residence: where a married couple lives with, or near, the husband's family. This typically occurs in patrilineal societies. See also **matriarchy / matriarchal family**, **patriarchy / patriarchal family** and **patrilineal system**.

Period total fertility rate: see **total fertility rate**.

Personal communities: a group that are tied together by relationships that are kin-like in terms of the meanings and commitments associated with them, despite the absence of actual **kin** relationships between members. The individual's **personal community** is usually chosen on the basis of egalitarianism and the quality of relationship provided by the members.

Polygamy: an individual being married to two or more people.

Post-modernism: aesthetic movement that originated in the arts during the early twentieth century in reaction to modernism. The post-modern movement emphasised a plurality of fragmentary forms while rejecting any claim to representational realism. In literature and social theory the movement is associated with post-structuralism. See also **post-modernist theory** and **late modernity**.

Post-modernist theory: in sociology of the family, Stacey (1990) argued that the post-modern family was not a single functional type, but rather a diversity and fluidity of forms as people moved in and out of different family settings, developing complex kin networks over the course of their lives. See also **post-modernism**.

Practices: actions and decisions that are governed to some extent by 'taken for granted' understandings or habit.

Primary research data: original data that is collected by a researcher, for example by conducting research 'in the field' such as interviewing or surveying people. See also **qualitative data**.

Primogeniture: an inheritance practice common in rural Ireland in the twentieth century where the eldest or first born son inherited the entire family estate upon his father's retirement. See also **stem-family system**.

Prospective data / prospective study: a prospective study is a cohort study that follows a group of research participants over time. Research participants may differ with respect to certain characteristics, and the

longitudinal data produced by this study is used to determine how these characteristics affect rates of a certain outcomes. See also **longitudinal data / longitudinal study, panel study** and **retrospective data / retrospective study.**

Pseudonym: the name given to an individual, which differs from his or her original or true name, to conceal the identity of that individual. A **pseudonym** can be given as a first name, or as both a first and surname.

Pyramid family structure: a term to describe a demographic profile where high rates of fertility give rise to larger families and long, overlapping generations. See also **beanpole family structure**.

Q

Qualitative approach: methodological approach to the collection and analysis of **qualitative data**. See also **qualitative data**.

Qualitative data: richly descriptive, non-numerical data that are usually collected through interview methods, observational methods or the thematic analysis of texts.

R

Radical feminism: radical feminist theorists developed an analogy between gender and social class, arguing that families were organized around the domination and exploitation of women's sexuality and reproductive capacities. See also **dual-systems theory, liberal feminism, Marxist-Feminism** and **structural-functionalism**.

Rational decision-making: usually refers to decision-making oriented towards maximizing economic or material well-being.

Relationships of choice: family-type relationships based on personal preferences rather than societal rules or conventions often used to describe family relationships of LGBT (see Weeks et al. 2001). See also **fictive kin**.

Resilience: the capacity to bounce back in the face of adverse circumstances.

Retrospective data / retrospective study: a retrospective study generally involves the research interviewee recounting events that have already taken place, for example **retrospective data** is collected during a life story interview. See also **prospective data / prospective study**.

Rules of alliance: societal rules which delineate the persons whom an individual is permitted to marry.

Role: the behaviour or expectations attached to the individual's social position.

S

Sandwich generation: term to describe a generation of adults in the early twenty-first century that are likely to experience greater pressures as a result of having to care for children and elderly parents at the same time, due to a combination of greater longevity in old age and the tendency for younger adults to postpone parenthood.

Secular shift in ageing: Peter Laslett (1987) termed the reduction in the risk of dying at all ages alongside reduced fertility that took place in most European societies between 1950 and 1960 as a **secular shift in ageing**. The transition occurred, according to Laslett, when two conditions were met: (1) a quarter of all adults had passed the age of 60; (2) at least half of all males surviving to age twenty-five can expect to live to age seventy. See also **longevity revolution**.

Selection bias: in social research if observations are selected so that they are not independent of outcome variables they may be affected by **selection bias** and this can result in biased and inaccurate inferences in the findings.

Social capital: refers to the idea that nature and quality of relationships between people can act as a resource for improving quality of life.

Social democratic welfare regime: in Gøsta Esping-Andersen's (1990) distinction amongst the 'three worlds' of welfare capitalism, the **social democratic welfare regime** is oriented towards de-emphasizing the market and reducing the inequalities arising under capitalism. See also **conservative welfare regime** and **liberal welfare regime**.

Social institution: see **institution**.

Socialization: process by which human's learn, starting from infancy, how to function in social life. **Socialization** is a central influence on the individual's behaviour, beliefs and actions.

Statistically representative: an unbiased indication of what entire population is like based on inferences about a sample from that population.

Stem-family system: a family system in which only one heir can marry in the family household. Sometimes this household involves three generations living together following the retirement of the older couple. In rural Ireland typically the couple's firstborn son remained in his parents' household after his marriage, and his spouse moved into the home of her in-laws. The younger couple then raised their own children in the family home alongside their grandparents. Other sons and daughters had to leave the parental household in order to start families of their own. However, sometimes unmarried brothers and sisters remained in the family home as unwaged labourers. See also **family systems**.

Structural-functionalism: classical sociological theory that saw society as a complex system whose parts work together to promote solidarity. Scholars within the tradition of **structural-functionalism** believed that the best way of explaining a particular social institution, such as the family, was to show what function or requirement it met for the preservation of society as a whole. See also **dual-systems theory**, **liberal feminism**, **Marxist-Feminist theory**, **radical feminism**.

T

Third Age: during the twentieth century a new phase emerged between adult independence and decrepitude – a comparatively healthy 'Third Age' with fewer immediate responsibilities and with opportunities for new forms of individual achievement and fulfilment. This new phase was made possible in part by the extension of life but also by the institutionalization of retirement through the introduction of old-age pensions (see Laslett 1987). See also **secular shift in ageing**.

Timing and sequencing of family life transitions: phrase to describe the stages by which an individual leaves the home of their family of origin to establish their own independent household, enters employment thereby gaining financial independence from their family of origin, marries and / or starts a family of their own. See also **formal adulthood** and **orderly transition to family formation**.

Total fertility rate (**TFR**): an estimate of annual rates of fertility. It is calculated as the average number of births a woman would have by the end of her reproductive years, if fertility levels at each age during her childbearing period remained constant at the levels prevailing at a given time.

Transformation of gender roles: refers to the significant change in customary roles for men and women that occurred from the 1970s onwards in most western societies.

Transnational familial networks: relationships amongst extended family members who are living in different countries due to migration.

U

Unbundling of family life transitions: whereas in the 1950s and 1960, young adults left home, entered employment, married and started a family in a tightly ordered sequence of events within a comparatively short period of time, today these transitions have become separated and prolonged, and their sequencing has become more variable. See also **formal adulthood** and **timing and sequencing of life transitions**.

Undifferentiated filiation / descent system: family system where ancestors from both the father's and the mother's lineage are recognized as part of the kinship group. See also **unilineal filiation / descent system**.

Unilineal filiation / descent system: family system where only ancestors and descendants from either the father's or mother's side are recognized as part of the kinship group. See also **matrilineal system, patrilineal system** and **undifferentiated filiation / descent system**.

Unstable family: according to Le Play in an unstable family the sons would leave their parents' households to marry and set up on their own 'as soon as they gain any confidence in themselves' (Le Play, 1872: 41). While this system favoured innovation, it failed to ensure the transmission of custom, values and practices from one generation to another, and could lead to the isolation and abandonment of people in old age (Mogey, 1955: 313).

V

Values: socially based, shared ideas about the proper or right way to live.

W

Welfare-state: term used to describe the state provision of services and supports that are funded by the state exchequer to ensure a basic standard of living for its citizens. Examples of services and supports include subsidised health care, unemployment support payments and subsidised education. See also **conservative welfare regime**, **liberal welfare regime** and **social democratic welfare regime**.

Technical information

Life Histories and Social Change

The *Life Histories and Social Change* (LHSC) project was a three-year project that was co-directed by Professor Seán Ó Riain and Dr Jane Gray of the Department of Sociology at NUI Maynooth. The senior research associates on the project were Dr Aileen O'Carroll and Dr James Monagle. The project was based in the Department of Sociology and at the National Institute for Regional and Spatial Analysis (NIRSA) at Maynooth University. The project received funding from the Irish Research Council for the Humanities and Social Sciences in 2005. The research team carried out detailed life story interviews with respondents who had participated in the Living in Ireland Survey, carried out by the Irish Economic and Social Research Institute (ESRI), as part of the European Community Household Panel survey between 1994 and 2001. With the assistance of the ESRI, respondents from three birth cohorts within the national sample were invited to opt in to the LHSC study.

Interviews were conducted in 2007 and 2008. In the years following data collection, the life story interviews were archived at the Irish Qualitative Data Archive at Maynooth University, Maynooth, Co. Kildare, Ireland (www.iqda. ie) and made available to bona fide researchers through application to the IQDA. The complete LHSC project database comprises 113 life story interviews, life history calendars, and simple retrospective social network schedules. The archival collection comprises 100 life story interviews – the remainder of the material was judged by the research team unsuitable for archiving (most often because the material was too sensitive) or was withheld from archiving by the interviewee. In 2015/2016 the IQDA will make available the collection of 100 interviews, plus a collection of audio files from these interviews through the Digital Repository of Ireland (www.dri.ie) as part of a demonstrator project entitled *Irish Lifetimes*, funded through the Irish Government Programme for Research in Third Level Institutions, Wave 5. Ruth Geraghty is leading the project to develop *Irish Lifetimes* at Maynooth University.

LHSC respondents were interviewed from within three birth cohorts of people who participated in the *Living in Ireland* study in each year from 1994 to 2001, as follows: Cohort 1 were born before 1935; Cohort 2 were born 1945–1954; Cohort 3 were born 1965–1974. The objective of the research was to obtain in-depth information of how, in the course of their lives, individual Irish people experienced and shaped social change in the twentieth century. The interviews gathered in this research became part of a significant database available to researchers interested in all aspects of how Irish society has changed. More information on the *Life Histories and Social Change* project is available at: www.iqda.ie.[1]

Growing Up in Ireland

Growing Up in Ireland: The National Longitudinal Study of Children was launched in 2006 and is being carried out by a consortium of researchers led by the ESRI and Trinity College Dublin. The principal investigator is Professor James Williams, Research Professor at the ESRI. The study is funded by the Department of Children and Youth Affairs, in association with the Department of Social Protection and the Central Statistics Office. The main aim of the study is to describe the lives of two representative samples of children in Ireland and how they are developing in the current social, economic and cultural environment. The project involves studying two main cohorts of children longitudinally with a view to improving our understanding of their development across a range of domains. In this book data from the nine-year-old 'child cohort' are presented.

A total of 120 families from the nine-year cohort participated in the first wave of data-collection for the qualitative study between April and August 2008. During the quantitative study, the families were invited to sign a consent form to have their names put forward for selection into the qualitative sample. Almost two-thirds (65.9 per cent) of the families forming the nine-year-old cohort (8,500 in total) gave their consent to be put forward for selection. Of these families, 120 families participated in the qualitative study. Two of these families included nine-year-old twin siblings, both of whom were interviewed, bringing the total number of child respondents to 122. The qualitative interviews took place in the children's homes within six months of the quantitative study. The children were aged between nine and ten when they were interviewed.

The qualitative sample was purposive and stratified according to socio-economic status (high, medium, and low income), urban/rural location, and

---

1   Source: Life History and Social Change Project User Guide to Archived Files
    (2012). Available at: http://na-srv-1dv.nuim.ie/iqda/archive/eserv/iqda:10028/
    LifeHistoryUserGuideV2.pdf. Accessed 30 March 2015.

family type (one or two resident parents). The largest category of children in the sample (17.2 per cent) corresponded to a two-parent family with high income in a rural area. A total of fifty-eight girls and sixty-four boys participated in the study. The qualitative sample included children from families with two resident parents (70.5 per cent) and one resident parent (29.5 per cent). Children from twenty-one of the twenty-six counties in the Republic of Ireland were represented, sixty-seven of whom were living in rural areas and fifty-five in urban areas. The areas explored in the qualitative study map onto the domains of the main quantitative study to provide a deeper understanding of the children's experiences of being nine years old in Ireland, and their parents' experiences of their parenting role. There were separate schedules for the child and the parents, each consisting of specific questions addressing the domains to be explored and probing questions which were used where appropriate to explore responses in more depth.[2]

Following data collection and analysis the qualitative collection were archived at the Irish Qualitative Data Archive at Maynooth University, Maynooth, Co. Kildare, Ireland (www.iqda.ie) and made available to bona fide researchers through application to the IQDA. The archival collection comprises all 120 family interviews, including interview transcripts, drawings and written materials from each child interview, transcripts from each parent interview, and interviewer field notes. More information on *Growing Up in Ireland* is available at: www.growingup.ie.

2   Source: Growing Up in Ireland: National Longitudinal Study of Children. Child Cohort – Qualitative Study. Technical Report on the 9-Year Qualitative Study. Technical Report Number 1. (2011). Available at: http://growingup.ie/fileadmin/user_upload/documents/Qual_Docs_Child_Cohort/Growing_Up_in_Ireland_-_Technical_Report_on_the_9-Year_Qualitative_Study.pdf. Accessed 30 March 2015.

List of participants

Participant's pseudonym	Archive ID number	Year of birth	Gender	Collection
Seamus	LHArchiveA02	1916	Male	LHSC Cohort 1
Joan	LHArchiveA03	1916	Female	LHSC Cohort 1
Evelyn	LHArchiveA06	1923	Female	LHSC Cohort 1
Rebecca	LHArchiveA07	1923	Female	LHSC Cohort 1
James	LHArchiveA09	1924	Male	LHSC Cohort 1
Kathleen	LHArchiveA11	1924	Female	LHSC Cohort 1
Clifford	LHArchiveA13	1926	Male	LHSC Cohort 1
Ben	LHArchiveA14	1926	Male	LHSC Cohort 1
Rosemary	LHArchiveA16	1927	Female	LHSC Cohort 1
Irene	LHArchiveA19	1928	Female	LHSC Cohort 1
Luke	LHArchiveA20	1928	Male	LHSC Cohort 1
Peter	LHArchiveA21	1928	Male	LHSC Cohort 1
Eileen	LHArchiveA22	1928	Female	LHSC Cohort 1
Simon	LHArchiveA23	1928	Male	LHSC Cohort 1
Laura	LHArchiveA24	1928	Female	LHSC Cohort 1
Mary	LHArchiveA25	1929	Female	LHSC Cohort 1
William	LHArchiveA26	1930	Male	LHSC Cohort 1
Lucy	LHArchiveA27	1930	Female	LHSC Cohort 1
Joseph	LHArchiveA28	1930	Male	LHSC Cohort 1
Deirdre	LHArchiveA29	1930	Female	LHSC Cohort 1
Nancy	LHArchiveA30	1930	Female	LHSC Cohort 1
Claire	LHArchiveA31	1931	Female	LHSC Cohort 1

Participant's pseudonym	Archive ID number	Year of birth	Gender	Collection
Graham	LHArchiveA32	1931	Male	LHSC Cohort 1
Nuala	LHArchiveA33	1931	Female	LHSC Cohort 1
Lillian	LHArchiveA34	1932	Female	LHSC Cohort 1
Rita	LHArchiveA35	1932	Female	LHSC Cohort 1
Monica	LHArchiveA36	1932	Female	LHSC Cohort 1
Mark	LHArchiveA37	1933	Male	LHSC Cohort 1
Clara	LHArchiveA38	1933	Female	LHSC Cohort 1
Patricia	LHArchiveA39	1933	Female	LHSC Cohort 1
Andrew	LHArchiveA40	1934	Male	LHSC Cohort 1
Delores	LHArchiveA41	1934	Female	LHSC Cohort 1
Patrick	LHArchiveA42	1934	Male	LHSC Cohort 1
Tony	LHArchiveA43	1934	Male	LHSC Cohort 1
Declan	LHArchiveA44	1934	Male	LHSC Cohort 1
Liam	LHArchiveA45	1934	Male	LHSC Cohort 1
Brenda	LHArchiveA46	1934	Male	LHSC Cohort 1
Doreen	LHArchiveB01	1945	Female	LHSC Cohort 2
David	LHArchiveB02	1945	Male	LHSC Cohort 2
Audrey	LHArchiveB03	1945	Female	LHSC Cohort 2
Denise	LHArchiveB04	1945	Female	LHSC Cohort 2
Desmond	LHArchiveB05	1945	Male	LHSC Cohort 2
Jillian	LHArchiveB06	1945	Female	LHSC Cohort 2
Linda	LHArchiveB07	1950s	Female	LHSC Cohort 2
Anthony	LHArchiveB08	1946	Male	LHSC Cohort 2
Geoff	LHArchiveB09	1946	Male	LHSC Cohort 2
Brigit	LHArchiveB10	1946	Female	LHSC Cohort 2
Daniel	LHArchiveB11	1947	Male	LHSC Cohort 2
Sarah	LHArchiveB12	1946	Female	LHSC Cohort 2
Phyllis	LHArchiveB13	1946	Female	LHSC Cohort 2
Liz	LHArchiveB15	1946	Female	LHSC Cohort 2
Owen	LHArchiveB16	1946	Male	LHSC Cohort 2
John	LHArchiveB17	1946	Male	LHSC Cohort 2
Jack	LHArchiveB18	1947	Male	LHSC Cohort 2
Judith	LHArchiveB20	1946	Female	LHSC Cohort 2
Betty	LHArchiveB21	1947	Female	LHSC Cohort 2

Participant's pseudonym	Archive ID number	Year of birth	Gender	Collection
Martin	LHArchiveB22	1947	Male	LHSC Cohort 2
Maire	LHArchiveB23	1949	Female	LHSC Cohort 2
Vincent	LHArchiveB24	1949	Male	LHSC Cohort 2
Sally	LHArchiveB25	1949	Female	LHSC Cohort 2
Siobhan	LHArchiveB26	1950	Female	LHSC Cohort 2
Edward	LHArchiveB27	1950	Male	LHSC Cohort 2
Nora	LHArchiveB28	1950	Female	LHSC Cohort 2
Enda	LHArchiveB29	1950	Male	LHSC Cohort 2
Bernard	LHArchiveB14	1951	Male	LHSC Cohort 2
Darren	LHArchiveB30	1951	Male	LHSC Cohort 2
Sharon	LHArchiveB31	1951	Female	LHSC Cohort 2
Rose	LHArchiveB32	1950s	Female	LHSC Cohort 2
Pauleen	LHArchiveB33	1952	Female	LHSC Cohort 2
Sean	LHArchiveB34	1952	Male	LHSC Cohort 2
Francis	LHArchiveB35	1952	Male	LHSC Cohort 2
Susan	LHArchiveB36	1953	Female	LHSC Cohort 2
Anne	LHArchiveB37	1953	Female	LHSC Cohort 2
Rob	LHArchiveB38	1953	Male	LHSC Cohort 2
Cormac	LHArchiveB39	1954	Male	LHSC Cohort 2
Barney	LHArchiveB41	1954	Male	LHSC Cohort 2
Marguerite	LHArchiveB42	1952	Female	LHSC Cohort 2
Marion	LHArchiveC02	1965	Female	LHSC Cohort 3
Mandy	LHArchiveC03	1965	Female	LHSC Cohort 3
Chris	LHArchiveC04	1965	Male	LHSC Cohort 3
Anne-Marie	LHArchiveC05	1966	Female	LHSC Cohort 3
Brian	LHArchiveC06	1966	Male	LHSC Cohort 3
Orla	LHArchiveC07	1966	Female	LHSC Cohort 3
Kevin	LHArchiveC08	1967	Male	LHSC Cohort 3
Niamh	LHArchiveC09	1960s	Female	LHSC Cohort 3
Aine	LHArchiveC11	1969	Female	LHSC Cohort 3
Lorraine	LHArchiveC12	1969	Female	LHSC Cohort 3
Elizabeth	LHArchiveC13	1970	Female	LHSC Cohort 3
Ruth	LHArchiveC14	1970s	Female	LHSC Cohort 3
Donal	LHArchiveC15	1970	Male	LHSC Cohort 3

Participant's pseudonym	Archive ID number	Year of birth	Gender	Collection
Grace	withheld	1970s	Female	LHSC Cohort 3
Louise	LHArchiveC17	1970	Female	LHSC Cohort 3
Emer	LHArchiveC19	1970s	Female	LHSC Cohort 3
Thomas	LHArchiveC20	1972	Male	LHSC Cohort 3
Karen	LHArchiveC23	1974	Female	LHSC Cohort 3
Cathy	LHArchiveC24	1974	Female	LHSC Cohort 3
Rachel	LHArchiveC25	1972	Female	LHSC Cohort 3
Janine	LHArchiveC26	1969	Female	LHSC Cohort 3
Angela	LHArchiveC27	1965	Female	LHSC Cohort 3
Maurice	LHArchiveC32	1966	Male	LHSC Cohort 3
Juliette	LHArchiveC37	1973	Female	LHSC Cohort 3
Shirley	GUI001	1999	Female	GUI, wave 1 at 9 years
Daniel	GUI002	1999	Male	GUI, wave 1 at 9 years
Emmanuelle	GUI003	1999	Female	GUI, wave 1 at 9 years
Mathew	GUI004	1999	Male	GUI, wave 1 at 9 years
Avril	GUI005	1999	Female	GUI, wave 1 at 9 years
Billy	GUI006	1999	Male	GUI, wave 1 at 9 years
Eoin	GUI007	1999	Male	GUI, wave 1 at 9 years
Jonathon	GUI008	1999	Male	GUI, wave 1 at 9 years
Daniel	GUI0010	1999	Male	GUI, wave 1 at 9 years
Luke	GUI0011	1999	Male	GUI, wave 1 at 9 years
Ronald	GUI0012	1999	Male	GUI, wave 1 at 9 years
Richard	GUI0013	1999	Male	GUI, wave 1 at 9 years
Sarah	GUI0014	1999	Female	GUI, wave 1 at 9 years
Melissa	GUI0015	1999	Female	GUI, wave 1 at 9 years
Debbie	GUI0016	1999	Female	GUI, wave 1 at 9 years
Nicola	GUI0017	1999	Female	GUI, wave 1 at 9 years
Audrey	GUI0018	1999	Female	GUI, wave 1 at 9 years
Audrina	GUI0019	1999	Female	GUI, wave 1 at 9 years
Amelie	GUI0020	1999	Female	GUI, wave 1 at 9 years
Louise	GUI0021	1999	Female	GUI, wave 1 at 9 years
Ruby	GUI0022	1999	Female	GUI, wave 1 at 9 years
Frank	GUI0023	1999	Male	GUI, wave 1 at 9 years
Christine	GUI0024	1999	Female	GUI, wave 1 at 9 years

Participant's pseudonym	Archive ID number	Year of birth	Gender	Collection
Sam	GUI0025	1999	Male	GUI, wave 1 at 9 years
Fiona	GUI0026	1999	Female	GUI, wave 1 at 9 years
Robert	GUI0027	1999	Male	GUI, wave 1 at 9 years
Henry	GUI0028	1999	Male	GUI, wave 1 at 9 years
Mary	GUI0029	1999	Female	GUI, wave 1 at 9 years
Declan	GUI0030	1999	Male	GUI, wave 1 at 9 years
Sam	GUI0031	1999	Female	GUI, wave 1 at 9 years
Ben	GUI0032	1999	Male	GUI, wave 1 at 9 years
Tina	GUI0033	1999	Female	GUI, wave 1 at 9 years
Charlotte	GUI0034	1999	Female	GUI, wave 1 at 9 years
Gemma	GUI0035	1999	Female	GUI, wave 1 at 9 years
Wendy	GUI0036	1999	Female	GUI, wave 1 at 9 years
Charlotte	GUI0037	1999	Female	GUI, wave 1 at 9 years
Damien	GUI0038	1999	Male	GUI, wave 1 at 9 years
Jason	GUI0039	1999	Male	GUI, wave 1 at 9 years
Mary	GUI0040	1999	Female	GUI, wave 1 at 9 years
Gavin	GUI0041	1999	Male	GUI, wave 1 at 9 years
Bill	GUI0042	1999	Male	GUI, wave 1 at 9 years
Helen	GUI0043	1999	Female	GUI, wave 1 at 9 years
Rachel	GUI0044	1999	Female	GUI, wave 1 at 9 years
Sam	GUI0045	1999	Male	GUI, wave 1 at 9 years
Dennis	GUI0046	1999	Male	GUI, wave 1 at 9 years
Eoin	GUI0047	1999	Male	GUI, wave 1 at 9 years
Naomi	GUI0048	1999	Female	GUI, wave 1 at 9 years
Karen	GUI0049	1999	Female	GUI, wave 1 at 9 years
Paul	GUI0050	1999	Male	GUI, wave 1 at 9 years
Damien	GUI0051	1999	Male	GUI, wave 1 at 9 years
Peter	GUI0052	1999	Male	GUI, wave 1 at 9 years
David	GUI0053	1999	Male	GUI, wave 1 at 9 years
Scott	GUI0054	1999	Male	GUI, wave 1 at 9 years
Susan	GUI0055	1999	Female	GUI, wave 1 at 9 years
Jackie	GUI0056	1999	Female	GUI, wave 1 at 9 years
Damien	GUI0057	1999	Male	GUI, wave 1 at 9 years
Jeff	GUI0058	1999	Male	GUI, wave 1 at 9 years

Participant's pseudonym	Archive ID number	Year of birth	Gender	Collection
Dylan	GUI0059	1999	Male	GUI, wave 1 at 9 years
Barry	GUI0060	1999	Male	GUI, wave 1 at 9 years
Laura	GUI0061	1999	Female	GUI, wave 1 at 9 years
Carly	GUI0062	1999	Female	GUI, wave 1 at 9 years
John	GUI0063	1999	Male	GUI, wave 1 at 9 years
Nick	GUI0064	1999	Male	GUI, wave 1 at 9 years
Gillian	GUI0065	1999	Female	GUI, wave 1 at 9 years
Sebastian	GUI0066	1999	Male	GUI, wave 1 at 9 years
Roisin	GUI0067	1999	Female	GUI, wave 1 at 9 years
Zenia	GUI0068	1999	Female	GUI, wave 1 at 9 years
Martin	GUI0069	1999	Male	GUI, wave 1 at 9 years
Sean	GUI0070	1999	Male	GUI, wave 1 at 9 years
Sally	GUI0071	1999	Female	GUI, wave 1 at 9 years
Amy	GUI0072	1999	Female	GUI, wave 1 at 9 years
Sarah	GUI0073	1999	Female	GUI, wave 1 at 9 years
Mark	GUI0074	1999	Male	GUI, wave 1 at 9 years
Ian	GUI0075	1999	Male	GUI, wave 1 at 9 years
Sophie	GUI0076	1999	Female	GUI, wave 1 at 9 years
Paula	GUI0077	1999	Female	GUI, wave 1 at 9 years
Simon	GUI0078	1999	Male	GUI, wave 1 at 9 years
Vicky	GUI0079	1999	Female	GUI, wave 1 at 9 years
Rachel	GUI0080	1999	Female	GUI, wave 1 at 9 years
Taylor	GUI0081	1999	Male	GUI, wave 1 at 9 years
Colm	GUI0082	1999	Male	GUI, wave 1 at 9 years
Leona	GUI0083	1999	Female	GUI, wave 1 at 9 years
Daniel	GUI0084	1999	Male	GUI, wave 1 at 9 years
Damien	GUI0085	1999	Male	GUI, wave 1 at 9 years
Graham	GUI0086	1999	Male	GUI, wave 1 at 9 years
Tania	GUI0087	1999	Female	GUI, wave 1 at 9 years
Erika	GUI0088	1999	Female	GUI, wave 1 at 9 years
Donal	GUI0089	1999	Male	GUI, wave 1 at 9 years
Maura	GUI0090	1999	Female	GUI, wave 1 at 9 years
Paul	GUI0091	1999	Male	GUI, wave 1 at 9 years
Etain	GUI0092	1999	Female	GUI, wave 1 at 9 years

Participant's pseudonym	Archive ID number	Year of birth	Gender	Collection
Peter	GUI0093	1999	Male	GUI, wave 1 at 9 years
Arthur	GUI0094	1999	Male	GUI, wave 1 at 9 years
Rory	GUI0095	1999	Male	GUI, wave 1 at 9 years
Paul	GUI0096	1999	Male	GUI, wave 1 at 9 years
Daniel	GUI0097	1999	Male	GUI, wave 1 at 9 years
Wesley	GUI0098	1999	Male	GUI, wave 1 at 9 years
Ann	GUI0099	1999	Female	GUI, wave 1 at 9 years
Noah	GUI0110	1999	Male	GUI, wave 1 at 9 years
Sean	GUI0101	1999	Male	GUI, wave 1 at 9 years
Jamie	GUI0102	1999	Female	GUI, wave 1 at 9 years
Kenny	GUI0103	1999	Male	GUI, wave 1 at 9 years
Damien	GUI0104	1999	Male	GUI, wave 1 at 9 years
Sarah	GUI0105	1999	Female	GUI, wave 1 at 9 years
Sandra	GUI0106	1999	Female	GUI, wave 1 at 9 years
Heidi	GUI0107	1999	Female	GUI, wave 1 at 9 years
Daniel	GUI0108	1999	Male	GUI, wave 1 at 9 years
Alan	GUI109	1999	Male	GUI, wave 1 at 9 years
John	GUI0110	1999	Male	GUI, wave 1 at 9 years
Roisin	GUI0111	1999	Female	GUI, wave 1 at 9 years
Rhona	GUI0112	1999	Female	GUI, wave 1 at 9 years
Freddy	GUI0113	1999	Male	GUI, wave 1 at 9 years
Lizzy	GUI0114	1999	Female	GUI, wave 1 at 9 years
Olivia	GUI0115	1999	Female	GUI, wave 1 at 9 years
Tiffany	GUI0116	1999	Female	GUI, wave 1 at 9 years
Simon	GUI0117	1999	Male	GUI, wave 1 at 9 years

Bibliography

Aboderin, I. (2004). Modernisation and Ageing Theory Revisited: Current Explanations of Recent Developing World and Historical Western Shifts in Material Family Support for Older People. *Ageing & Society*, 24 (1): 29–50.

Aboim, S. (2010). Gender Cultures and the Division of Labour in Contemporary Europe: A Cross-National Perspective. *The Sociological Review*, 58 (2): 171–196.

Alwin, D. F. (1996). From Childbearing to Childrearing: The Link Between Declines in Fertility and Changes in the Socialization of Children. *Population and Development Review*, 22 (Supplement: Fertility in the United States: New Patterns, New Theories): 176–196.

Amato, P. R. (2005). The Impact of Family Formation Change on the Cognitive, Social, and Emotional Well-Being of the Next Generation. *The Future of Children*, 15 (2): 75–96.

Amen (2015). *Fighting the Myths*. Available at: www.amen.ie/victims.html#2. Accessed: 15 October 2015.

Andersson, G. (2002). Children's Experience of Family Disruption and Family Formation: Evidence from 16 FFS countries. *Demographic Research*, 7 (7): 343–364.

Arber, S. & Timonen, V. (2012). *Contemporary Grandparenting: Changing Family Relationships in Global Contexts*. Bristol: Policy Press.

Arensberg, C. M. (1988). *The Irish Countryman: An Anthropological Study*. Long Grove, IL: Waveland Press [First published 1937].

Arensberg, C. M. & Kimball, S. T. (2001). *Family and Community in Ireland*. Ennis, County Clare: Clasp Press [First published 1940].

Ariès, P. (1962). *Centuries of Childhood: A Social History of Family Life*. New York: Vintage Books.

Attias-Donfut, C. & Segalen, M. (2002). The Construction of Grandparenthood. *Current Sociology*, 50 (2): 281–294.

Attias-Donfut, C., Ogg, J. & Wolff, F.-C. (2005). European Patterns of Intergenerational Financial and Time Transfers. *European Journal of Ageing*, 2 (3): 161–173.

Becker, G. S. (1991). *A Treatise on the Family, Enlarged Edition*. Cambridge, Mass.: Harvard University Press [First published 1981].

Beck-Gernsheim, E. (1998). On the Way to a Post-Familial Family: From a Community of Need to Elective Affinities. *Theory, Culture & Society*, 15 (3): 53–70.

Bengtson, V. L. (2001). Beyond the Nuclear Family: The Increasing Importance of Multigenerational Bonds. *Journal of Marriage and Family*, 63 (1): 1–16.

Bengtson, V., Giarrusso, R., Mabry, J. B. & Silverstein, M. (2002). Solidarity, Conflict, and Ambivalence: Complementary or Competing Perspectives on Intergenerational Relationships? *Journal of Marriage and Family*, 64 (3): 568–576.

Bernstein, S. (2005). The Changing Discourse on Population and Development: Toward a New Political Demography. *Studies in Family Planning* 36 (2): 127–132.

Bianchi, S. M. & Milkie, M. A. (2010). Work and Family Research in the First Decade of the 21st Century. *Journal of Marriage and Family*, 72 (3): 705–725.

Bianchi, S. M., Sayer, L. C., Milkie, M. A. & Robinson, J. P. (2012). Housework: Who Did, Does Or Will Do It, And How Much Does It Matter? *Social Forces*, 91 (1): 55–63.

Billari, F. C. & Liefbroer, A. C. (2010). Towards a New Pattern of Transition to Adulthood? *Advances in Life Course Research*, 15 (2–3): 59–75.

Birdwell-Pheasant, D. (1992). The Early Twentieth-Century Irish Stem Family: A Case Study from County Kerry. In Silverman, M. and Gulliver, P. H., eds. *Approaching the Past: Historical Anthropology through Irish Case Studies*. New York: Columbia University Press.

Bittman, M., England, P., Sayer, L., Folbre, N. & Matheson, G. (2003). When Does Gender Trump Money? Bargaining and Time in Household Work. *American Journal of Sociology*, 109 (1): 186–214.

Boh, K. (1989). European Family Life Patterns: A Reappraisal. In Boh, K., ed. *Changing Patterns of European Family Life: A Comparative Analysis of 14 European Countries*. London: Routledge.

Bourdieu, P. (1977). *Outline of a Theory of Practice*. Cambridge: Cambridge University Press.

Bourke, J. (1987). Women and Poultry in Ireland, 1881–1914. *Irish Historical Studies* 25 (99): 293–310.

Bourke, J. (1990). Dairywomen and Affectionate Wives: Women in the Irish Dairy Industry, 1890–1914. *Agricultural History Review*, 38 (2): 149–164.

Bourke, J. (1993). *Husbandry to Housewifery: Women, Economic Change, and Housework in Ireland, 1890–1914*. Oxford: Oxford University Press.

Bourke, J. (1994). *Working Class Cultures in Britain, 1890–1960: Gender, Class, and ethnicity*. London: Routledge.

Bradley, F., Smith, M., Long, J. & O'Dowd, T. (2002). Reported Frequency of Domestic Violence: Cross Sectional Survey of Women Attending General Practice. *BMJ*, 324 (7332): 271–277.

Brady, D. & Burroway, R. (2012). Targeting, Universalism, and Single-Mother Poverty: A Multilevel Analysis Across 18 Affluent Democracies. *Demography*, 49 (2): 719–746.

Brannen, J. (1995). Young People and their Contribution to Household Work. *Sociology*, 29 (2): 317–338.

Breen, R. (1983). Farm Servanthood in Ireland, 1900–40. *The Economic History Review*, 36 (1): 87–102.

Breen, R. & Cooke, L. P. (2005). The Persistence of the Gendered Division of Domestic Labour. *European Sociological Review*, 21 (1): 43–57.

Breheny, M., Stephens, C. & Spilsbury, L. (2013). Involvement Without Interference: How Grandparents Negotiate Intergenerational Expectations in Relationships With Grandchildren. *Journal of Family Studies*, 19 (2): 174–184.

Brody, H. (1986). *Inishkillane: Change and Decline in the West of Ireland*. London: Faber and Faber [First published 1973].

Bunreacht na hÉireann. (1937). *The Constitution of Ireland*. Dublin: Stationery Office.

Burgess, E. W. (1948). The Family in a Changing Society. *The American Journal of Sociology*, 53 (6), 417–422.

Byrne, A., Edmondson, R. & Farley, T. (2001). Introduction to the Third Edition of C. Arensberg and S. Kimball, *Family and Community in Ireland*. Ennis, County Clare: Clasp Press, pp. i–ci.

Callan, T., Nolan, B. & Keane, C. (2010). Inequality and the Crisis: The Distributional Impact of Tax Increases and Welfare and Public Sector Pay Cuts. *Economic and Social Review* 41 (4): 461–471.

Callan, T., van Soest, A. & Walsh, J. R. (2007). *Tax Structure and Female Labour Market Participation: Evidence from Ireland*. Working Paper No. 208. Dublin: ESRI.

Carney, F. J. (1980), Household Size and Structure in Two Areas of Ireland, 1821 and 1911.In Cullen, L. M. and Furet, F., eds. *Ireland and France 17th–20th Centuries: Towards a Comparative Study of Rural History*, Paris: L'Ecole Des Hautes Etudes.

Cashin, A. M. & Payne, D. (2006). *What 'World of Welfare' Fits? Ireland in a Comparative Perspective*. Working Paper No. 200604, Geary Institute, University College Dublin.

Castles, F. (2002). Three Facts about Fertility: Cross-National Lessons for the Current Debate. *Family Matters* 63: 22–27.

Census of Ireland (1940). *Census 1936 Volume 5-Ages, Orphanhood and Conjugal Conditions, Part II*, Table 1B. Available at: www.cso.ie/en/media/csoie/census/census1936results/volume5/C,1936,Vol,5,part,2,T1b.pdf. Accessed 27 October 2015.

Chambaz, C. (2001). Lone-Parent Families in Europe: A Variety of Economic and Social Circumstances. *Social Policy & Administration*, 35 (6): 658–671.

Charmaz, K. (2014). *Constructing Grounded Theory*. London: Sage, 2nd edn.

Cheadle, J. E. & Amato, P. R. (2011). A Quantitative Assessment of Lareau's Qualitative Conclusions About Class, Race, and Parenting. *Journal of Family Issues*, 32 (5): 679–706.

Cherlin, A. J. (1990). Recent Changes in American Fertility, Marriage, and Divorce. *The ANNALS of the American Academy of Political and Social Science*, 510 (1): 145–154.

Cherlin, A. J. (1992). *Marriage, Divorce, Remarriage, Revised and Enlarged Edition*. Cambridge, Mass.: Harvard University Press [First published 1981].

Cherlin, A. J. (1999). Going to Extremes: Family Structure, Children's Well-Being, and Social Science. *Demography*, 36 (4): 421–428.

Cherlin, A. J. (2003). Should the Government Promote Marriage? *Contexts*, 2 (4), 22–29.

Cherlin, A. J. (2004). The Deinstitutionalization of American Marriage. *Journal of Marriage and Family*, 66 (4): 848–861.

Cherlin, A. J. (2012). Goode's World Revolution and Family Patterns: A Reconsideration at Fifty Years. *Population and Development Review* 38 (4): 577–607.

CME Info (2015). Child Mortality Estimates: Inter-Agency Group for Child Mortality Estimation. Available online at: www.childmortality.org/index.php?r=site/index/ Accessed 27 October 2015.

Cohen, P. N. (2015). Divergent Responses to Family Inequality. In Amato, P. R., Booth,

A., McHale, S. M. & Van Hook, J., eds. Families in an Era of Increasing Inequality. Switzerland: Springer International Publishing.

Coleman, D. A. (1992). The Demographic Transition in Ireland in International Context. In Goldthorpe, J. H. and Whelan, C. T., eds. *The Development of Industrial Society in Ireland*. Oxford: British Academy.

Collier, J., Rosaldo, M. & Yanagisako, S. (1992). Is there a Family? New Anthropological Views. In B. Thorne and M. Yalom, eds. *Rethinking the Family: Some Feminist Questions*. Boston: Northeastern University Press.

Collins, B. (1982). Proto-Industrialization and Pre-Famine emigration. *Social History*, 7 (2), 127–146.

Coltrane, S. (2000). Research on Household Labor: Modeling and Measuring the Social Embeddedness of Routine Family Work. *Journal of Marriage and Family*, 62 (4):1208–1233.

Commission to Inquire Into Child Abuse (2009). Final Report of the Commission to Inquire Into Child Abuse. Retrieved from www.childabusecommission.com/rpt/pdfs/ [12 May 2015].

Condon, J. (2000). The Patriotic Children's Treat: Irish Nationalism and Children's Culture at the Twilight of Empire. *Irish Studies Review*, 8 (2): 167–178.

Conlon, C., Timonen, V., Carney, G. & Scharf, T. (2014). Women (Re)Negotiating Care Across Family Generations: Intersections of Gender and Socioeconomic Status. *Gender & Society*, 28 (5): 729–751.

Connidis, I. A. & McMullin, J. A. (2002). Sociological Ambivalence and Family Ties: A Critical Perspective. *Journal of Marriage and Family*, 64 (3): 558–567.

Cooke, L. P. (2006). 'Doing' Gender in Context: Household Bargaining and Risk of Divorce in Germany and the United States. *American Journal of Sociology*, 112 (2): 442–472.

Coontz, S. (1995). The American Family and the Nostalgia Trap. *Phi Delta Kappan*, 76 (7): 1–20.

Corcoran, M. (2003). 'Global Cosmopolites: Issues of Self-Identity and Collective Identity Among the Transnational Irish elite'. *Etudes Irlandaises, Special issue on Ireland and America in the Twentieth Century*, 28 (2): 135–150.

Corcoran, M. P., Gray, J. & Peillon, M. (2010). *Suburban Affiliations: Social Relations in the Greater Dublin Area*. University College Dublin Press.

Corden, A. & Millar, J. (2007). Qualitative Longitudinal Research for Social Policy – Introduction to Themed Section. *Social Policy and Society*, 6 (4): 529–532.

Cornwell, B., Laumann, E. O. & Schumm, L. P. (2008). The Social Connectedness of Older Adults: A National Profile. *American Sociological Review*, 73 (2): 185–203.

Corrigan, C. (1993). Household Structure in Early Twentieth Century Ireland. *Irish Journal of Sociology*, 3: 56–78.

Coulter, C. (1995). Researchers Dispute No campaign's Assertion of Damage Inflicted by Divorce on Children. *Irish Times*, 25 October. Dublin, Ireland. Retrieved from http://search.proquest.com.jproxy.nuim.ie/hnpirishtimes/docview/525455183/citation/39FE5BBFF4834416PQ/8?accountid=12309 [30 March 2015].

Courts Service Ireland. *A Guide to Judicial Separation*. Available at: www.courts.ie/Courts.ie/library3.nsf/pagecurrent/2182B4805D0CD318802577EA003FF141?opendocument. Accessed: 27 March 2015.

Crawford, W. H. (1991). Women in the Domestic Linen Industry. In McCurtain, M. And O'Dowd, M., eds. *Women in Early Modern Ireland*. Dublin: Wolfhound Press.

CSO (Central Statistics Office). Statbank CD2017. Persons in Private Households by Sex, Composition of Private Household, Census Year and Statistic. Available at: www.cso.ie/px/pxeirestat/Statire/SelectVarVal/Define.asp?Maintable=CD217&Planguage=0. Accessed 12 May 2015.

CSO (2009). *Community Involvement and Social Networks. Results from the Social Capital module and the Quarterly National Household Survey Q3 2006 and the Social & Cultural Participation module of the Survey on Income and Living Conditions 2006*. Dublin: The Stationery Office. Available at: www.cso.ie/en/media/csoie/releasespublications/documents/labourmarket/2006/comsoc06.pdf. Accessed 12 May 2015.

CSO (2012a). *Profile 3. At Work – Employment, Occupations and Industry*. Dublin: The Stationery Office. Available at: www.cso.ie/en/census/census2011reports/census2011profile3atwork-employmentoccupationsandindustry/. Accessed 12 May 2015.

CSO (2012b). *Profile 6. Migration and Diversity*. Dublin: The Stationery Office. Available at: www.cso.ie/en/census/census2011reports/census2011profile6migrationand diversity-aprofileofdiversityinireland/. Accessed 12 May 2015.

CSO (2013). Population and Migration Estimates, April 2013. Available at: www.cso.i.e/en/releasesandpublications/er/pme/populationandmigrationestimatesapril2013/ Accessed 27 October 2015.

CSO (2014a). *Garda Recorded Crime Statistics 2008–2012*. Dublin: The Stationery Office. Available at: www.cso.ie/en/media/csoie/releasespublications/documents/crimejustice/2012/gardacrimestats_2012.pdf. Accessed 13 July 2015.

CSO (2014b). *Marriages and Civil Partnerships 2013*. Dublin: The Stationery Office. Available at: www.cso.ie/en/releasesandpublications/er/mcp/marriagesandcivil partnerships2013/#.VRr3n_nF840. Accessed 31 March 2015.

CSO (2014c). *Vital Statistics, Fourth Quarter and Yearly Summary, 2013*. Dublin: The Stationery Office. Available at: www.cso.ie/en/media/csoie/releasespublications/documents/vitalstats/2013/vstats_q42013.pdf. Accessed 13 July 2015.

CSO (2014d). *Women and Men in Ireland 2013*. Dublin: The Stationery Office. Available at: www.cso.ie/en/releasesandpublications/ep/p-wamii/womenandmeninireland 2013/#.VRr3RvnF840. Accessed 13 July 2015.

CSO (2015). Statbank CNA15. Population by Age Group, Sex, Year and Statistic. Available at: www.cso.ie/px/pxeirestat/statire/SelectVarVal/Define.asp?Maintable =CNA15&Planguage=0 Accessed 27 October 2015.

Cunningham, H. (1995). *Children and Childhood in Western Society Since 1500*. London: Routledge.

Daly, M. E. (1981). Women in the Irish Workforce from Pre-Industrial to Modern Times. *Saothar*, 7: 74–83.

Daly, M. E. (1995). Women in the Irish Free State: The Interaction between Economics and Ideology. *Journal of Women's History* 7 (1) 99–116.

Daly, M. & Lewis, J. (2000). The Concept of Social Care and the Analysis of Contemporary Welfare States. *The British Journal of Sociology*, 51 (2): 281–298.

Davis, A. 2012. *Modern Motherhood: Women and Family in England, 1945–2000*. Manchester: Manchester University Press.

Day, A. & McWilliams, P. (1992). *Ordnance Survey Memoirs of Ireland. Parishes of County Fermanagh II: 1834–5*. Belfast: Institute of Irish Studies.

Delaney, E. (2007). *The Irish in Post-War Britain*. Oxford: Oxford University Press.

Demos, J. & Demos, V. (1969). Adolescence in Historical Perspective. *Journal of Marriage and the Family*, 31 (4): 632–638.

De Vries, J. (1994). The Industrial Revolution and the Industrious Revolution. *The Journal of Economic History*, 54 (2): 249–270.

Dobash, R. E. & Dobash, R. P. (1998). *Rethinking Violence Against Women*. London: Sage.

Donovan, C., Heaphy, B. & Weeks, J. (2003). *Same Sex Intimacies: Families of Choice and Other Life Experiments*. London: Routledge.

Doyle, M., O'Dywer, C. & Timonen, V. (2010). 'How Can You Just Cut Off a Whole Side of the Family and Say Move On?' The Reshaping of Paternal Grandparent-Grandchild Relationships Following Divorce or Separation in the Middle Generation. *Family Relations*, 59 (5): 587–598.

Duncan, S. (1995). Theorizing European Gender Systems. *Journal of European Social Policy*, 5 (4): 263–284.

Duncan, S. (2011). Personal Life, Pragmatism and Bricolage. *Sociological Research Online*, 16 (4): 13. Available at: www.socresonline.org.uk/16/4/13.html. Accessed 10 July 2015.

Duncan, S. & Edwards, R. (1997). Lone Mothers and Paid Work – Rational Economic Man or Gendered Moral Rationalities? *Feminist Economics*, 3 (2): 29–61.

Duncan, S. & Irwin, S. (2004). The Social Patterning of Values and Rationalities: Mothers' Choices in Combining Caring and Employment. *Social Policy and Society*, 3 (4): 391–399.

Duncan, S., Edwards, R., Reynolds, T. & Alldred, P. (2003). Motherhood, Paid Work and Partnering: Values and Theories. *Work, Employment & Society*, 17 (2): 309–330.

Dykstra, P. A. & Fokkema, T. (2011). Relationships Between Parents and Their Adult Children: A West European Typology of Late-Life Families. *Ageing & Society*, 31 (4): 545–569.

Elder, G. H. E., Jr. (1994). Time, Human Agency, and Social Change: Perspectives on the Life Course. *Social Psychology Quarterly*, 57 (1): 4–15.

Elliot, F. R. (1996). *Gender, Family and Society*. London: Macmillan.

Ellwardt, L., Peter, S., Präg, P. & Steverink, N. (2014). Social Contacts of Older People in 27 European Countries: The Role of Welfare Spending and Economic Inequality. *European Sociological Review*, 30 (4): 413–430.

Engels, F. (1972). *The Origin of the Family, Private Property, and the State, in the Light of the Researches of Lewis H. Morgan*. Edited by E. B. Leacock. New York: International Publishers [First published 1884].

Esping-Andersen, G. (1990). *The Three Worlds of Welfare Capitalism*. John Wiley & Sons.

ESS Round 3: European Social Survey Round 3 Data (2006). Data file edition 3.5. Norwegian Social Science Data Services, Norway – Data Archive and distributor of ESS data.

Eurobarometer (2007). *Health and Long-Term Care in the European Union*. Special Eurobarometer 283, Wave 67.3. http://ec.europa.eu/public_opinion/archives/ebs/ebs_283_en.pdf. Accessed 10 July 2015.

Eurostat (1999). Demographic Statistics: Data 1960–99. Luxembourg: Office for Official Publications of the European Communities.

Eurostat (2013). Household Composition, Poverty and Hardship Across Europe. Statistical Working Papers, Theme: Population and Social Conditions. Luxembourg: Publications of the European Union http://ec.europa.eu/eurostat/documents/3888793/5856569/KS-TC-13–008–EN.PDF. Accessed 22 April 2015.

Eurostat (2014a) *European Community Health Indicators (ECHI) Health Expectancy: Healthy Life Years (HLY) at Age 65, From 2004 Onwards.* Heidi data tool 2010. Available at: http://ec.europa.eu/health/indicators/indicators/index_en.htm. Accessed 13 July 2015.

Eurostat (2014b). Online database: Life Expectancy by Age and Sex [demo_mlexpec]. http://ec.europa.eu/eurostat/web/population-demography-migration-projections/deaths-life-expectancy-data/database. Accessed 22 April 2015.

EVS (2011): European Values Study Longitudinal Data File 1981–2008 (EVS 1981–2008). GESIS Data Archive, Cologne. ZA4804 Data file Version 2.0.0, doi:10.4232/1.11005.

Fagan, P. (2011). *Missing Pieces: A Comparison of the Rights and Responsibilities Gained from Civil Partnership Compared to the Rights and Responsibilities Gained through Civil Marriage in Ireland.* Dublin: Marriage Equality.

Fahey, T. (1992). State, Family and Compulsory Schooling in Ireland. *Economic & Social Review,* 23 (4): 369–395.

Fahey, T. (1998). Family Policy in Ireland: A Strategic Overview. In Commission on the Family, *Strengthening Families for Life: Final Report to the Minister for Social, Community and Family Affairs.* Dublin: Stationery Office.

Fahey, T. (2012). Small Bang? The Impact of Divorce Legislation on Marital Breakdown in Ireland. *International Journal of Law, Policy and the Family,* 26 (2), 242–258.

Fahey, T. (2014). The Family in Ireland in the New Millennium. In Connolly, L., ed. *The 'Irish' Family.* London: Routledge.

Fahey, T. & Field, C. A. (2008). *Families in Ireland an Analysis of Patterns and Trends.* Dublin: Stationery Office.

Fahey, T. & Layte, R. (2007). Family and Sexuality. In Fahey, T., Russell, H. & Whelan, C. T., eds. *Quality of Life in Ireland.* Dordrecht: Springer.

Fahey, T., Hayes, B. C. & Sinnott, R. (2005). *Conflict and Consensus: A Study of Values and Attitudes in the Republic of Ireland and Northern Ireland.* Dublin: Institute of Public Administration.

Fahey, T., Keilthy, P. & Polek, E. (2012). *Family Relationships and Family Well-Being: A Study of the Families of Nine-Year Olds in Ireland.* Dublin: Family Support Agency and University College Dublin.

Fahey, T., Maitre, B., Nolan, B. & Whelan, C. T. (2007). *A Social Portrait of Older People in Ireland.* Dublin: Stationery Office.

Fahey, T., Russell, H. & Smyth, E. (2000). Gender Equality, Fertility Decline and Labour Market Patterns Among Women in Ireland. In Nolan, B., O'Connell, P. J. and Whelan, C. T., eds. *Bust to Boom: The Irish Experience of Growth and Inequality.* Dublin: Institute of Public Administration.

Ferguson, H. (2007). Abused and Looked After Children as 'Moral Dirt': Child Abuse and Institutional Care in Historical Perspective. *Journal of Social Policy,* 36 (1): 123–139.

Finch, J. (2007). Displaying Families. *Sociology,* 41 (1): 65–81.

Fine-Davis, M. (2011). *Attitudes to Family Formation in Ireland: Findings from the*

Nationwide Study. Dublin: Family Support Agency and Social Attitude and Policy Research Group, Trinity College.

Finkle, J. L. and McIntosh, C. A. (1994). The New Politics of Population. *Population and Development Review*, 20 (Supplement): 3–34.

Fisher, K. (2000). Uncertain Aims and Tacit Negotiation: Birth Control Practices in Britain, 1925–50. *Population and Development Review*, 26 (2): 295–317.

Fitzpatrick, D., Gibbon, P., Curtin, C. & Varley, A. (1983). The Stem Family in Ireland: A Debate. *Comparative Studies in Society and History*, 25 (2): 339–395.

Flaherty, E. (2013). Geographies of Communality, Colonialism, and Capitalism: Ecology and the World-System. *Historical Geography*, 41: 59–79.

Flaherty, R. (2014, 7 February). Most Adults Support Ban on Slapping Children. *Irish Times*. Retrieved from www.irishtimes.com/news/crime-and-law/most-adults-support-ban-on-slapping-children-1.1682517. Accessed 4 March 2014.

Folbre, N. (2004). Sleeping Beauty Awakes: Self-Interest, Feminism and Fertility in the Early Twentieth Century. *Social Research*, 71 (2): 343–356.

Forste, R. & Fox, K. (2012). Household Labor, Gender Roles, and Family Satisfaction: A Cross-National Comparison. *Journal of Comparative Family Studies*, 43 (5): 613–631.

Fox, R. (1978). *The Tory Islanders: A People of the Celtic Fringe*. Cambridge: Cambridge University Press.

FRA (European Agency for Fundamental Rights). (2014). Violence Against Women: An EU Wide Survey. Main Results Report. Available at: http://fra.europa.eu/en/publication/2014/violence-against-women-eu-wide-survey-main-results-report. Accessed 12 May 2015.

Fuller-Thomson, E., Minkler, M. & Driver, D. (1997). A Profile of Grandparents Raising Grandchildren in the United States. *The Gerontologist*, 37 (3): 406–411.

Furstenberg, F. F., Jr. (2007). The Making of the Black Family: Race and Class in Qualitative Studies in the Twentieth Century. *Annual Review of Sociology*, 33 (1): 429–448.

Furstenberg, F. F., Jr. (2010). On a New Schedule: Transitions to Adulthood and Family Change. *The Future of Children*, 20 (1): 67–87.

Furstenberg, F.F., Jr. (2013). Transitions to Adulthood: What We Can Learn from the West. *Annals of the American Academy of Political and Social Science*, 646 (1): 28–41.

Furstenberg, F. F., Jr., Kennedy, S., McLoyd, V. C., Rumbaut, R. G. & Settersten, R. A. (2004). Growing Up is Harder to Do. *Contexts*, 3 (3): 33–41.

Fuwa, M. (2004). Macro-Level Gender Inequality and the Division of Household Labor in 22 Countries. *American Sociological Review*, 69 (6): 751–767.

Gallagher, C. (2012). Connectedness in the Lives of Older People in Ireland: A Study of the Communal Participation of Older People in Two Geographic Localities. *Irish Journal of Sociology*, 20 (1): 84–102.

Geraghty, R., Gray, J. and Ralph, R. (2014). 'One of the Best Members of the Family': Continuity and Change in Young Children's Relationships with their Grandparents. In Connolly, L., ed. *The 'Irish' Family*. London: Routledge.

Gerstel, N. & Sarkisian, N. (2006). Marriage: the Good, the Bad, and the Greedy. *Contexts*, 5 (4): 16–21.

Gibbon, P. (1973). 'Arensberg and Kimball revisited', *Economy and Society* (2) 4: 479–498.

Giddens, A. (1991). *Modernity and Self-Identity: Self and Society in the Late Modern Age.* Stanford: Stanford University Press.

Gilham, A. K. (2012). Serving up a Little Family Stability. *Irish Times*, 3 April. Retrieved from: http://search.proquest.com/docview/963549761?accountid=12309 [12 May 2015].

Gillis, J. R. (2004). Marriages of the Mind. *Journal of Marriage and Family*, 66 (4): 988–991.

Goffman, E. (1959). *The Presentation of Self in Everyday Life.* New York: Doubleday.

Goode, W. J. (1963). *World Revolution and Family Patterns.* New York: Free Press.

Gordon, L. (1988). *Heroes of Their Own Lives: The Politics and History of Family Violence.* New York: Viking.

Gordon, M. (1977). Kinship Boundaries and Kinship Knowledge in Urban Ireland. *International Journal of Sociology of the Family*, 7 (1): 1–14.

Gourdon, V. (1999). Are Grandparents Really Absent From the Family Tradition? *The History of the Family*, 4 (1): 77–91.

Gray, A. (2005). The Changing Availability of Grandparents as Carers and its Implications for Childcare Policy in the UK. *Journal of Social Policy*, 34 (4), 557–577.

Gray, B. (2011). Becoming Non-Migrant: Lives Worth Waiting For. *Gender, Place & Culture*, 18 (3), 417–432.

Gray, J. (2005). *Spinning the Threads of Uneven Development: Gender and Industrialization in Ireland During the Long Eighteenth Century.* Lanham, MD: Lexington Books.

Gray, J. (2010). Poverty and the Life Cycle in 20th Century Ireland: Changing Experiences of Childhood, Education and the Transition to Adulthood. Combat Poverty Agency Working Paper Series 10 (4): 1–59.

Gray, J. (2014). The Circulation of Children in Rural Ireland During the First Half of the Twentieth Century. *Continuity and Change*, 29 (3): 399–421.

Gray, J. and Geraghty, R. (2013). Fertility and the Transformation of Parental Values in Ireland. Paper presented at the Annual Conference of the European Sociological Association, Torino, 28–31 August.

Gray, J., Geraghty, R. & Ralph, D. (2013). Young Grandchildren and Their Grandparents: A Secondary Analysis of Continuity and Change Across Four Birth Cohorts. *Families, Relationships and Societies*, 2 (2): 289–298.

Growing Up in Ireland (2012). Key Findings: Thirteen Year Olds, No. 3. The Family and Financial Circumstances of 13 Year Olds. Available online at: www.growingup.ie/fileadmin/user_upload/Conference_2012/GUI_KF_A4_3_Family.pdf/ Accessed 27 October 2015.

Guinnane, T. (1997). *The Vanishing Irish: Households, Migration, and the Rural Economy in Ireland, 1850–1914.* Princeton, NJ: Princeton University Press.

Guinnane, T. (2011). The Historical Fertility Transition: A Guide for Economists. *Journal of Economic Literature*, 49 (3): 589–614.

Hajnal, J. (1982). Two Kinds of Preindustrial Household Formation System. *Population and Development Review*, 8 (3): 449–494.

Hakim, C. (2002). Lifestyle Preferences as Determinants of Women's Differentiated Labor Market Careers. *Work and Occupations*, 29 (4): 428–459.

Halpin, B. & Chan, T. W. (2003). Educational Homogamy in Ireland and Britain: Trends and Patterns. *The British Journal of Sociology*, 54 (4): 473–495.

Halpin, B. & O'Donoghue, C. (2004). Cohabitation in Ireland: Evidence From Survey Data. University of Limerick Working Paper Series WP2004-01: 1–11.

Hank, K. (2007). Proximity and Contacts Between Older Parents and Their Children: A European Comparison. *Journal of Marriage and Family*, 69 (1): 157–173.

Hanlon, N. (2012). *Masculinities, Care and Equality: Identity and Nurture in Men's Lives*. London: Palgrave Macmillan.

Hannan, C. (2008). The Changing Nature of Family Formation in Ireland. Unpublished PhD thesis, University of Oxford.

Hannan, C. (2014). Marriage, Fertility and Social Class in Twentieth-Century Ireland. In Connolly, L., ed. *The 'Irish' Family*. Abingdon: Routledge.

Hannan, C., Halpin, B. & Coleman, C. (2013). *Growing Up in a One-Parent Family*. Dublin: Family Support Agency.

Hannan, D. F. (1972). Kinship, Neighbourhood and Social Change in Irish Rural Communities. *Economic and Social Review* 3 (2): 163–188.

Hannan, D. F. (1979). *Displacement and Development: Class, Kinship and Social Change in Irish Rural Communities*. ESRI Research Series, 96. Dublin: ESRI.

Hannan, D. F. and Commins, P. (1992). The Significance of Small-Scale Landholders in Ireland's Socio-Economic Transformation. In Goldthorpe, J. H. and Whelan, C. T., eds. *The Development of Industrial Society in Ireland*. Oxford: British Academy.

Hannan, D. F. & Katsiaouni, L. A. (1977). *Traditional Families? From Culturally Prescribed to Negotiated Roles in Farm Families*. ESRI Research Series, 87. Dublin: ESRI.

Hannan, D. F. and Ó Riain, S. (1993). *Pathways to Adulthood in Ireland: Causes and Consequences of Success and Failure in Transitions Among Irish Youth*. Economic and Social Research Institute, Research Series 161. Dublin: ESRI.

Hansen, K. V. (2004). *Not-So-Nuclear Families: Class, Gender, and Networks of Care*. New Brunswick, NJ: Rutgers University Press.

Hansen, T. (2012). Parenthood and Happiness: A Review of Folk Theories Versus Empirical Evidence. *Social Indicators Research*, 108 (1): 29–64.

Hareven, T. K. (1993). *Family Time & Industrial Time: The Relationship Between the Family and Work in a New England Industrial Community*. Lanham, MD: University Press of America.

Hareven, T. K. (1994). Aging and Generational Relations: A Historical and Life Course Perspective. *Annual Review of Sociology*, 20 (1): 437–461.

Harper, S. (2003). Changing Families as European Societies Age. *European Journal of Sociology/Archives Européennes de Sociologie*, 44 (2): 155–184.

Hartmann, H. I. (1979). The Unhappy Marriage of Marxism and Feminism: Towards a More Progressive Union. *Capital & Class*, 3 (2): 1–33.

Hawkins, A. J., Amato, P. R. & Kinghorn, A. (2013). Are Government-Supported Healthy Marriage Initiatives Affecting Family Demographics? A State-Level Analysis. *Family Relations*, 62 (3): 501–513.

Heanue, M. (2000). Matters of Life and Death. In Redmond, A., ed. *That Was Then, This is Now. Change in Ireland 1949–1999. A Publication to Mark the 50th Anniversary of the Central Statistics Office*. Dublin: Stationery Office.

Hegewisch, A. & Gornick, J. C. (2011). The Impact of Work-Family Policies on Women's Employment: A Review of Research from OECD countries. *Community, Work & Family*, 14 (2): 119–138.

Herlofson, K. & Hagestad, G. (2011). Challenges in Moving From Macro to Micro:

Population and Family Structures in Ageing Societies. *Demographic Research*, 25 (10): 337–370.

Heywood, C. (2001). *A History of Childhood: Children and Childhood in the West from Medieval to Modern Times*. Hoboken, NJ: Wiley.

Hilliard, B. (2007). Changing Irish Attitudes to Marriage and Family in Cross-National Comparison. In Hilliard, B. & Nic Ghiolla Phádraig, M., eds. *Changing Ireland in International Comparison*. Dublin: Liffey Press.

Hochschild, A. R. (1989). *The Second Shift*. London: Penguin Books.

Holland, J. (2011). Timescapes: Living a Qualitative Longitudinal Study. *Forum Qualitative Sozialforschung / Forum: Qualitative Social Research*, 12 (3). Retrieved from www.qualitative-research.net/index.php/fqs/article/view/1729.

Holland, J. & Edwards, R. (2014). *Understanding Families Over Time: Research and Policy*. Basingstoke: Palgrave Macmillan.

Holloway, S. L. & Valentine, G. (2000). Spatiality and the New Social Studies of Childhood. *Sociology*, 34 (4): 763–783.

Holmquist, K. (2010, 16 October). No Place Like the Mammy's Home. *Irish Times*. Retrieved from: http://search.proquest.com/irishtimes/docview/758467022/DD0 207A3A5A243B2PQ/1?accountid=12309 [12 May 2015].

Honeyman, K. & Goodman, J. (1991). Women's Work, Gender Conflict, and Labour Markets in Europe, 1500–1900. *The Economic History Review*, 44 (4): 608–628.

Horgan, J., Muhlau, P., McCormack, P. & Roder, A. (2008). *Attitudes to Domestic Abuse in Ireland*. Dublin: Cosc The National Office for the Prevention of Domestic, Sexual and Gender Based Violence.

Horsfall, B. & Dempsey, D. (2013). Grandparents Doing Gender: Experiences of Grandmothers and Grandfathers Caring for Grandchildren in Australia. *Journal of Sociology*. Published online before print. http://doi: 10.1177/1440783313498945.

Humphreys, A. J. (1966). *New Dubliners: Urbanization and the Irish Family*. London: Routledge and Kegan Paul.

Humphries, J. (2003). Child Labor: Lessons from the Historical Experience of Today's Industrial Economies. *The World Bank Economic Review*, 17 (2): 175–196.

Humphries, J. (2010). *Childhood and Child Labour in the British Industrial Revolution*. Cambridge: Cambridge University Press.

Humphries, N., Brugha, R. & McGee, H. (2009). 'I Won't be Staying Here for Long': A Qualitative Study on the Retention of Migrant Nurses in Ireland. *Human Resources for Health*, 7 (1), 68. http://doi.org/10.1186/1478–4491–7–68.

Hunnicutt, G. (2009). Varieties of Patriarchy and Violence Against Women Resurrecting 'Patriarchy' as a Theoretical Tool. *Violence Against Women*, 15 (5): 553–573.

Inglis, T. (1998). *Lessons in Irish Sexuality*. Dublin: University College Dublin Press.

Inglis, T. (2014). Family and the Meaning of Life in Contemporary Ireland. In Connolly, L., ed. *The 'Irish' Family*. Abingdon: Routledge.

Irish Examiner (2014). Traditional Family Farm Under Threat. *Irish Examiner*, 6 February. Retrieved from: www.irishexaminer.com/farming/news/traditional-family-farm-under-threat-257748.html [12 May 2015].

Irwin, S. (2009). Locating Where the Action Is: Quantitative and Qualitative Lenses on Families, Schooling and Structures of Social Inequality. *Sociology*, 43 (6): 1123–1140.

Jackson, A. (2011). Premarital Cohabitation as a Pathway into Marriage. An Investigation into how Premarital Cohabitation is Transforming the Institution of Marriage in Ireland. Athlone as a Case Study. Unpublished PhD thesis, Maynooth University

Jackson, P., Olive, S. & Smith, G. (2009). Myths of the Family Meal: Re-Reading Edwardian Life Histories. In Jackson, P., ed. *Changing Families, Changing Food.* London: Palgrave.

Jamieson, L., Morgan, D. Crow, G. And Allan, G. (2006). Friends, Neighbours and Distant Partners: Extending or Decentring Family Relationships? Sociological Research Online 11 (3). www.socresonline.org.uk/11/3/jamieson.html.

Jenks, C. (1996). *Childhood.* Hoboken, NJ: Psychology Press.

Johnson, M. P. & Ferraro, K. J. (2000). Research on Domestic Violence in the 1990s: Making Distinctions. *Journal of Marriage and Family,* 62 (4): 948–963.

Kamiya, Y. and Timonen, V. (2011). Older People as Members of their Families and Communities. In Barrett, A., Savva, G., Timonen, V. And Kenny, R.A., eds. *Fifty Plus in Ireland (2011): First Results from* The Irish LongituDinal Study on Ageing (TILDA). Dublin: The Irish LongituDinal Study on Ageing.

Karsten, L. (2001). Mapping Childhood in Amsterdam: The Spatial and Social Construction of Children's Domains in the City. *Tijdschrift voor Economische en Sociale Geografie,* 93 (3): 231–241.

Kasearu, K. And Kutsar, D. (2011). Patterns Behind Unmarried Cohabitation Trends in Europe. *European Societies,* 13 (2): 307–325.

Kearns, N., Coen, L. & Canavan, J. (2008). *Domestic Violence in Ireland: An Overview of National Strategic Policy and Relevant International Literature on Prevention and Intervention Initiatives in Service Provision.* Galway: Child and Family Research Centre.

Kefalas, M. J., Furstenberg, F. F., Carr, P. J. & Napolitano, L. (2011). 'Marriage Is More Than Being Together': The Meaning of Marriage for Young Adults. *Journal of Family Issues,* 32 (7): 845–875.

Kelly, J. B. & Johnson, M. P. (2008). Differentiation Among Types of Intimate Partner Violence: Research Update and Implications for Interventions. *Family Court Review,* 46 (3): 476–499.

Kennedy, F. (1989). *Family, Economy and Government in Ireland.* Economic and Social Research Institute Research Series, 143. Dublin: ESRI

Kennedy, F. (2001). *Cottage to Crèche: Family Change in Ireland.* Dublin: Institute of Public Administration.

Kiernan, K. (2002). Cohabitation in Western Europe: Trends, Issues, and Implications. In Booth, A. & Crouter, A. C., eds. *Just Living Together: Implications of Cohabitation on Families, Children, and Social Policy.* Mahwah, NJ: Lawrence Erlbaum Associates.

King-O'Riain, R. C. (2014). Transconnective Space, Emotions and Skype: The Transnational Emotional Practices of Mixed International Couples in the Republic of Ireland. In Bensky, T. & Fisher, E., eds. *Internet and Emotions.* New York: Routledge.

Kohli, M. (2006). Ageing and Justice. In Binstock, R. H., George, L. K., Cutler, S. J., Hendricks, J., and Schulz, J. H., *Handbook of Aging and the Social Sciences.* London: Academic Press.

Kohli, M. (2007). The Institutionalization of the Life Course: Looking Back to Look Ahead. *Research in Human Development,* 4 (3–4): 253–271.

Kohli, M., Hank, K. & Künemund, H. (2009). The Social Connectedness of Older Europeans: Patterns, Dynamics and Contexts. *Journal of European Social Policy*, 19 (4): 327–340.

Kohn, M. (1977). *Class and Conformity: A Study in Values, with a Reassessement, 1977*. Chicago: University of Chicago Press.

Kok, J. & Mandemakers, K. (2012). Nuclear Hardship in the Nuclear Heartland? Families and Welfare in the Netherlands, 1850–1940. Working Paper WOG: KNAW.

Korpi, W., Ferrarini, T. & Englund, S. (2013). Women's Opportunities Under Different Family Policy Constellations: Gender, Class, and Inequality Tradeoffs in Western Countries Re-examined. *Social Politics: International Studies in Gender, State & Society*, 20 (1), 1–40.

Lachance-Grzela, M. & Bouchard, G. (2010). Why Do Women Do the Lion's Share of Housework? A Decade of Research. *Sex Roles*, 63 (11–12): 767–780.

Lareau, A. (2003). *Unequal Childhoods: Class, Race, and Family Life*. Berkeley: University of California Press.

Lasch, C. (1997). *Women and the Common Life: Love, Marriage, and Feminism*. New York: W. W. Norton.

Laslett, P. (1977). *Family Life and Illicit Love in Earlier Generations: Essays in Historical Sociology*. Cambridge: Cambridge University Press.

Laslett, P. (1987). The Emergence of the Third Age. *Ageing & Society*, 7 (2): 133–160.

Laslett, P. (1988). Family, Kinship and Collectivity as Systems of Support in Pre-Industrial Europe: A Consideration of the 'Nuclear-Hardship' Hypothesis. *Continuity and Change*, 3 (Special Issue 2): 153–175.

Leonard, M. (2005). Children, Childhood and Social Capital: Exploring the Links. *Sociology*, 39 (4): 605–622.

Leonard, M. (2009). Helping with Housework: Exploring Teenagers' Perceptions of Family Obligations. *Irish Journal of Sociology*, 17 (1): 1–18.

Le Play, F. (1872). *The Organization of Labor in Accordance with Custom and the Law of the Decalogue: With a Summary of Comparative Observations Upon Good and Evil in the Regime of Labor, the Causes of Evils Existing at the Present Time, and the Means Required to Effect Reform; with Objections and Answers, Difficulties and Solutions*. New York: Claxton, Remsen & Haffelfinger. Available as free eBook from the Internet Archive: http://archive.org/details/organizationofla00lepl.

Lesthaeghe, R. (2010). The Unfolding Story of the Second Demographic Transition. *Population and Development Review* 36 (2): 211–251.

Lewis, J. (1992). Gender and the Development of Welfare Regimes. *Journal of European Social Policy*, 2 (3): 159–173.

Lister, R. (1994). 'She Has Other Duties': Women, Citizenship and Social Security. In Baldwin, S. and Falkingham, J., eds. *Social Security and Social Change: New Challenges*. Hemel Hempstead: Harvester Wheatsheaf.

Luescher, K. & Pillemer, K. (1998). Intergenerational Ambivalence: A New Approach to the Study of Parent-Child Relations in Later Life. *Journal of Marriage and the Family*, 60 (2): 413–425.

Lundström, Francesca. (2001). *Grandparenthood in Modern Ireland*. Dublin: Age Action Ireland.

Lunn, P. & Fahey, T. (2011). *Households and Family Structures in Ireland: A Detailed Statistical Analysis of Census 2006*. Dublin: Family Support Agency and ESRI.

Lunn, P., Fahey, T. & Hannan, C. (2010). *Family Figures: Family Dynamics and Family Types in Ireland, 1986–2006*. Dublin: Family Support Agency and ESRI.

Macfarlane, A. (1986). *Marriage and Love in England: Modes of Reproduction*. Oxford: Blackwell.

Maguire, M. J. & Cinnéide, S. Ó. (2005). 'A Good Beating Never Hurt Anyone': The Punishment and Abuse of Children in Twentieth-Century Ireland. *Journal of Social History*, 38 (3): 635–652.

Manning, W. D., Fettro, M. N. & Lamidi, E. (2014). Child Well-Being in Same-Sex Parent Families: Review of Research Prepared for American Sociological Association Amicus Brief. *Population Research and Policy Review*, 33 (4): 485–502.

Margolis, R. & Myrskylä, M. (2011). A Global Perspective on Happiness and Fertility. *Population and Development Review*, 37 (1): 29–56.

Marquardt, E., Blankenhorn, D., Lerman, R. I, Malone-Colón, L. & Bradford Wilcox, W. (2012). The President's Marriage Agenda for the Forgotten Sixty Percent in *The State of Our Unions* (Charlottesville, VA: National Marriage Project and Institute for American Values).

Mason, K. O. (1997). Explaining Fertility Transitions. *Demography*, 34 (4): 443–454.

Mason, K. O. (2001). Gender and Family Systems in the Fertility Transition. *Population and Development Review*, 27: 160–176.

Mason, J., May, V. & Clarke, L. (2007). Ambivalence and the Paradoxes of Grandparenting. *The Sociological Review*, 55 (4): 687–706.

McCoy, S., Byrne, D. & Banks, J. (2012). Too Much of a Good Thing? Gender, 'Concerted Cultivation' and Unequal Achievement in Primary Education. *Child Indicators Research*, 5 (1):155–178.

McCoy, S. & Smyth, E. (2007). So Much To Do, So Little Time. Part-Time Employment Among Secondary Students in Ireland. *Work, Employment & Society*, 21 (2): 227–246.

McDonagh, M. (2014, 21 June). Romance Endures in Leitrim Ballroom. *Irish Times*.

McGarrigle, C. and Kenny, R. A. (2013). *Profile of the Sandwich Generation and Intergenerational Transfers in Ireland*. Dublin: The Irish Longitudinal Study on Ageing.

McGinnity, F. & Russell, H. (2007). Work Rich, Time Poor? Time Use of Women and Men in Ireland. *Economic and Social Review*, 38 (3): 325–354.

McGinnity, F. & Russell, H. (2008). *Gender Inequalities in Time Use: The Distribution of Caring, Housework and Employment Among Women and men in Ireland*. Dublin: Equality Authority and ESRI.

McGinnity, F., Murray, A. & McNally, S. (2013). *Mother's Return to Work and Childcare Choices for Infants in Ireland. Growing Up in Ireland*, Infant Cohort, Report 2. Dublin: Stationery Office.

McGinnity, F., Russell, H. & Smyth, E. (2007). Gender, Work-Life Balance and Quality of Life. In Fahey, T., Russell, H. & Whelan, C. T., eds. *Quality of Life in Ireland. Social Indicators Research Series*, 32. Springer Netherlands.

McKeown, K., Ferguson, T. H., Ferguson, H. & Rooney, D. (1998). *Changing Fathers? Fatherhood and Family Life in Modern Ireland*. Cork: Collins Press.

McKeown, K., Lehane, P., Rock, R., Haase, T. & Pratschke, J. (2002). *Unhappy Marriages: Does Counselling Help?* Maynooth: ACCORD.

McLanahan, S. & Percheski, C. (2008). Family Structure and the Reproduction of Inequalities. *Annual Review of Sociology*, 34 (1): 257–276.

McRae, S. (2003). Constraints and Choices in Mothers' Employment Careers: A Consideration of Hakim's Preference Theory. *The British Journal of Sociology*, 54 (3): 317–338.

Medick, H. (1984). Village Spinning Bees: Sexual Culture and Free Time Among Rural Youth in Early Modern Germany. In Medick, H. And Sabean, D., eds. *Interest and Emotion: Essays on the Study of Family and Kinship*. Cambridge: Cambridge University Press.

Merchant, E. R., Gratton, B. & Gutmann, M. P. (2012). A Sudden Transition: Household Changes for Middle Aged U.S. Women in the Twentieth Century. *Population Research and Policy Review*, 31 (5): 703–726.

Messenger, B. (1980). *Picking up the Linen Threads: A Study in Industrial Folklore*. Belfast: Blackstaff Press.

Messenger, J. (1969). *Inis Beag: Isle of Ireland*. New York: Holt, Rhinehart and Winston.

Miller, D. W. (1983). The Armagh Troubles 1784–95. In Clark, S. & Donnelly, J. S., *Irish Peasants: Violence and Political Unrest 1780–1914*. Madison: University of Wisconsin Press.

Mills, C. W. (1959). *The Sociological Imagination*. Oxford: Oxford University Press.

Minkler, M. (1999). Intergenerational Households Headed by Grandparents: Contexts, Realities, and Implications for Policy. *Journal of Aging Studies*, 13 (2): 199–218.

Mogey, J. M. (1955). The Contribution of Frederic Le Play to Family Research. *Marriage and Family Living*, 17 (4): 310–315.

Mokyr, J. (1980). Industrialization and Poverty in Ireland and the Netherlands. *Journal of Interdisciplinary History*, 10 (3): 429–458.

Morgan, D. (2011). *Rethinking Family Practices*. Basingstoke: Palgrave Macmillan.

Morrow, V. (1996). Rethinking Childhood Dependency: Children's Contributions to the Domestic Economy. *The Sociological Review*, 44 (1): 58–77.

Morrow, V. (1999). Conceptualising Social Capital in Relation to the Well-Being of Children and Young People: A Critical Review. *The Sociological Review*, 47 (4): 744–765.

Murcott, A. (1983). *The Sociology of Food and Eating: Essays on the Sociological Significance of Food*. Aldershot: Gower.

Murphy, C., Keilthy, P. And Caffrey, L. (2008). *Lone Parents and Employment. What are the Real Issues?* Dublin: One Family.

Murphy, E. M. (2011). Children's Burial Grounds in Ireland (Cillíní) and Parental Emotions Toward Infant Death. *International Journal of Historical Archaeology*, 15 (3): 409–428.

Murphy, M. (2010). Family and Kinship Networks in the Context of Ageing Societies. In S. Tuljapurkar, N. Ogawa & A. H. Gauthier, eds. *Ageing in Advanced Industrial States*. Dordrecht: Springer Netherlands.

Murphy, M. P. (2011). A Caring Society. *Studies*, 100 (397): 80–92.

Murphy, M. P. (2012). The Politics of Irish Labour Activation, 1980–2010. *Administration*, 60 (2): 20–32.

Murphy, M. P. (2012). *Careless to Careful Activation: Making Activation Work for Women*. Dublin: National Women's Council of Ireland.

Myrskylä, M., Kohler, H.-P. & Billari, F. C. (2009). Advances in Development Reverse Fertility Declines. *Nature*, 460 (7256): 741–743.

Nazroo, J. (1995). Uncovering Gender Differences in the Use of Marital Violence: The Effect of Methodology. *Sociology*, 29 (3): 475–494.

Neale, B. & Flowerdew, J. (2003). Time, Texture and Childhood: The Contours of Longitudinal Qualitative Research. *International Journal of Social Research Methodology*, 6 (3): 189–199.

Neale, B., Henwood, K. & Holland, J. (2012). Researching Lives Through Time: An Introduction to the Timescapes Approach. *Qualitative Research*, 12 (1): 4–15.

Neilson, J. & Stanfors, M. (2014). It's About Time! Gender, Parenthood, and Household Divisions of Labor Under Different Welfare Regimes. *Journal of Family Issues*, 35 (8): 1066–1088.

NESC (National Economic and Social Council) (2013). *The Social Dimensions of the Crisis: The Evidence and its Implications*. NESC Report No. 134. Dublin: National Economic and Social Council.

Ní Laoire, C. (2011). Narratives of 'Innocent Irish Childhoods': Return Migration and Intergenerational Family Dynamics. *Journal of Ethnic and Migration Studies*, 37 (8): 1253–1271.

Ní Laoire, C. (2014). Children, Cousins and Clans: The Role of the Extended Family And kinship in the Lives of Children in Returning Irish Migrant Families. In Connolly, L., ed. *The 'Irish' Family*. Abingdon: Routledge.

Ní Laoire, C., Carpena-Méndez, F., Tyrrell, N. & White, A. (2011). *Childhood and Migration in Europe: Portraits of Mobility, Identity and Belonging in Contemporary Ireland*. Farnham: Ashgate Publishing, Ltd.

Nolan, P. & Lenski, G. E. (1999). *Human Societies: An Introduction to Macrosociology*. New York: McGraw Hill College.

O'Connor, P. (2008). *Irish Children and Teenagers in a Changing World: The National* Write Here Write Now *Project*. Manchester: Manchester University Press.

O'Connor, P. M. (2010). Bodies In and Out of Place: Embodied Transnationalism Among Invisible Immigrants – the Contemporary Irish in Australia. *Population, Space and Place*, 16 (1): 75–83.

Ogilvie, S. (2004). How Does Social Capital Affect Women? Guilds and Communities in Early Modern Germany. *The American Historical Review*, 109 (2): 325–359.

Ó Gráda, C. (1980). Primogeniture and Ultimogeniture in Rural Ireland. *Journal of Interdisciplinary History*, 10 (3): 491–497.

Ó Gráda, C. (2006). *Jewish Ireland in the Age of Joyce: A Socioeconomic History*. Princeton, NJ: Princeton University Press.

Olagnero, M., Meo, A. & Corcoran, M. P. (2005). Social Support Networks in Impoverished European Neighbourhoods. *European Societies*, 7 (1): 53–79.

O'Sullivan, S. (2012). 'All Changed, Changed Utterly'? Gender Role Attitudes and the Feminisation of the Irish Labour Force. *Women's Studies International Forum*, 35 (4): 223–232.

Pahl, R. & Pevalin, D. J. (2005). Between Family and Friends: A Longitudinal Study of Friendship Choice. *The British Journal of Sociology*, 56 (3), 433–450.

Pahl, R. & Spencer, L. (2004). Personal Communities: Not Simply Families of 'Fate' or 'Choice'. *Current Sociology*, 52 (2): 199–221.

Parreñas, R. (2005). Long Distance Intimacy: Class, Gender and Intergenerational Relations Between Mothers and Children in Filipino Transnational Families. *Global Networks*, 5 (4): 317–336.

Parsons, T. & Bales, R. F. (1956). *Family Socialization and Interaction Process*. London: Routledge and Kegan Paul.

Payne, D. & McCashin, A. (2005). *Welfare State Legitimacy: The Republic of Ireland in Comparative Perspective*. Geary Discussion Paper Series 2005, 10.

Pfau-Effinger, B. (1998). Gender Cultures and the Gender Arrangement: A Theoretical framework for Cross-National Gender Research. *Innovation: The European Journal of Social Science Research*, 11 (2): 147–166.

Phillipson, C., Bernard, M., Phillips, J. & Ogg, J. (1998). The Family and Community Life of Older People: Household Composition and Social Networks in Three Urban Areas. *Ageing & Society*, 18 (3): 259–289.

Plakans, A. (1977). Identifying Kinfolk Beyond the Household. *Journal of Family History*, 2 (1): 3–27.

Plane, D. A., Henrie, C. J. & Perry, M. J. (2005). Migration Up and Down the Urban Hierarchy and Across the Life Course. *Proceedings of the National Academy of Sciences of the United States of America*, 102 (43): 15313–15318.

Pollock, L. A. (1983). *Forgotten Children: Parent-Child Relations from 1500 to 1900*. Cambridge: Cambridge University Press.

Popenoe, D. (1993). American Family Decline, 1960–1990: A Review and Appraisal. *Journal of Marriage and the Family*, 55 (3): 527–542.

Putnam, R. (2000). *Bowling Alone: The Collapse and Revival of American Community*. New York: Simon and Schuster.

Quail, A., Murray, A. & Williams, J. (2011). *Support from Grandparents to Families with Infants*. ESRI Research Bulletin 2011/1/4.

Quinn, D. (2011). Traditional Family Unit Dying Away. *Irish Independent*, 16 December. Available at: www.independent.ie/opinion/analysis/david-quinn-traditional-family-unit-dying-away-26802726.html. Accessed 12 May 2015.

Raftery, M. (1999). *States of Fear*. Television Documentary. Dublin: RTÉ.

Ragin, C. C. & Amoroso, L. M. (2010). *Constructing Social Research: The Unity and Diversity of Method*. London: Sage.

Ralph, D. (2013). 'It was a bit like the Passover': Recollections of Family Mealtimes During Twentieth Century Irish Childhoods. *Children's Geographies*, 11 (4): 422–435.

Ralph, D. (2015). 'Who should do the caring'? Involved Fatherhood and Ambivalent Gendered Moral Rationalities Among Cohabiting/Married Irish Parents. *Community, Work & Family*, Published online before print. http://doi.org/10.1080/13668803.2014.1000266.

Ramsey, C. B. (2013). Exit Myth: Family Law, Gender Roles, and Changing Attitudes Toward Female Victims of Domestic Violence, *Michigan Journal of Gender & Law*, 20 (1). http://repository.law.umich.edu/mjgl/vol20/iss1/1/.

Reher, D. S. (1998). Family Ties in Western Europe: Persistent Contrasts. *Population and Development Review*, 24 (2): 203–234.

Reher, D. S. (2007). Towards Long-Term Population Decline: A Discussion of Relevant Issues. *European Journal of Population / Revue Européenne de Démographie*, 23 (2): 189–207.

Rose, S. O. (1993). *Limited Livelihoods: Gender and Class in Nineteenth-Century England*. Berkeley: University of California Press.

Ruggles, S. (2007). The Decline of Intergenerational Coresidence in the United States, 1850 to 2000. *American Sociological Review*, 72 (6): 964–989.

Ruggles, S. (2009). Reconsidering the Northwest European Family System: Living Arrangements of the Aged in Comparative Historical Perspective. *Population and Development Review*, 35 (2): 249–273.

Ruggles, S. (2011). Intergenerational Coresidence and Family Transitions in the United States, 1850–1880. *Journal of Marriage and Family*, 73 (1): 136–148.

Russell, H., McGinnity, F., Callan, T. & Keane, C. (2009). *A Woman's Place – Female Participation in the Irish Labour Market*. Dublin: The Equality Authority and the ESRI.

Ryan, L. (2004). Family Matters: (E)migration, Familial Networks and Irish Women in Britain. *The Sociological Review*, 52 (3): 351–370.

Ryan, L. (2007). Migrant Women, Social Networks and Motherhood: The Experiences of Irish Nurses in Britain. *Sociology*, 41 (2): 295–312.

Ryan, P. (2012). [As King-O'Riain] *Angela Macnamara: An Intimate History of Irish Lives*. Dublin: Irish Academic Press.

Ryan-Flood, R. (2014). Staying Connected: Irish Lesbian and Gay Narratives of Family. In L. Connolly, ed., *The 'Irish' Family*. Abingdon: Routledge.

Sabean, D. W. (1990). *Property, Production, and Family in Neckarhausen, 1700–1870*. Cambridge: Cambridge University Press.

Safe Ireland. (2013). *On Just One Day: A National One Day Count of Women and Children Accessing SAFE IRELAND Domestic Violence Services*. Dublin: Safe Ireland.

Saxonberg, S. (2013). From Defamilialization to Degenderization: Toward a New Welfare Typology. *Social Policy & Administration*, 47 (1): 26–49.

Sayer, A. (2011). *Why Things Matter to People: Social Science, Values and Ethical Life*. Cambridge: Cambridge University Press.

Scanzoni, J. (2000). *Designing Families: The Search for Self and Community in the Information Age*. Thousand Oaks, CA: Pine Forge Press.

Scheper-Hughes, N. (1992). *Death Without Weeping: The Violence of Everyday Life in Brazil*. Berkeley: University of California Press.

Scott, J. and Marshall, G., eds. (2009). *A Dictionary of Sociology*. 3rd Edition. Oxford: Oxford University Press.

Seccombe, W. (1990). Starting to Stop: Working-Class Fertility Decline in Britain. *Past & Present*, 126 (1): 151–188.

Segalen, M. (1983). *Love and Power in the Peasant Family: Rural France in the Nineteenth Century*. Oxford: Blackwell.

Segalen, M. (1986). *Historical Anthropology of the Family*. Cambridge: Cambridge University Press.

Sen, A. K. (1990). Gender and Cooperative Conflicts. In Tinker, I., ed. *Persistent Inequalities: Women and World Development*. New York: Oxford University Press.

Settersten, R. A., Jr. (2012). The Contemporary Context of Young Adulthood in the USA: From Demography to Development, From Private Troubles to Public Issues. In Booth, A., Brown, S. L., Landale, N. S., Manning, W. D. & McHale, S. M. (Eds.), *Early Adulthood in a Family Context*. New York: Springer.

Seward, R. R., Stivers, R. A., Igoe, D. G., Amin, I. & Cosimo, D. (2005). Irish Families in the Twentieth Century: Exceptional or Converging? *Journal of Family History*, 30 (4): 410–430.

Shimizu, Yoshifumi. (2014). Changes in Families in Ireland from the 19th Century to the Early 20th Century. *St. Andrew's University Sociological Review* 47 (2): 1–24.

Shirani, F., Henwood, K. & Coltart, C. (2012). Meeting the Challenges of Intensive Parenting Culture: Gender, Risk Management and the Moral Parent. *Sociology*, 46 (1): 25–40.

Shortall, S. (1991). The Dearth of Data on Irish Farm Wives: A Critical Review of the Literature. *Economic & Social Review* 22 (4): 311–332.

SIMon (2015). SIMon Social Indicators Monitor. GESIS: Leibniz Institut fur Sozialwissenschaften. Available at: www.gesis.org/en/social-indicators/products/simon-social-indicators-monitor/ Accessed 27 October 2015

Skeggs, B. & Loveday, V. (2012). Struggles for Value: Value Practices, Injustice, Judgment, Affect and the Idea of Class. *The British Journal of Sociology*, 63 (3): 472–490.

Skehill, C. (2003). Social Work in the Republic of Ireland A History of the Present. *Journal of Social Work*, 3 (2): 141–159.

Smart, C. & Shipman, B. (2004). Visions in Monochrome: Families, Marriage and the Individualization Thesis. *The British Journal of Sociology*, 55 (4): 491–509.

Sommerville, C. J. (1982). *The Rise and Fall of Childhood*. London: Sage.

Stacey, J. (1990). *Brave New Families: Stories of Domestic Upheaval in Late-Twentieth-Century America*. Berkeley: University of California Press.

Stack, C. B. (1975). *All Our Kin: Strategies for Survival in a Black Community*. New York: Basic Books.

Steiner-Scott, E. (1997). 'To Bounce a Boot Off Her Now and Then': Domestic Violence in Post-Famine Ireland. In Valiulis, M. G. And O'Dowd, M., eds. *Women and Irish History: Essays in Honour of Margaret MacCurtain*. Dublin: Wolfhound Press.

Stone, L. (1977). *The Family, Sex and Marriage in England 1500–1800*. London: Weidenfeld & Nicolson.

Straus, M. A. & Gelles, R. J. (1986). Societal Change and Change in Family Violence from 1975 to 1985 as Revealed by Two National Surveys. *Journal of Marriage and the Family*, 48 (3): 465–479.

Survival (2015). Understanding Uncertainty: Survival animation. Available at: http://understandinguncertainty.org/survival/ Accessed 27 October 2015.

Swisher, R., Sweet, S. & Moen, P. (2004). The Family-Friendly Community and Its Life Course Fit for Dual-Earner Couples. *Journal of Marriage and Family*, 66 (2): 281–292.

Tadmor, N. (2010). Early Modern English Kinship in the Long Run: Reflections on Continuity and Change. *Continuity and Change*, 25 (Special Issue 1): 15–48.

Thane, P. (2003). Social Histories of Old Age and Aging. *Journal of Social History*, 37 (1): 93–111.

Thane, P. (2006). Women and Ageing in the Twentieth Century. *L'Homme*, 17 (1): 59–74.

Tilly, C. (1984). *Big Structures, Large Processes, Huge Comparisons*. New York: Russell Sage Foundation.

Tilly, L. & Scott, J. W. (1987). *Women, Work, and Family*. New York: Routledge [First published 1978].

Timonen, V. & Doyle, M. (2008). From the Workhouse to the Home: Evolution of Care Policy for Older People in Ireland. *International Journal of Sociology and Social Policy*, 28 (3/4): 76–89.

Timonen, V., Conlon, C., Scharf, T. & Carney, G. (2013). Family, State, Class and

Solidarity: Re-Conceptualising Intergenerational Solidarity Through the Grounded Theory Approach. *European Journal of Ageing*, 10 (3): 171–179.

Tong, R. (2014). *Feminist Thought: A More Comprehensive Introduction*. Boulder, Colorado: Westview Press.

Uhlenberg, P. (1980). Death and the Family. *Journal of Family History*, 5 (3): 313–320.

Valentine, G. (1996). Children Should Be Seen and Not Heard: The Production and Transgression of Adults' Public Space. *Urban Geography*, 17 (3): 205–220.

Van Bavel, J. & Winter, T. D. (2013). Becoming a Grandparent and Early Retirement in Europe. *European Sociological Review*, 29 (6): 1295–1308.

Van de Kaa, D. (1987). Europe's Second Demographic Transition. *Population Bulletin*, 42 (1): 1–63.

Van Gaalen, R. I. & Dykstra, P. A. (2006). Solidarity and Conflict Between Adult Children and Parents: A Latent Class Analysis. *Journal of Marriage and Family*, 68 (4), 947–960.

Wall, K. & Gouveia, R. (2014). Changing Meanings of Family in Personal Relationships. *Current Sociology*, 62 (3): 352–373.

Walsh, K., O'Shea, E., Scharf, T. & Murray, M. (2012). Ageing in Changing Community Contexts: Cross-Border Perspectives From Rural Ireland and Northern Ireland. *Journal of Rural Studies*, 28 (4): 347–357.

Watson, D. & Parsons, S. (2005). *Domestic Abuse of Women and Men in Ireland: Report on the National Study of Domestic Abuse*. Dublin: National Crime Council.

Watson, D., Maitre, B. & Whelan, C. T. (2012). *Work and Poverty in Ireland: An Analysis of CSO Survey on Income and Living Conditions 2004–2010*. Dublin: Social Inclusion Division of Department of Social Protection and the ESRI.

Watson, D., Maitre, B., Whelan, C. T. and Williams, J. (2014). *Growing Up in Ireland: Dynamics of Child Economic Vulnerability and Socio-Emotional Development – An Analysis of the First Two Waves of the* Growing Up in Ireland *Study*. Dublin: Stationery Office.

Weeks, J., Heaphy, B. & Donovan, C. (2001). *Same-Sex Intimacies: Families of Choice and Other Life Experiments*. London: Routledge.

Weininger, E. B. & Lareau, A. (2009). Paradoxical Pathways: An Ethnographic Extension of Kohn's Findings on Class and Childrearing. *Journal of Marriage and Family*, 71 (3): 680–695.

West, C. & Zimmerman, D. H. (1987). Doing Gender. *Gender & Society*, 1 (2): 125–151.

Widmer, E. & Jallinoja, R. (2008). *Beyond the Nuclear Family: Families in a Configurational Perspective*. Bern: Peter Lang.

Wilmott, P. & Young, M. D. (1960). *Family and Class in a London Suburb*. London: Routledge and Kegan Paul.

Women's Aid (2015). *Myths about domestic violence*. Available at: www.womensaid.ie/help/whatisdomesticviolence/myths.html. Accessed: 15 October 2015.

Wood, R. G., McConnell, S., Moore, Q., Clarkwest, A. & Hsueh, J. (2012). The Effects of Building Strong Families: A Healthy Marriage and Relationship Skills Education Program for Unmarried Parents. *Journal of Policy Analysis and Management*, 31 (2): 228–252.

Young, Arthur. 1892. *Arthur Young's Tour in Ireland (1776–1779)*, ed. Arthur W. Hutton. London: George Bell and Sons.

Young, M. D. & Wilmott, P. (1957). *Family and Kinship in East London*. London: Routledge and Kegan Paul.

Zelizer, V. A. R. (1985). *Pricing the Priceless Child: The Changing Social Value of Children.* Princeton, NJ: Princeton University Press.

Zinnecker, J. (1995). The Cultural Modernization of Childhood. In Chisholm, L., Buchner, P., Kruger, H. and Du Bois-Reymond, M., eds. *Growing Up in Europe.* Berlin: Walter De Gruyter.

Index